IMAGES
of America

SAN ANTONIO'S HISTORIC MARKET SQUARE

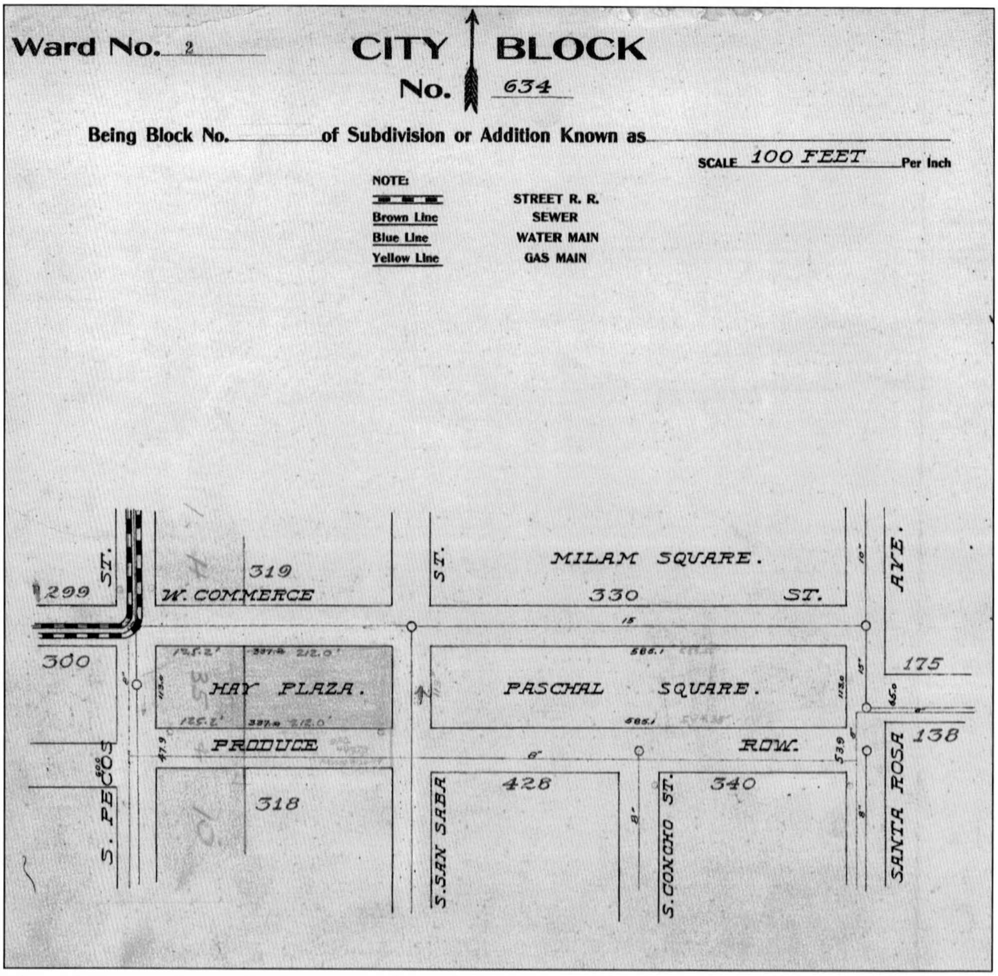

This 1908 map shows the location of Paschal Square and Hay Plaza, the area now known as Market Square. This area has been a market for over a century. Market Square consists of Centro de Artes, El Mercado, Farmers Market, and businesses along the pedestrian malls of Mariachi Plaza, Madero Plaza, and Hidalgo Plaza. (Courtesy of the City of San Antonio, Office of the City Clerk Municipal Archives & Records.)

On the Cover: In 1946, a vendor works from her cart parked across the street from the market house in Milam Park. In the background is Santa Rosa Hospital. In the early days, the market area was much larger and included Milam Park and Washington Square. The present-day parameters for Market Square were set in the 1970s during urban renewal. (Courtesy of UTSA Special Collections–ITC, photograph MS389-000027.)

IMAGES
of America

SAN ANTONIO'S HISTORIC MARKET SQUARE

Edna Campos Gravenhorst

ARCADIA
PUBLISHING

ISBN 978-1-4671-2669-4

Published by Arcadia Publishing
Charleston, South Carolina

Printed in the United States of America

Library of Congress Control Number: 2017932824

For all general information, please contact Arcadia Publishing:
Telephone 843-853-2070
Fax 843-853-0044
E-mail sales@arcadiapublishing.com
For customer service and orders:
Toll-Free 1-888-313-2665

Visit us on the Internet at www.arcadiapublishing.com

To the people of San Antonio, especially to the business owners and employees of Market Square.
Also to all visitors, "Mi casa es su casa."

Contents

Acknowledgments

I wish to thank the vendors and business owners of Market Square, many of whom are third and fourth generation. All the people who are running businesses today are contributing to the preservation of San Antonio as a market town. A special thank-you to La Familia Cortez Restaurants, which has been in Market Square since 1941. Through their contributions of community support, political involvement, and as an employer, the Cortez family has been an instigator in the preservation of Market Square and Mexican American history. In keeping with the conservation of San Antonio as a bicultural city, a big thank-you goes to Cecilia Matilla Murrieta for translating this book to Spanish.

There have been many people who have contributed to this book. I apologize in advance that not everyone is listed; the list was too long. I wish to thank some of the major contributors: Sylvia Reyna, Texana at San Antonio Public Libraries; Tom Shelton, the Institute of Texan Cultures; Beth Standifird, San Antonio Conservation Society Foundation; Elvira Sanchez Kisser, City of San Antonio, Office of the City Clerk Municipal Archives & Records; Angela Camarillo, San Antonio River Authority; Al Rendon, Rendon Photography & Fine Art; Rueben M. Perez, coauthor of *Laredito*; Lionel and Kathy Sosa, Sosa & Sosa; and Michael Cortez, Pete Cortez, and Cariño Cortez-Haass, La Familia Cortez Restaurants. I would also like to thank the following for supplying information and photographs: Yolix Luna, Thelma Gonzalez, Jaime and Connie Herrejon, Joanne Gonzales, Mary Perales Valdez, Alice and Phillip Leon, Henry Gomez, Francisco Perez, Beatriz Llamas, Gabriella Albright, Alicia Reyes, Michael Douglas, Victor and Sandra Dominguez, David Peché, and Melessa Rodriguez.

I also wish to thank my editor at Arcadia Publishing, Liz Gurley, who has guided and supported me through this process with her patience and expertise. I am grateful to my friends and *comadres*—Carol Hawkins, Nancy Lara, and Mary Roland. They helped me with interviews and appointments and provided moral support. This gratitude list cannot be complete without mentioning my siblings and my deceased parents: Alejandro Campos, Roel Campos, Linda Graves, Andrea Bierstedt, Alejandro Campos (1932–1994), and Consuelo Sendejo Campos (1933–2015).

The biggest thank-you goes to my husband, Ted Gravenhorst Jr., who supports my writing career.

Introduction

San Antonio celebrates its 300th anniversary in 2018. In that year, we also pay tribute to the 118th anniversary of Market Square. In 1900, the Municipal Market House was completed. The construction of the building and decades of development in the surrounding area marked the beginning of the market zone in this part of the city. There have been many changes to the market; the most significant was the 1976 renovation. The 40th anniversary of Market Square's renovation was celebrated in 2016.

In 1988, Mary Ann Noonan Guerra published *The History of San Antonio's Market Square*. Thirty years later, her book has been a great source of information for *San Antonio's Historic Market Square*.

Early plazas with their open-air markets were the centers of community. Vendors drove their wagons filled with produce and household goods to the squares before dawn. When the day's market was over, the Chili Queens set up their stands where they fed locals and visitors. Besides Mexican food, there was music and dancing. As San Antonio grew, the market locations moved farther from the city's center.

Municipal Market House and areas surrounding Paschal Square and Hay Market Plaza became the city market. In the 1920s, the Municipal Market House Annex buildings were constructed to provide better sanitary conditions and modern vendor stalls. In 1938, the old Municipal Market House was demolished. In its place, a metal structure with open sides was built. Trucks could drive in, and vendors sold their wares from the backs of the trucks. This building provided little protection from the weather. Eventually it was enclosed, but still had no heat or air-conditioning. That would come later, when Farmers Market Plaza was remodeled.

As construction of supermarkets in the city and suburbs increased, traffic at the city market decreased. In the 1950s and 1960s, between prostitution and drugs, the area was dangerous. Many families moved on to other jobs and locations around the city, but some persevered and went from selling produce to selling souvenir products to tourists who came from all over the world.

The Cortez family stayed and played a major role in the preservation of Market Square. In the 1970s, Market Square went through renovations and became a popular market again. In 2016, the Cortez family celebrated the 75th anniversary of Mi Tierra Café & Bakery. This iconic San Antonio destination was founded by Pedro and Cruz Cortez, who started their business with a three-table market café in 1941.

Market Square is comprised of Farmers Market, El Mercado, and Centro de Artes and includes businesses, offices, and studios along Produce Row at Concho and Dolorosa Streets. San Antonio's bilingual and bicultural personality comes to life in Market Square. There are events here year-round. During events, there are food booths, arts, crafts, and live entertainment with music, singing, and dancing. Some of the major fiestas scheduled in the past were the Chocolate Festival, Rodeo Roundup, March Market Madness, Fiesta Primavera/Spring Break, Tejano Music Awards Fan Fair (with over 100 bands), Cascarones, Fiesta de los Reyes, Cinco de Mayo, Mother's Day

Weekend, Return of the Chili Queens Memorial Day Weekend Celebration, SA Pride Fest, Father's Day Weekend, Freedom Fest, Back to School, Annual Salsa Salsa Street Fest (salsa making and salsa dancing contests), Labor Day Weekend, Fiesta Patrias, Hispanic Heritage Weekend Celebration, Annual Car Show, Texas BBQ Tour Event, Dia de los Muertos, Tamalada (tamale making and eating), Feria de Santa Cecilia, Blessing of the Animals, Winter Wonderland, and College Football Fan Fiesta.

The journey in writing this book has not been easy, but the education it has provided me is priceless. As a storyteller of working-class Americans, it is difficult to locate vintage photographs and information in institutions. To tell a more complete story, I must go to people willing to share their memories.

Looking back through the history of most Americans, the "good old days" were not so good! The first hurdle in locating vintage photographs of Market Square and the people of the market community was that most people were poor. They were too busy earning a living to take pictures, and pictures cost money they needed for necessities. The second hurdle was that most vendors at Market Square were and still are identified as Mexican Americans. For decades, their ancestors were excluded from most of recorded Texas history. The Chicano Movement of the 1960s sparked change.

Gustavo C. Garcia, a Mexican American civil rights lawyer, did his part to bring about change before 1960. He served the League of United Latin American Citizens as legal advisor from 1939 to 1940 and was elected to the San Antonio Independent School District Board of Education in 1948. He went on to serve as legal advisor to the American GI Forum from 1951 to 1952. By the mid-1950s, Garcia's personal struggles were affecting his career. On June 3, 1964, he had a seizure in an office in the old Farmers Market and died. He is buried at Fort Sam Houston National Cemetery.

Emma Tenayuca also brought about change. In 1938, she led the strike for better wages and working conditions for pecan shellers at Southern Pecan Shelling Company at 135 East Cevallos Street. In 1927, the company was located at 1223 West Commerce Street. As a young child, Tenayuca witnessed the struggles of working people when she visited the Plaza de Zacate (Hay Market). As an adult, these memories fueled her passion for minority rights. In late 1938, Tenayuca was blacklisted and forced to leave San Antonio because of an incident at the Municipal Market House Auditorium. She was to speak at a small gathering for the Communist party when a crowd of 5,000 people attacked the auditorium "huntin' Communists." In the 1940s, Tenayuca went to San Francisco to earn a college degree, and the Pecan Workers Union No. 172 set up its offices in the market area, at 109 South Santa Rosa Avenue.

As of February 2017, officials for the City of San Antonio and Market Square are Ivy Taylor, mayor; Sheryl Sculley, city manager; Roberto C. Treviño, city councilman, District 1; Mark Jenkins, manager of Market Square; Yvette Ramirez, president of Farmers Market Plaza; and Greg Peña, president of El Mercado Merchants Association.

The San Antonio Tricentennial Celebration Commission headquarters are located at Centro de Artes. Commission chairs are Robert Thrailkill, Dr. Alfonso Chiscano, Fr. David Garcia, Dr. Katie Luber, and Lionel Sosa. Commission members are Hon. Tommy Adkisson, Hector Cardenas, Joe Linson, Brenda Pacheco, Dr. Cynthia Teniente-Matson, Faith Radle, Jim Landers, Cristina Bazaldua, Blayne Tucker, Frieda Wright, Luke Holland, Dr. Felix D. Almaraz Jr., Tommy Calvert Sr., and Carrie Baker. Other subcommittee members and chairs are Tim Hedgepeth, Aaron Zimmerman, Rene Barilleaux, Art Ordoqui, Amy Shaw, Angelica Docog, Dan Yoxall, and Vanessa Hurd. Honorary commission chairs are the current mayor, Ivy Taylor, along with former mayors Phil Hardberger, Edward D. Garza, Howard Peak, William Thorton, Nelson Wolff, Henry Cisneros, and Lila Cockrell.

Happy 300th anniversary to the city that embraces change and diversity. Viva San Antonio!

One

Early Plazas

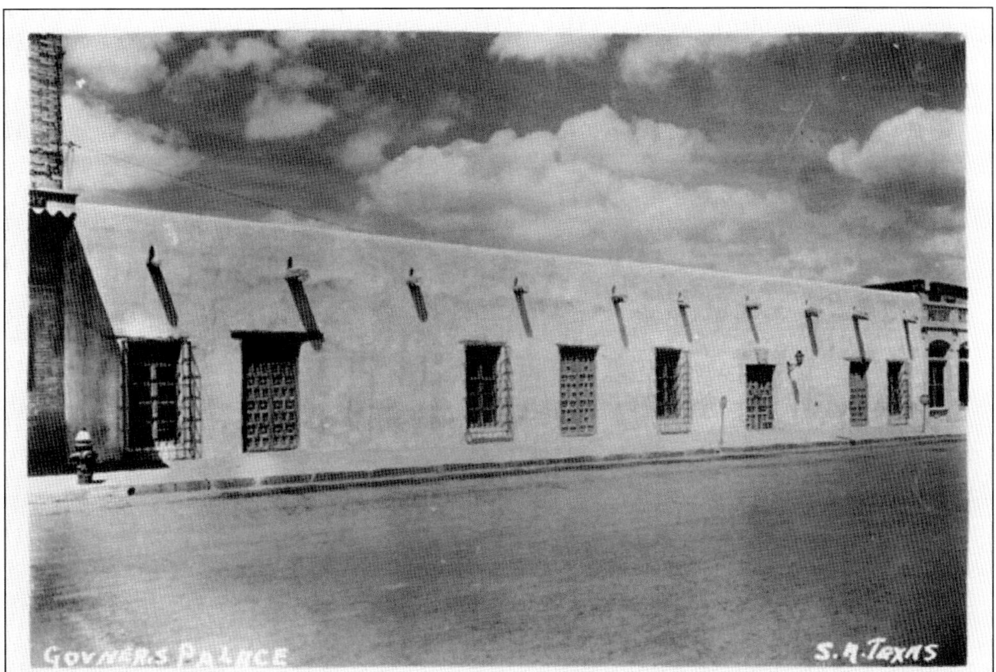

Military Plaza, or Plaza de Armas, was established in 1722; it is the oldest plaza in San Antonio. The *presidio* provided parade grounds and a market for the Spanish soldiers. Their captain lived in the Governor's Palace, which was also his working office. The palace served as office and residence for captains from 1722 to the early 1800s. (Courtesy of Texana Division, San Antonio Public Libraries, Postcard Collection.)

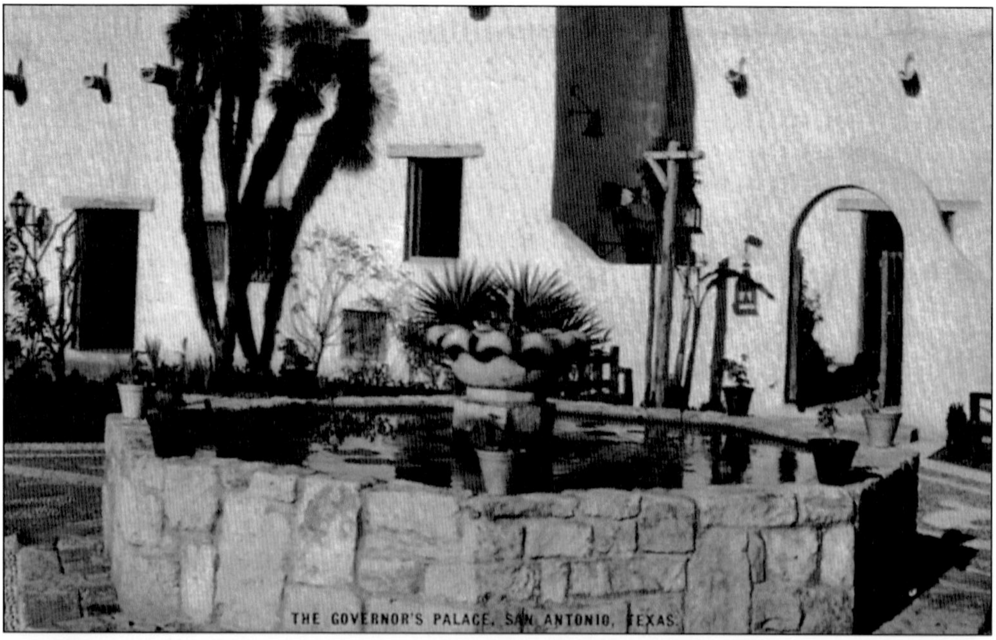

A military presence continued in Military Plaza through the early 19th century. After Texas gained its independence, the plaza became a stopping point for cowboys, rangers, and passersby who wanted to catch up with the latest local news. After the Civil War, it was the site of a busy outdoor market where the Chili Queens fed hungry locals and people passing through. (Author's collection.)

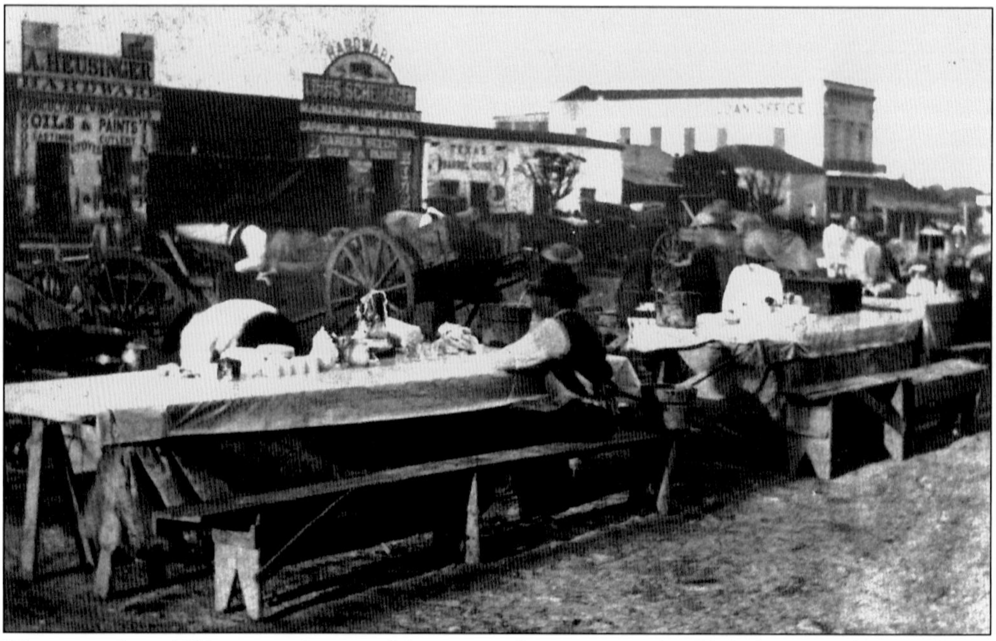

This scene from 1872 gives a glimpse of the seating for visitors at the Chili Queen stalls in Military Plaza. The Chili Queens were young Mexican women who served their customers at tables in the open-air market. The tables and lamps were set up at night and taken down before the market vendors arrived to set up their produce stands in the morning. (Courtesy of the San Antonio Conservation Society Foundation, Raba Collection.)

Aside from produce, the market vendors sold other goods residents needed for their daily lives. In this photograph of Military Plaza in 1879, hay for sale is evident. Other wagons are loaded with animal skins, earthenware, and other wares needed at home and on the range. It was customary to receive a *pilon* (a bonus, a little extra) after making a purchase. (Courtesy of the San Antonio Conservation Society Foundation, Raba Collection.)

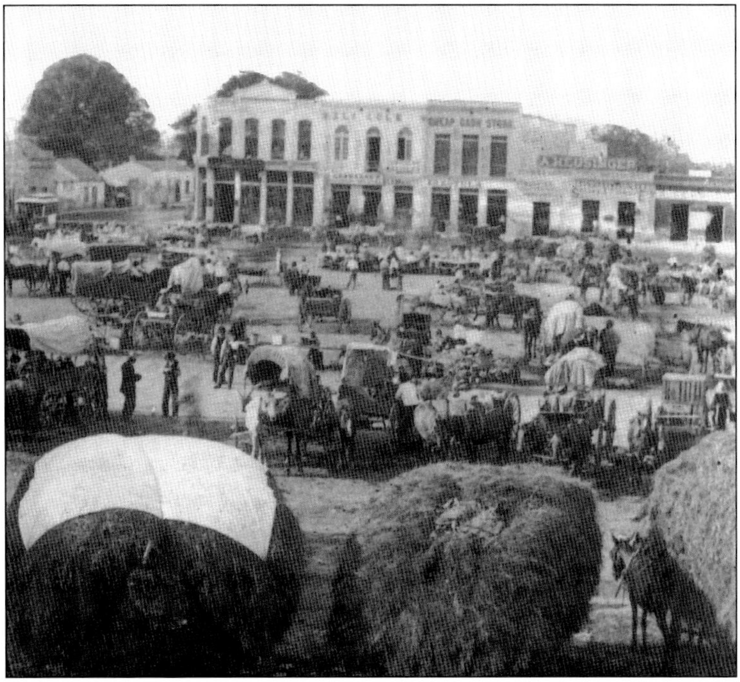

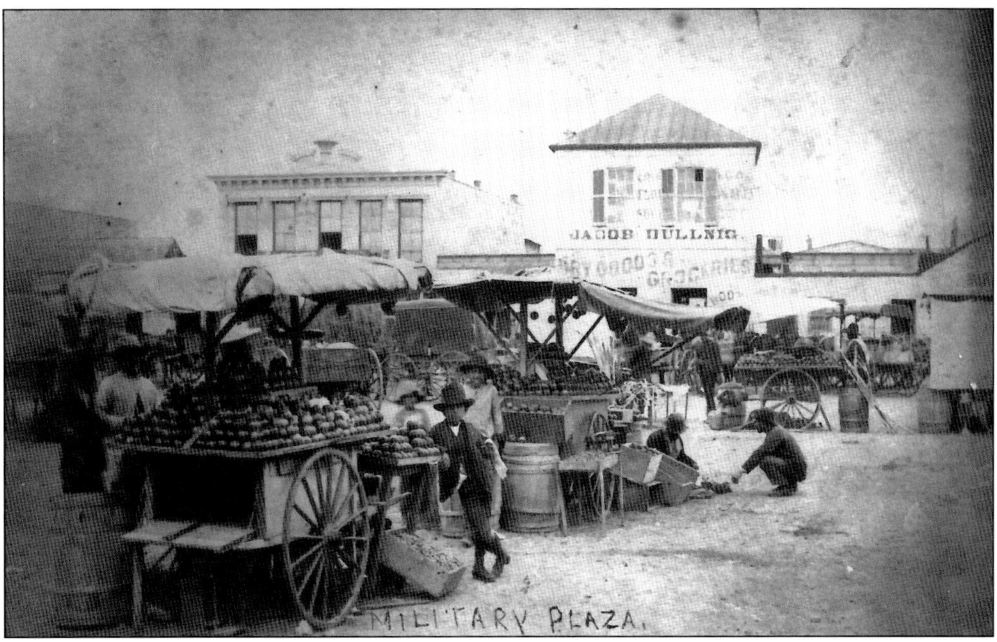

In 1883, most of the wagon vendors at Military Plaza were Mexican, but there were also Belgians, Germans, French, Italians, and a few Anglo-Americans. The peddlers started at dawn, and their customers came in shifts. First were the hotel caterers wanting the best food for their customers, then the boardinghouse cooks haggling for bargains, followed by the housewives. By 10:00 a.m., the market was over. (Courtesy of the San Antonio Conservation Society Foundation, Raba Collection.)

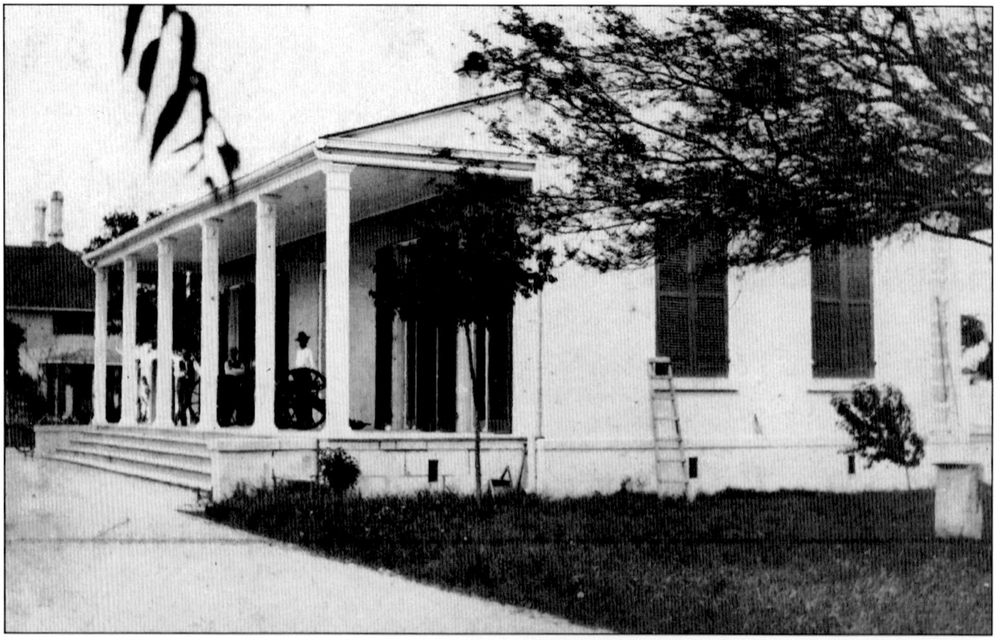

The San Antonio Arsenal was founded in 1859 and closed in 1949. This c. 1870s image shows the Administration Building for the arsenal. In 1982, H-E-B Grocery Company bought 10 acres of arsenal property for its corporate headquarters. In 1985, remodeling was completed and H-E-B moved in. Today, the former Arsenal Administration Building is the H-E-B visitor center. (Courtesy of UTSA Special Collections–ITC, negative 106-0387.)

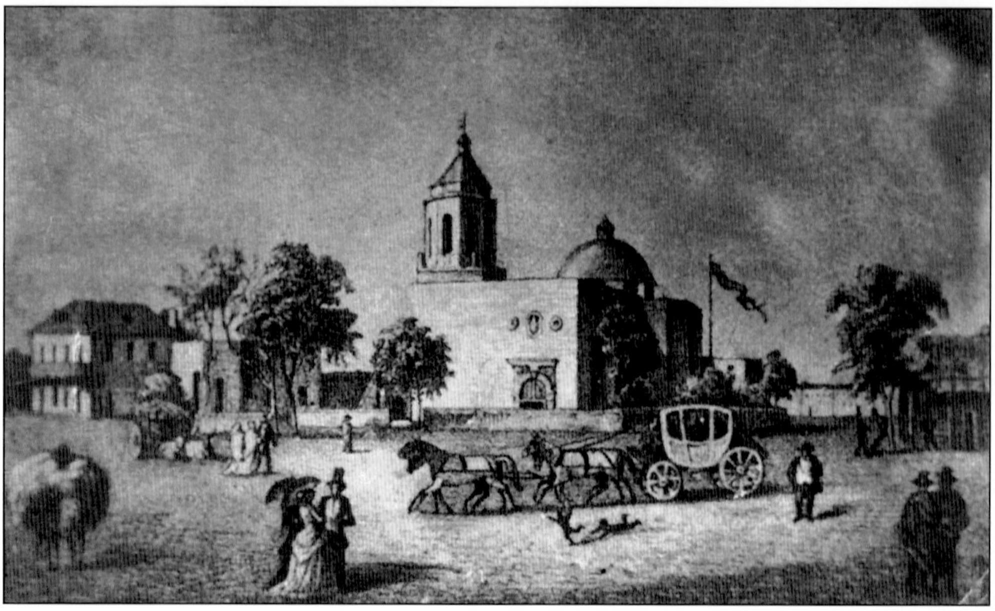

In 1731, Don Juan de Acuna, the 37th viceroy of New Spain, issued orders to establish Villa de San Fernando. Acuna provided maps and supplies for the settlers coming from the Canary Islands. His orders set land aside for the entertainment and use of the people in the form of squares, parks, and plazas. This illustration of Main Plaza is from 1854. (Courtesy of the San Antonio Conservation Society Foundation, Raba Collection.)

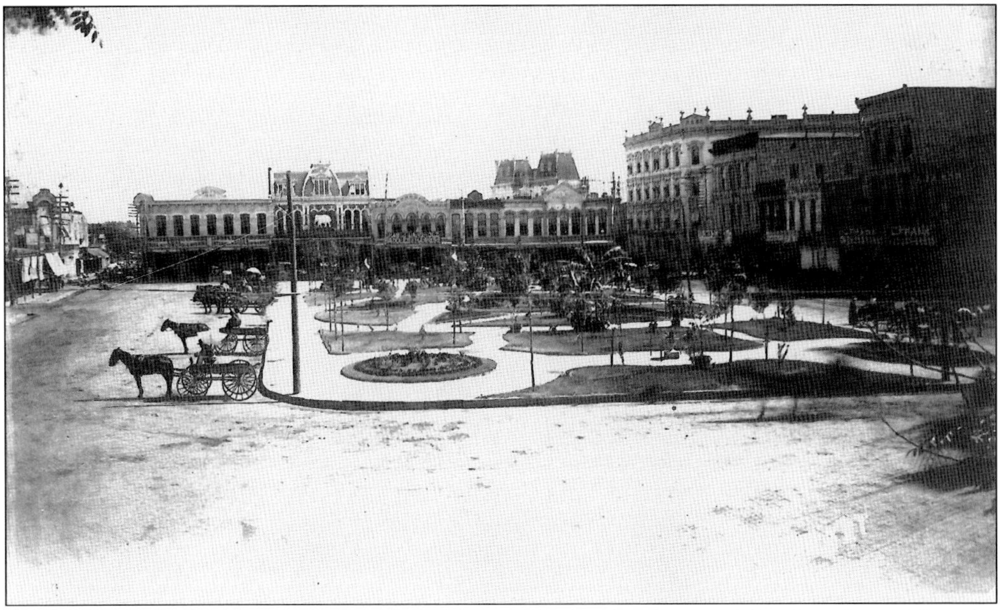

Main Plaza was originally named Plaza de Las Islas by the Canary Island settlers. After the independence of Texas, it became known as Main Plaza. Of the many industries and activities around the square, gambling was one of the most popular. This 1886 photograph shows the White Elephant Saloon and Gambling House, where it was rumored that entire ranches were lost to gambling. (Courtesy of the San Antonio Conservation Society Foundation, Raba Collection.)

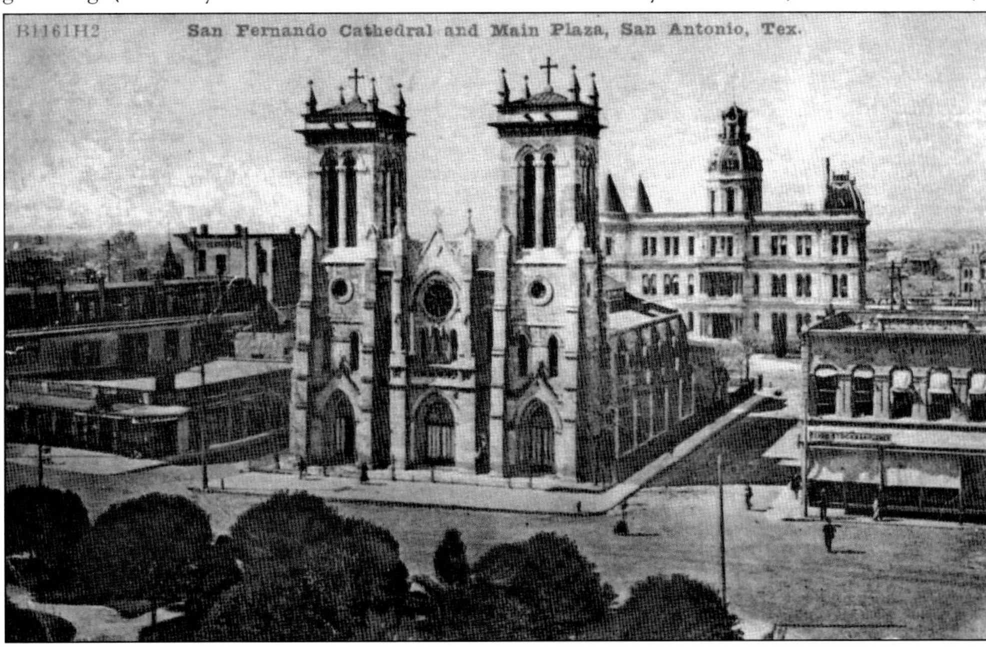

The building of San Fernando Church started in 1738; today, it is the oldest cathedral in Texas. King Philip V recruited 16 families, totaling 52 people, from the Canary Islands to settle the area for the colonization of New Spain. Surveyors laid out the town from the church and marked the square. Later, the streets were lined with government buildings, stores, and individual houses. (Author's collection.)

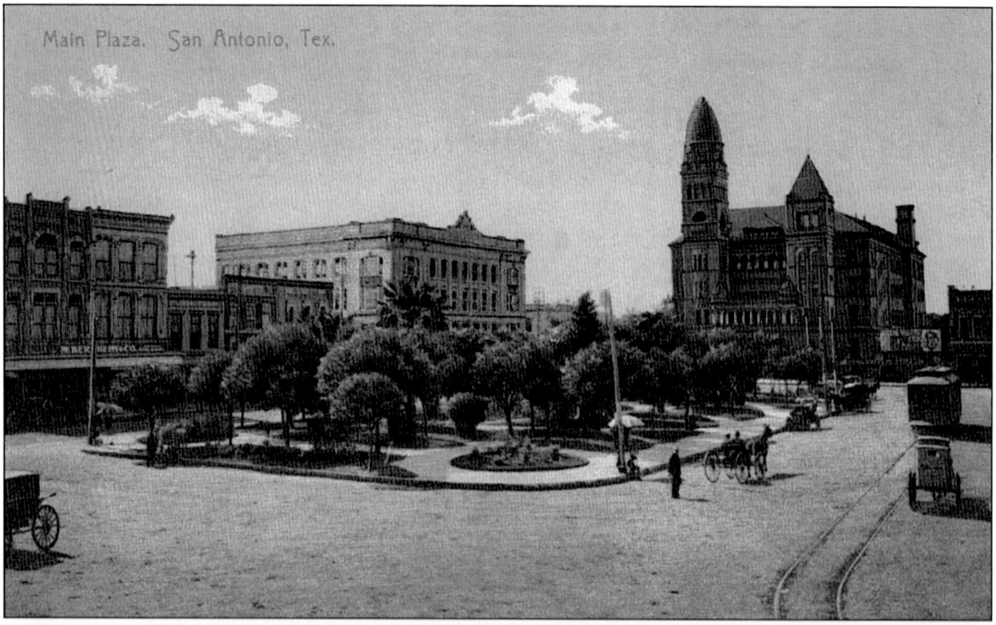

For over a century, the streets surrounding Main Plaza were dirt and grass. Eventually, they were improved with graded gravel, and by 1890, the streets were paved with mesquite blocks. Lighting also improved—from torchlights in the 1870s, to calcium lights in the 1880s, and electric streetlights in the 1890s. With the improvements, the square buzzed with activity day and night. (Author's collection.)

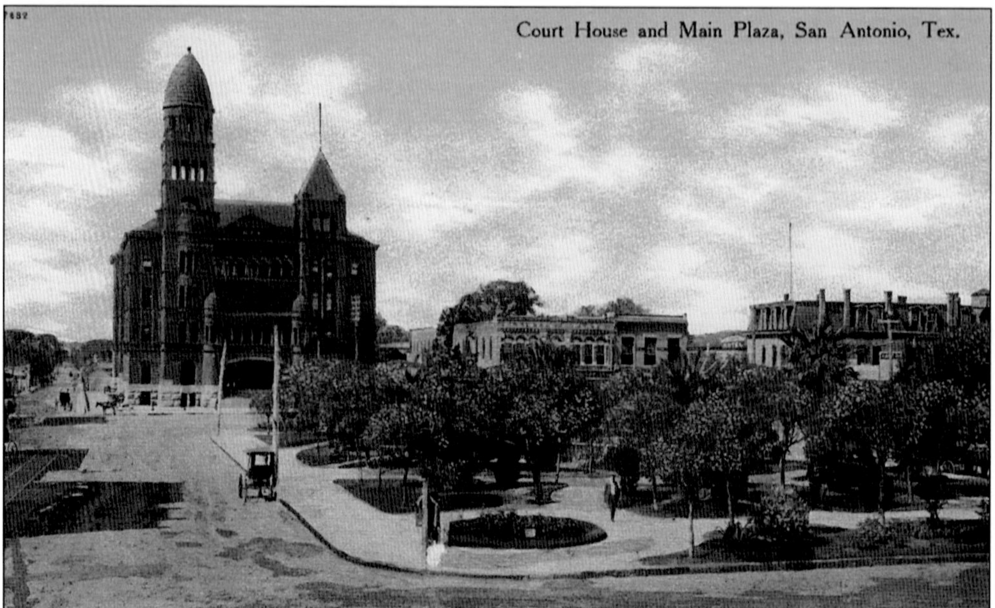

In 1892, the cornerstone for Bexar County Courthouse was laid in Main Plaza. The granite and red sandstone Romanesque Revival building was designed by James R. Gordon. Today, it is the oldest courthouse in continuous use in Texas. Since it was built, the courthouse has gone through four expansions, totaling 300,000 square feet. It is the largest courthouse in Texas. (Author's collection.)

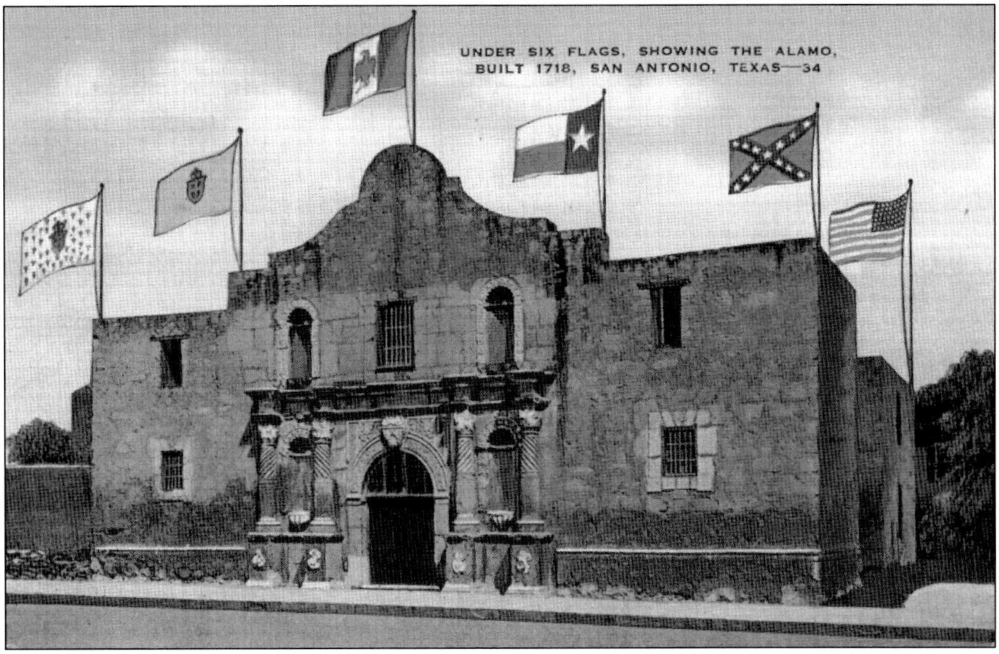

Part of the courtyard of Mission San Antonio de Valero, known today as the Alamo, later became Alamo Plaza. In 1836, from February 23 to March 6, it was the site of the Battle of the Alamo, where Texans fought against Mexican soldiers led by Gen. Santa Anna. In 2015, the Alamo became part of San Antonio Missions UNESCO World Heritage Site. (Author's collection.)

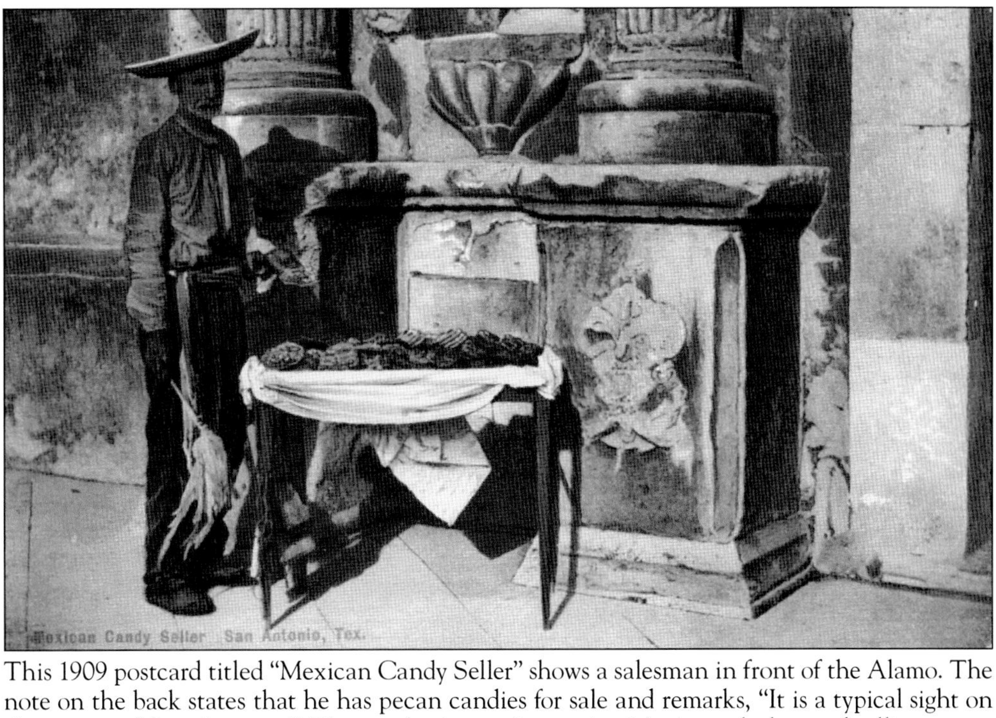

This 1909 postcard titled "Mexican Candy Seller" shows a salesman in front of the Alamo. The note on the back states that he has pecan candies for sale and remarks, "It is a typical sight on the streets of San Antonio." The vendor is wearing native Mexican clothes and selling pecan pralines, like the ones sold in Mexico. (Author's collection.)

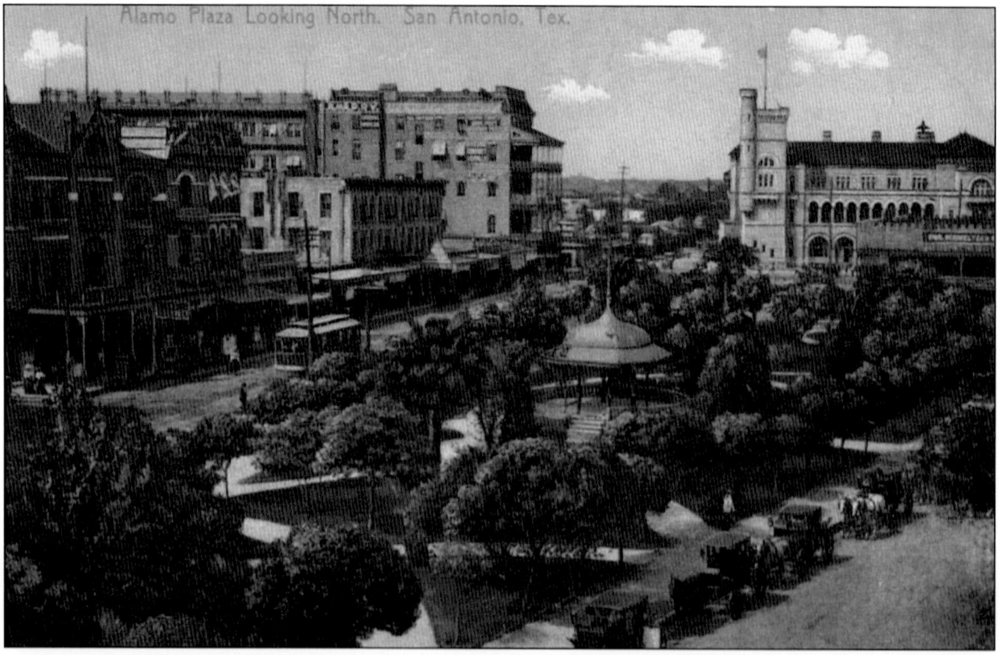

In this early 1900s postcard, Alamo Plaza is surrounded by buildings from the late 1800s and early 1900s. Facing the plaza is the post office and opera house; the Alamo and the Menger Hotel are not visible. This commercial area in the center of downtown began before the Civil War and boomed in the late 1800s. Today, it is still buzzing with business activity. (Author's collection.)

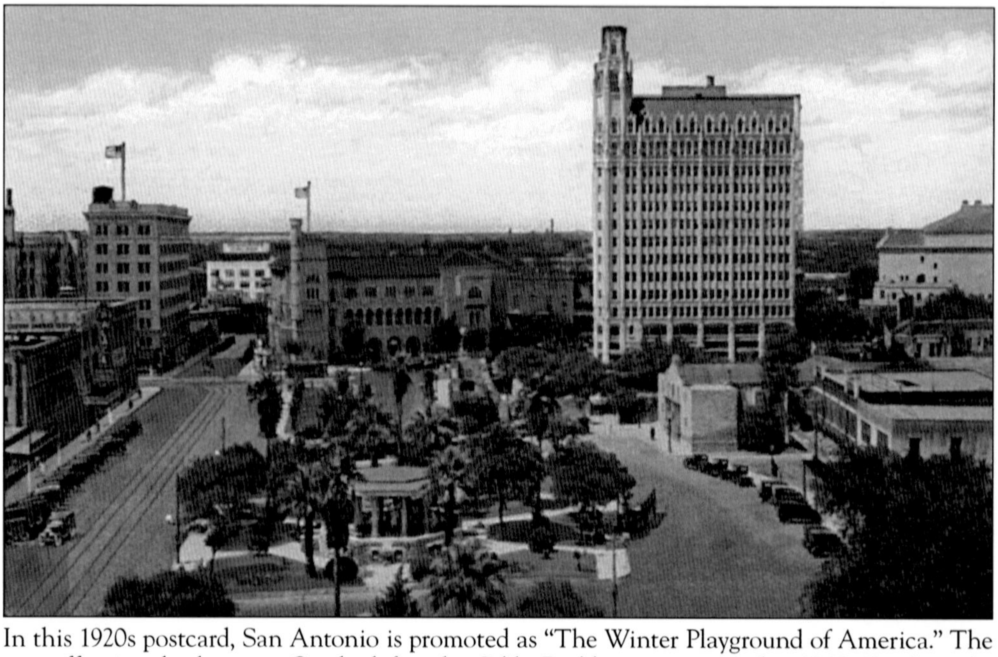

In this 1920s postcard, San Antonio is promoted as "The Winter Playground of America." The post office is at back center. On the left is the Gibbs Building, constructed in 1909. On the right is the Medical Arts Building, completed in 1926. Today, the Gibbs Building is the Indigo Hotel, and the medical building is the Emily Morgan Hotel. Both hotels are rumored to be haunted. (Author's collection.)

Two

Municipal Market House

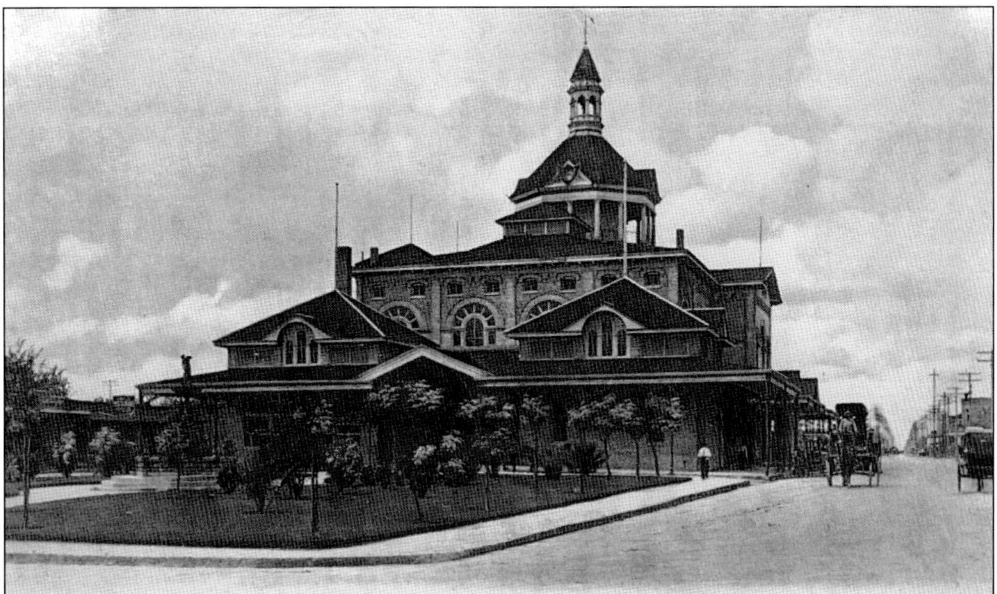

With the construction of the Municipal Market House, the surrounding area became a center for commerce. The Municipal Market House was designed by Alfred Giles in 1899 and completed in 1900 at a cost of $55,000. A notice to contractors that ran in the May 7, 1899, *Sunday Light Newspaper* asked for bids to construct the market house and convention center in Paschal Plaza. (Author's collection.)

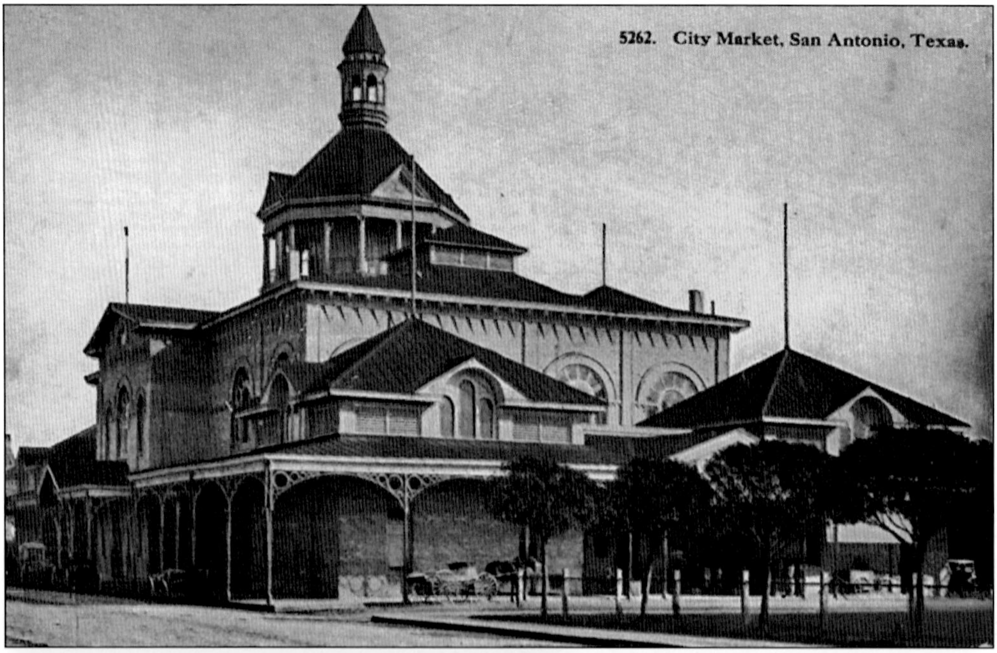

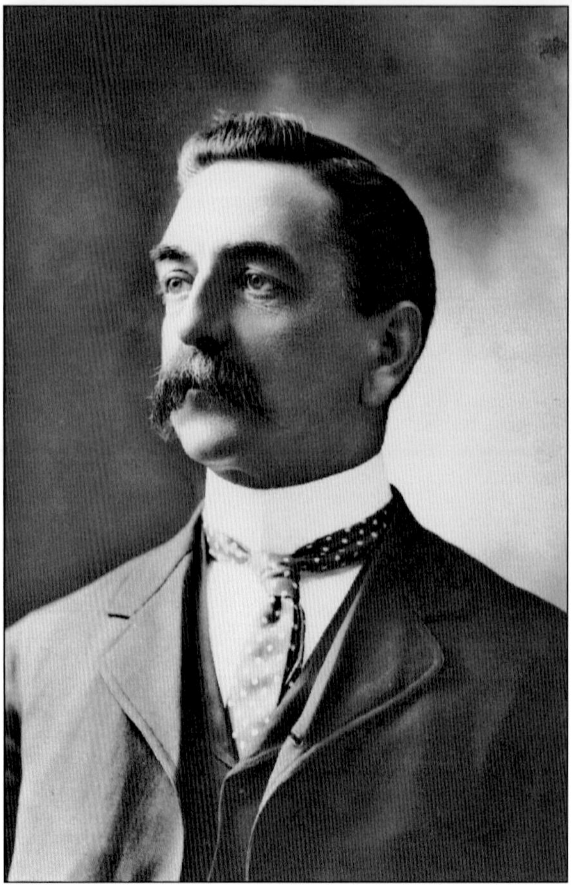

The first floor of City Market was designed to house the produce market. On the second floor, the convention hall could seat 4,000 people. On May 15, 1899, city council decreed, "100 feet off of west end of Paschal Square next to and adjoining S. Pecos Street set aside as a stand for all wagons, carts and other vehicles offering any produce for sale." (Author's collection.)

Alfred Giles, architect of City Market, was born in England in 1853. He received his architectural training in London and immigrated to America in 1873. He arrived in San Antonio in 1874 and went to work for John H. Kampmann, a successful local contractor. In 1876, Giles established his own firm. By 1900, he had designed 40 structures centrally located in the city. (Courtesy of UTSA Special Collection–ITC, negative 071-0549.)

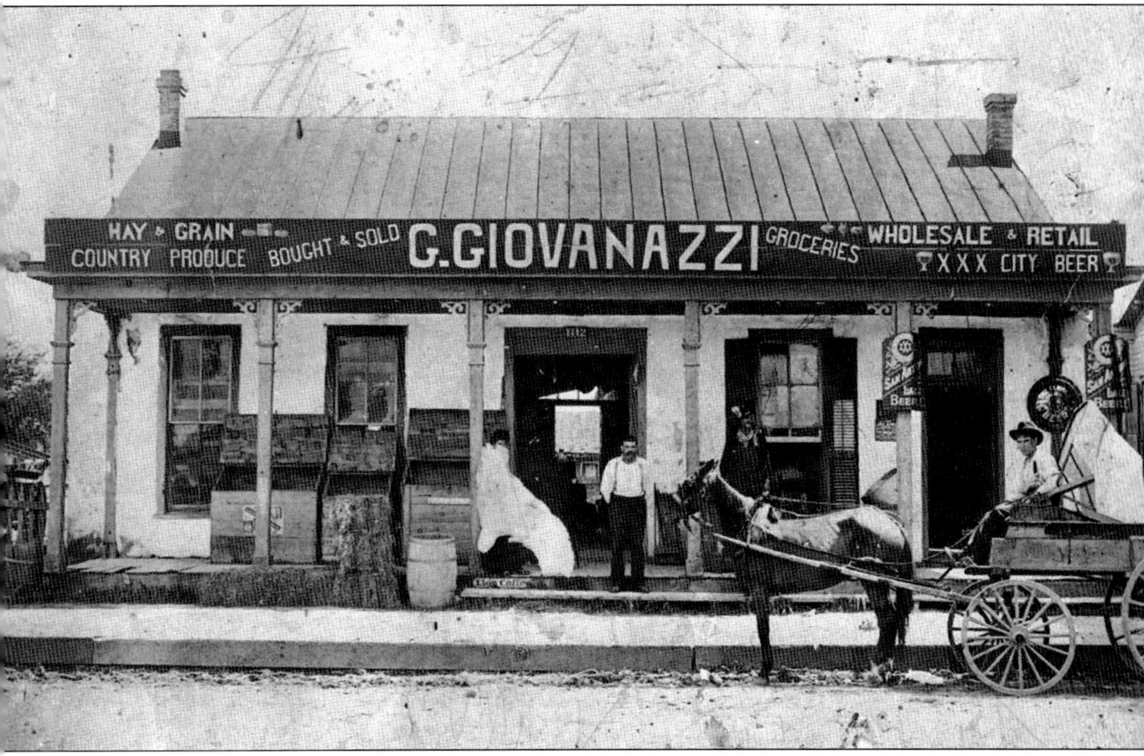

This photograph of the Giovanazzi grocery store's new location in Hay Market Plaza at 1112 West Commerce Street was taken in 1905 or 1906. Giovanni Giovanazzi is standing on the steps at the entrance. In the 1900 census records, Giovanazzi was listed as a naturalized citizen who came to America from Hungary in 1881, at the age of 19. His occupation was listed as a grocer residing at 1025 South Pecos Street with his wife, Louise; his daughters F., A., and Mary; and sons Joe and John (Giovanni Jr.). In the 1901 city directory, Giovanazzi's is listed as a grocery and saloon at 1025 South Laredo Street. By the late 1920s, Giovanazzi's was gone, and its address no longer listed in the city directory. The entire block of 1100 West Commerce Street was listed as Market Square. (Courtesy of UTSA Special Collection–ITC, photograph 98-285.)

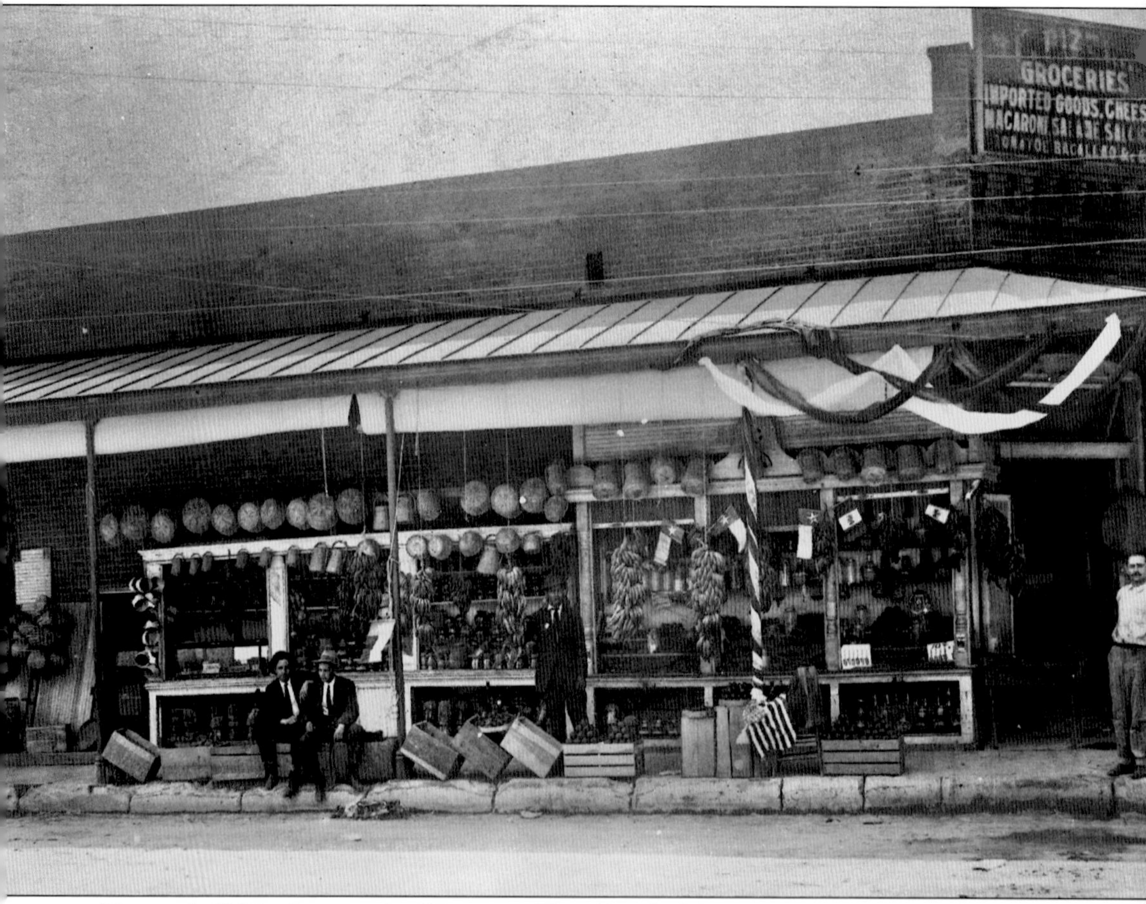

This early 1900s photograph of Francisco "Don Poncho" Pizzini's grocery store at the southwest corner of Produce Row and Concho Street proudly displays the Texas and Mexico flags. An Italian, Pizzini had lived in Mexico for 14 years before making his way to San Antonio in the early 1870s. He worked for an Italian merchant before opening his own store in 1891. In the late 1920s, Frank Pizzini was listed at 202–204 Produce Row. In the 1948 city directory, Pizzini was listed as a grocer at 202 Produce Row. Jamaica 1 (restaurant), Jamaica 2 (tortillas), and Jamaica 3 (restaurant) were listed at 204 Produce Row, and Jamaica 5 (restaurant) was listed at 204 ½ Produce Row. In October 1974, Pizzini Mexican Products was listed in *Texas Monthly Magazine* at 202 Produce Row. The magazine mentioned that Pizzini's had an assortment of hundreds of herbs and teas and stated, "Go armed with an herb book to find out exactly what to buy." (Courtesy of UTSA Special Collection–ITC, photograph 88-117.)

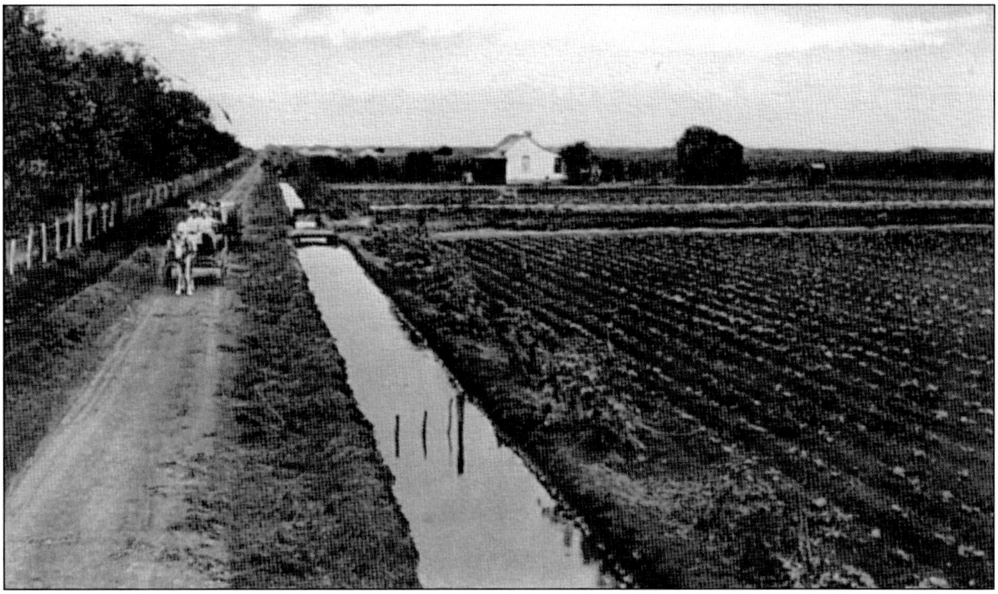

Belgians who came to San Antonio from the 1860s to the 1920s contributed to the area's fresh produce markets. They are credited with improving irrigation and introducing new crops to area farmers. One of the new crops was cauliflower. Fresh produce was sold in the market areas for decades. After urban renewal in the 1970s, there was less and less produce offered in the Farmers Market. (Author's collection.)

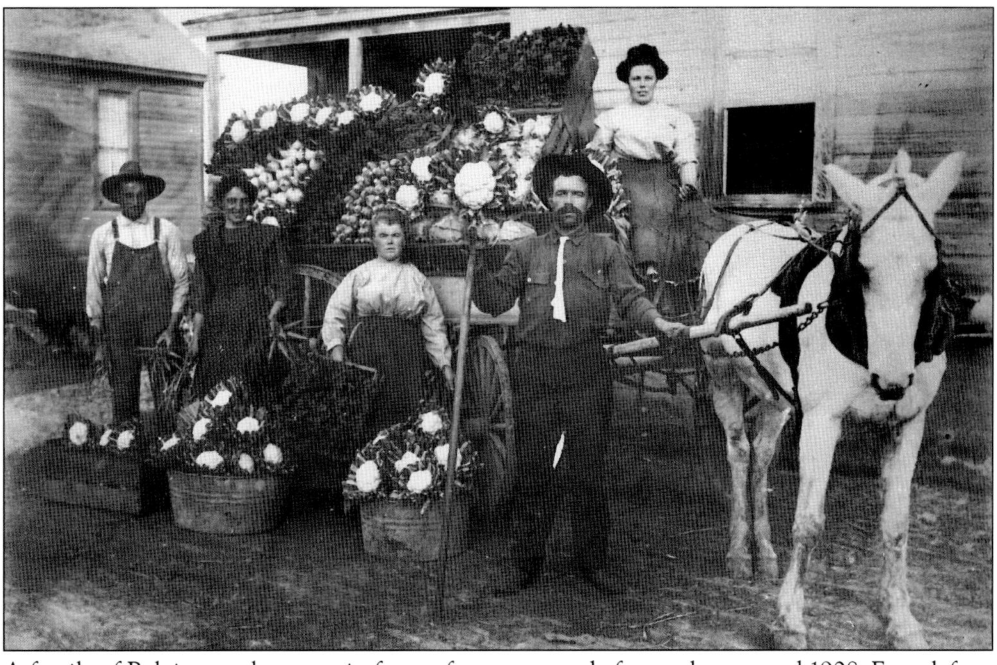

A family of Belgian settlers pose in front of a wagon ready for market around 1908. From left to right are Emma and Prosper Vervaet, Delphina Bauwens (Aviel's mother), and Mary and Aviel Bauwens. Aviel Bauwens and Prosper Vervaet were brothers-in-law. Aviel's wife, Mary, was Prosper's sister. Aviel and Prosper were both gardeners at Steves Gardens on South Flores Street. (Courtesy of UTSA Special Collection–ITC, negative 68-3183.)

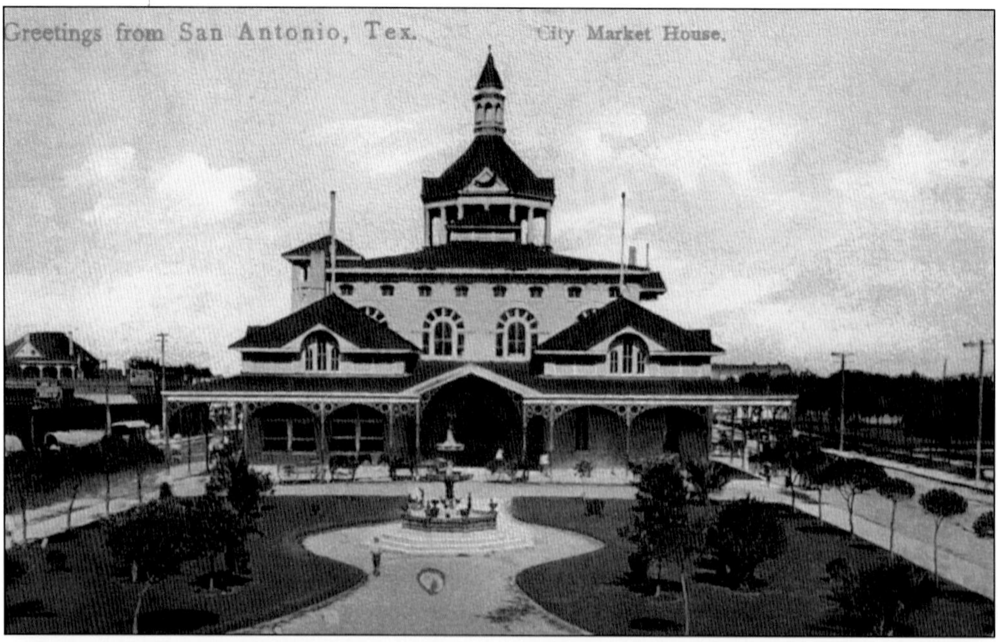

In 1910, this postcard printed for the Joske Brothers Company was mailed to Elgin, Illinois. At this time, City Market House was buzzing with the activity of many different ethnic groups, including Chinese immigrants. The market was a place where they were welcomed and found work, later establishing their own businesses. Many had come to San Antonio in the 1880s to work on the Southern Pacific Railroad. (Author's collection.)

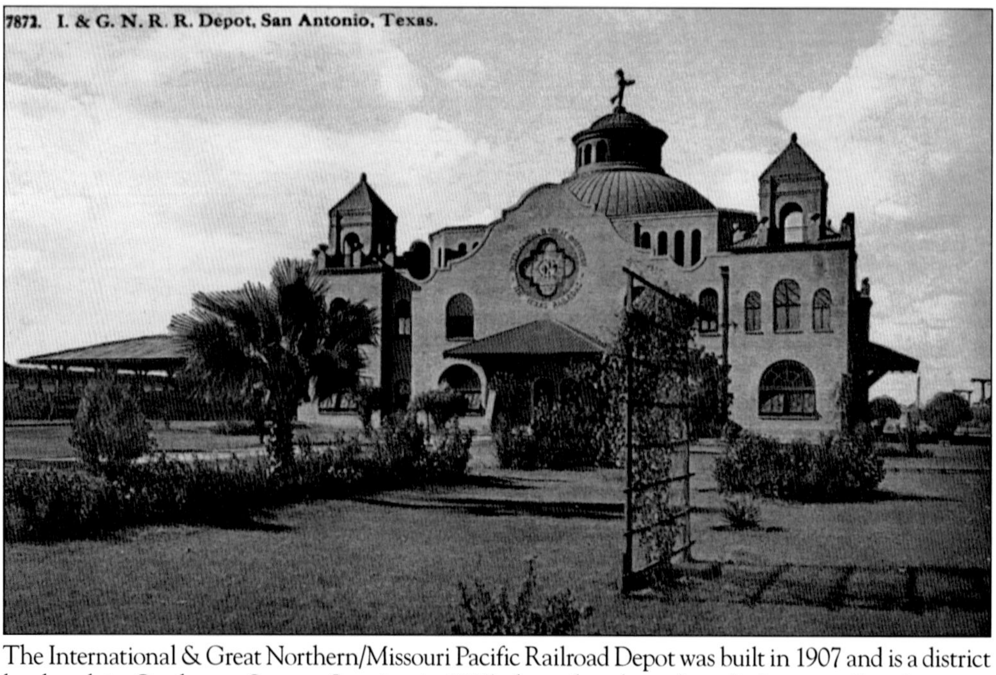

The International & Great Northern/Missouri Pacific Railroad Depot was built in 1907 and is a district landmark in Cattleman Square. Starting in 1885, the railroad ran from St. Louis to San Antonio, shipping cattle from the city stockyards to the Midwest. The former I&GN Hotel constructed in 1909 is across the street; the hotel later became the Heimann Building. (Author's collection.)

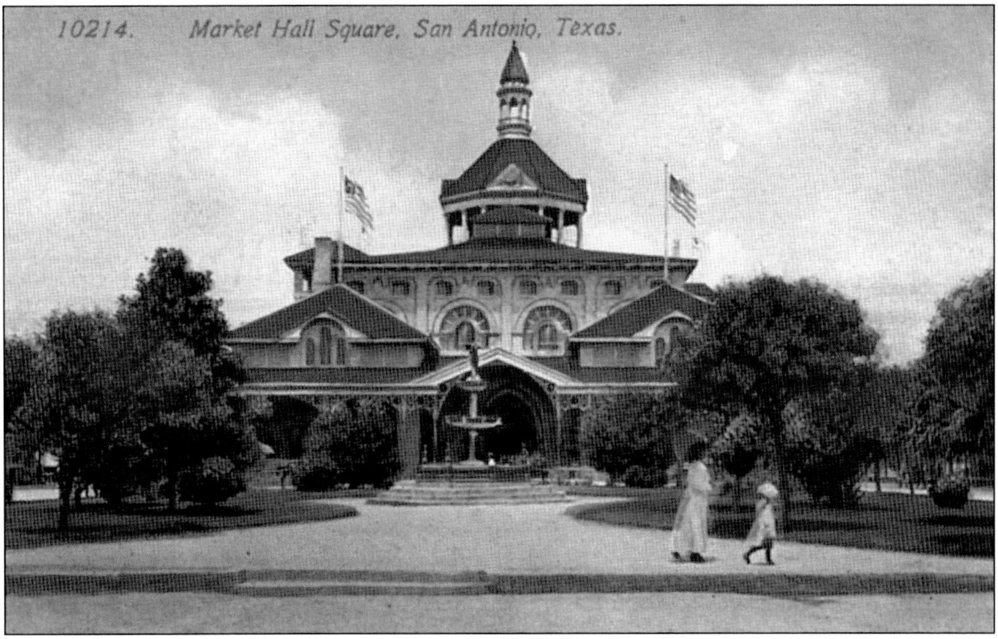

In 1915, this card was printed for S.H. Kress & Company, a five-and-dime department store, and mailed to Los Angeles, California. Each time a new postcard was printed, the City Market House was called by a different name; this time it was listed as Market Hall Square. Other names used were City Market and Municipal Market House. (Author's collection.)

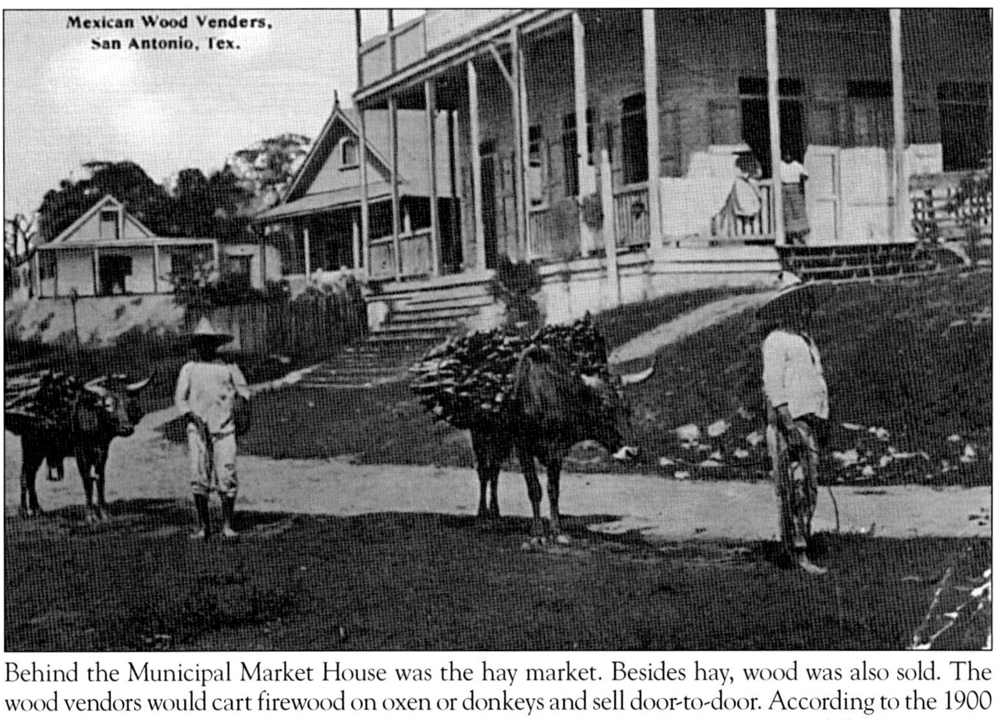

Behind the Municipal Market House was the hay market. Besides hay, wood was also sold. The wood vendors would cart firewood on oxen or donkeys and sell door-to-door. According to the 1900 census, San Antonio was the fastest growing city in Texas. It is hard to imagine city folks viewing San Antonio as progressive when this card was mailed to New York in 1916. (Author's collection.)

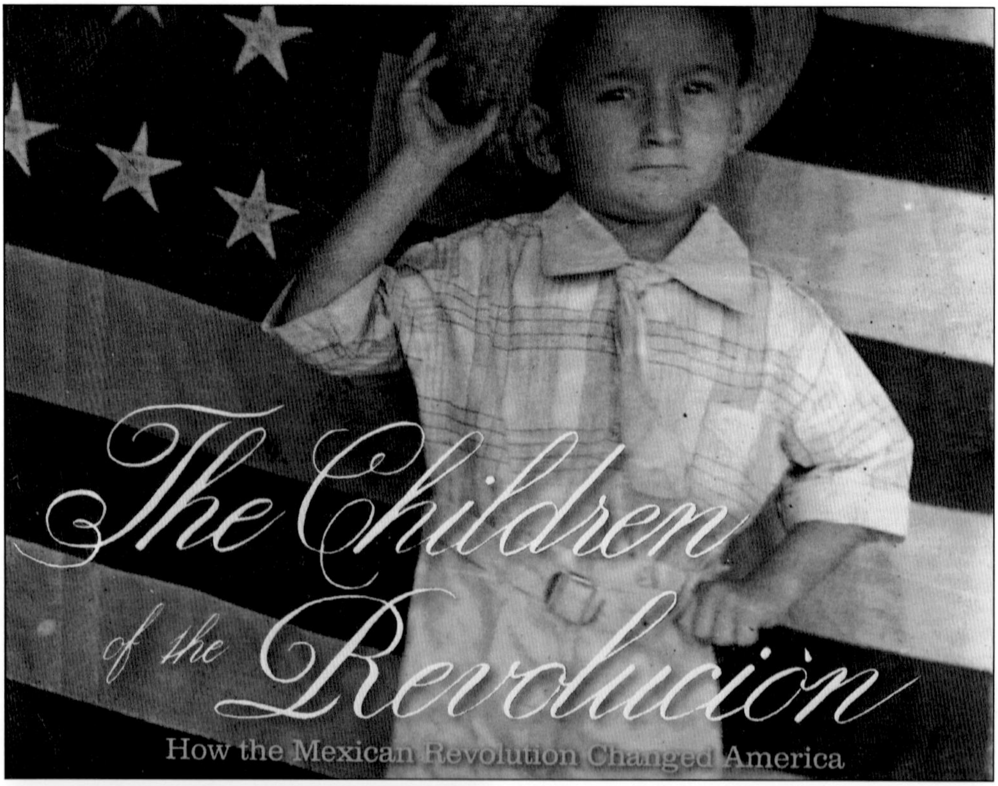

During the Mexican Revolution (1910–1920), close to one million people fled Mexico. These families seized opportunities in the United States and went to work creating better lives. The book *The Children of the Revolución*, edited by Lionel Sosa with historical narrative by Neftalí García, tells the story of this Mexican migration to America. There is also a 20-part documentary series at www.childrenoftherevolucion.org. (Courtesy of Lionel Sosa.)

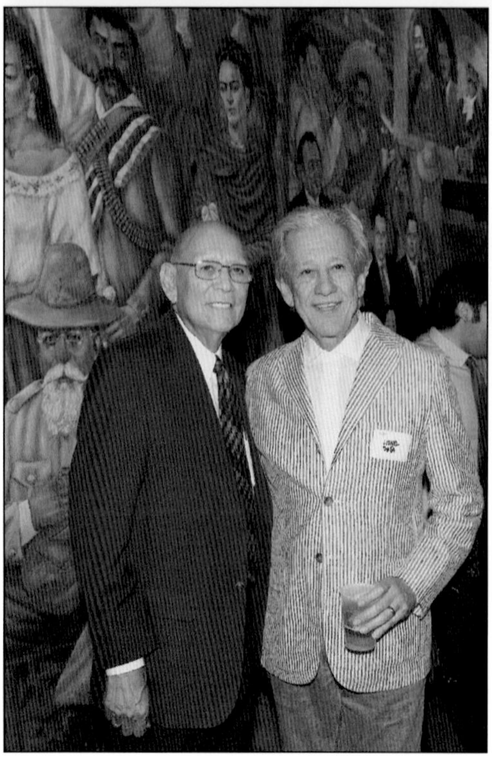

Lionel Sosa, marketing executive and political consultant, and Tino Duran, founder and publisher of *La Prensa* bilingual newspaper, stand in front of a mural at Mi Tierra Café & Bakery. Sosa and Duran, along with the Cortez family, owners of La Familia Cortez Restaurants, are leaders in the community and advocates in preserving Mexican American culture and traditions. (Photograph by Al Rendon; courtesy of La Familia Cortez Restaurants.)

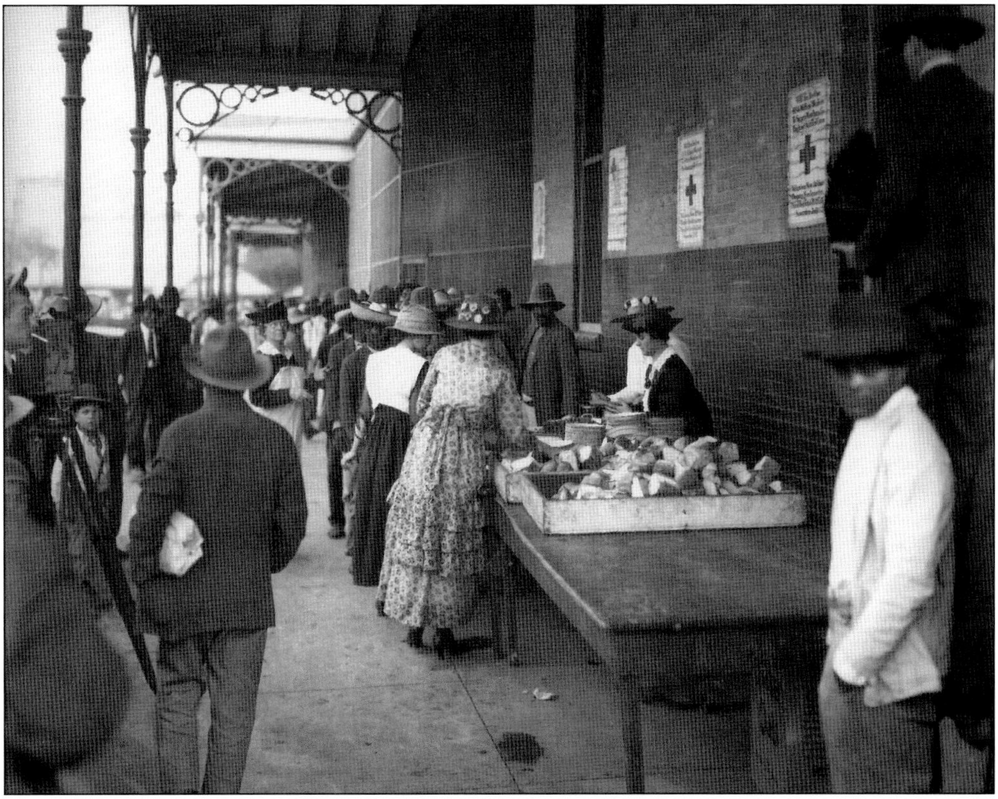

Many Mexicans came to San Antonio to escape the violence and political unrest during the Mexican Revolution. Since San Antonio is 859 miles from Mexico City and 156 miles from the Mexican border town of Laredo, Texas, the city was a destination for refugees. In this photograph of Market Square, volunteers are distributing food to refugees. (Courtesy of UTSA Special Collections–ITC, negative 101-0711.)

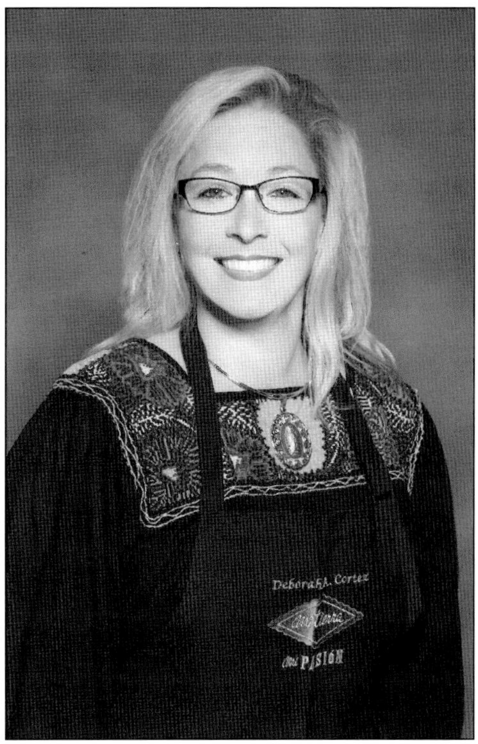

Deborah Cortez and other members of the Cortez family tell their story in the documentary series *The Children of the Revolución, A Commitment to Mi Tierra*, which can be found online. The Cortez family, owners of three restaurants in Market Square and another in close proximity, was instrumental in saving Market Square from destruction during the urban renewal movement in the 1960s and early 1970s. (Photograph by Al Rendon; courtesy of La Familia Cortez Restaurants.)

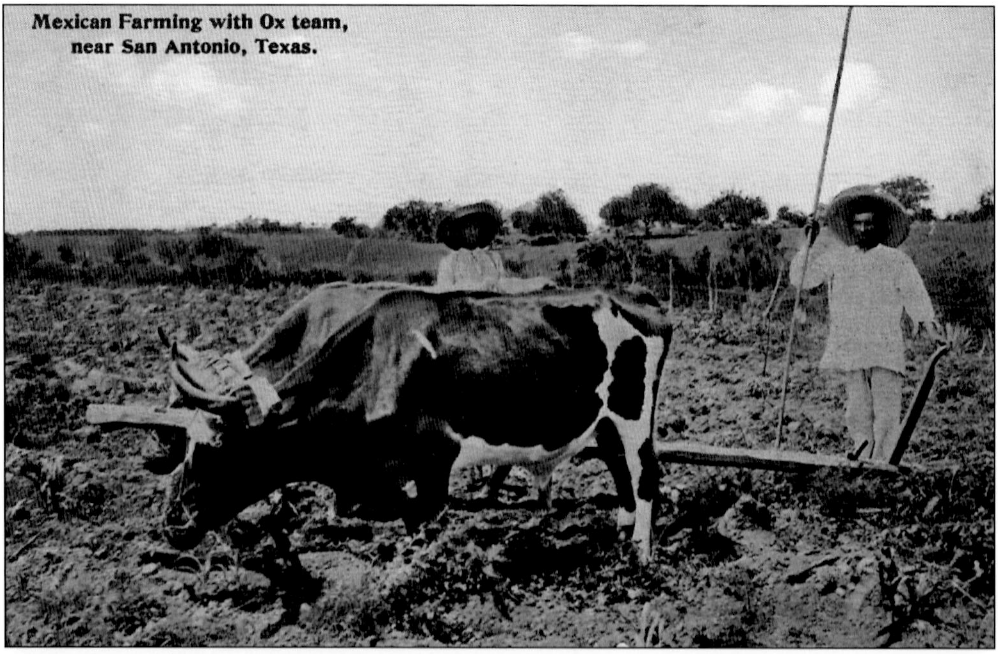

While some of the Mexican refugees found work in the city, others labored in farms surrounding San Antonio. From the early days of settlement in Bexar County to World War II, agriculture drove the economy, providing food for farmers, ranchers, and city dwellers. This early 1900s postcard shows men plowing a field wearing traditional work garments and hats. (Author's collection.)

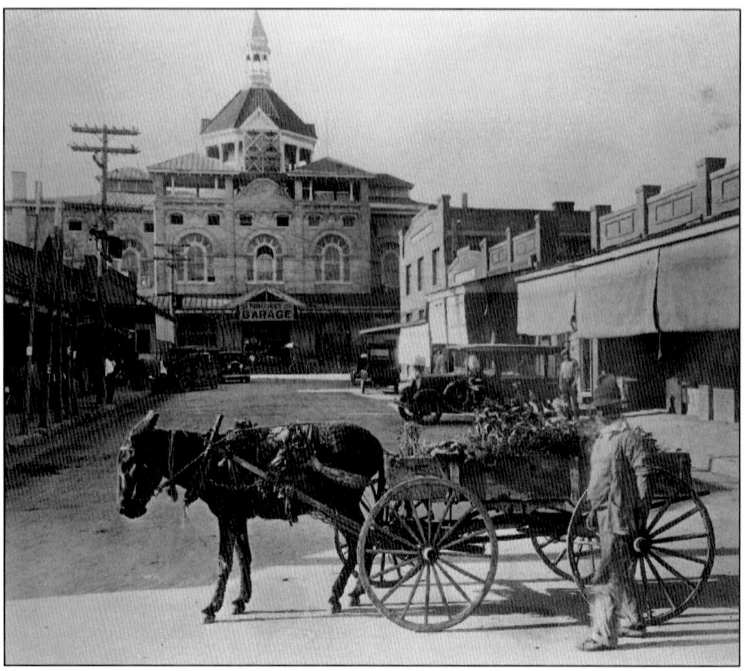

Wagons filled with produce left the farms at dawn to arrive in time for their earliest customers, the hotel cooks. In this c. 1920s photograph of Market House, City Market is visible looking north on South Concho Street from Buena Vista Street. In 1924, the market was open until 10:00 p.m. on Saturdays. No business was allowed after 9:00 a.m. on Sundays. (Courtesy of UTSA Special Collections–ITC, photograph 89-24.)

Around 1925, there was a Pony Express riders reunion on the grounds of the Municipal Market House. These riders, men and boys, were hired at $50 a month to deliver mail on horseback. The Pony Express was short-lived, operating from April 1860 to October 1861. The most famous Pony Express rider was Buffalo Bill. (Courtesy of the San Antonio Conservation Society Foundation; Raba Collection.)

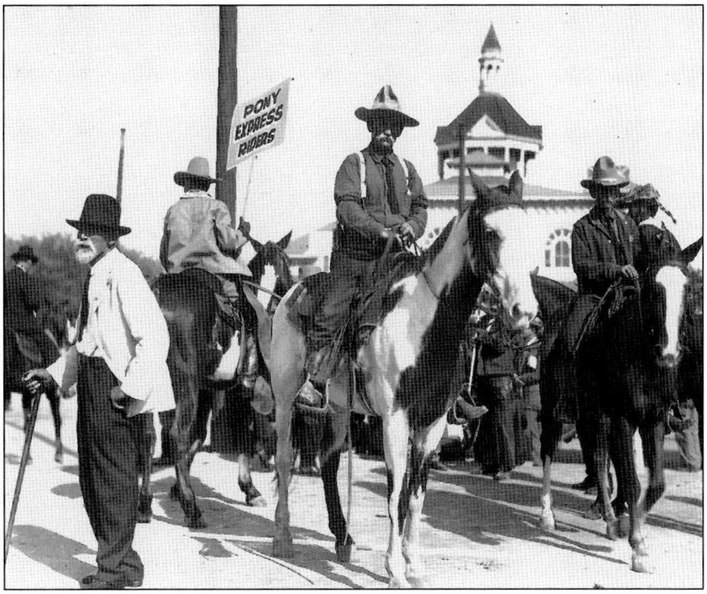

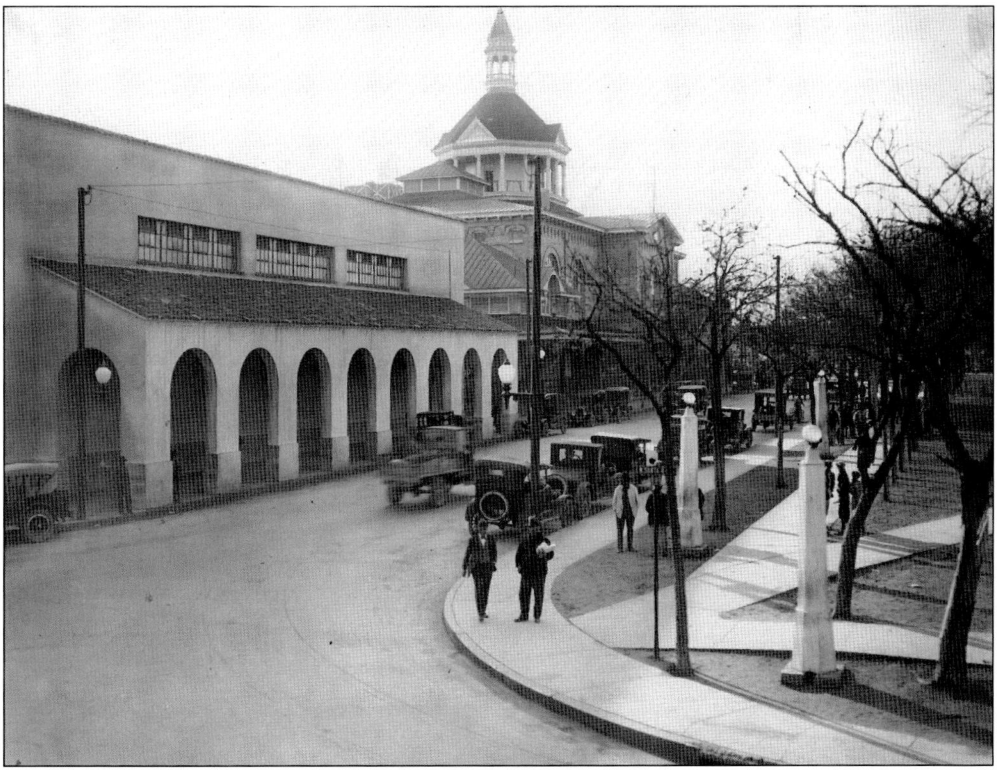

Across Commerce Street from the market, to the right, is Milam Square. In the 1927 San Antonio City Directory, Municipal Market House Annex (the building with the arches) was listed at South Santa Rosa Avenue and the southwest corner of West Commerce Street. The large building, City Market, was listed at West Commerce Street and the corner of Paschal Square, formerly known as Presidio Square. (Courtesy of Texana Division, San Antonio Public Libraries, Photograph Collection.)

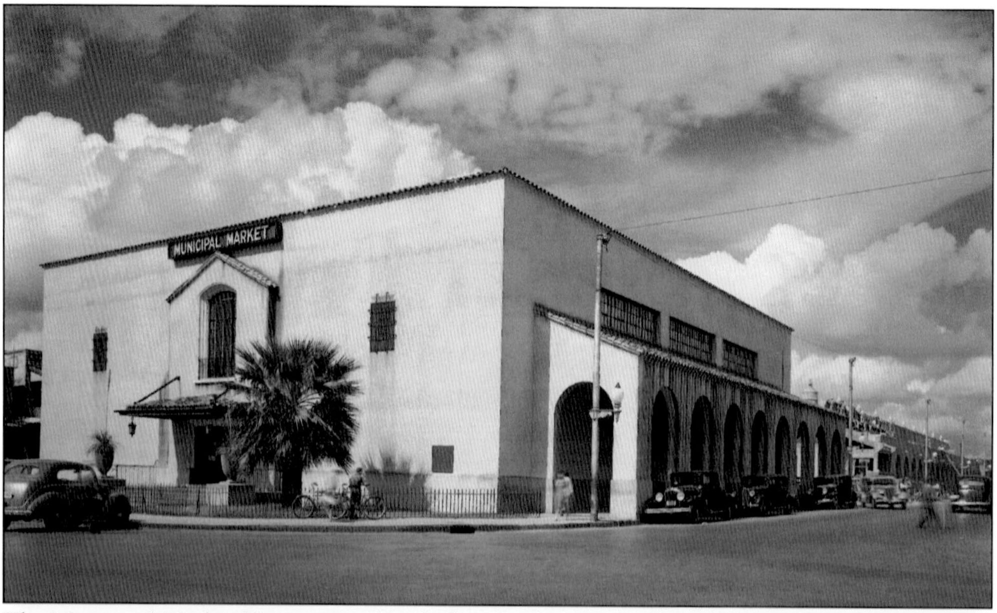

The Municipal Market House started to decline in the 1920s and was demolished in 1938. In this photograph from the early 1930s of the building designated as Municipal Market, the structure directly behind it was the annex to the market, constructed in the 1920s. The cupola of the old Municipal Market House is barely visible between the two buildings. (Courtesy of UTSA Special Collections–ITC, photograph Z-2128-A-01.)

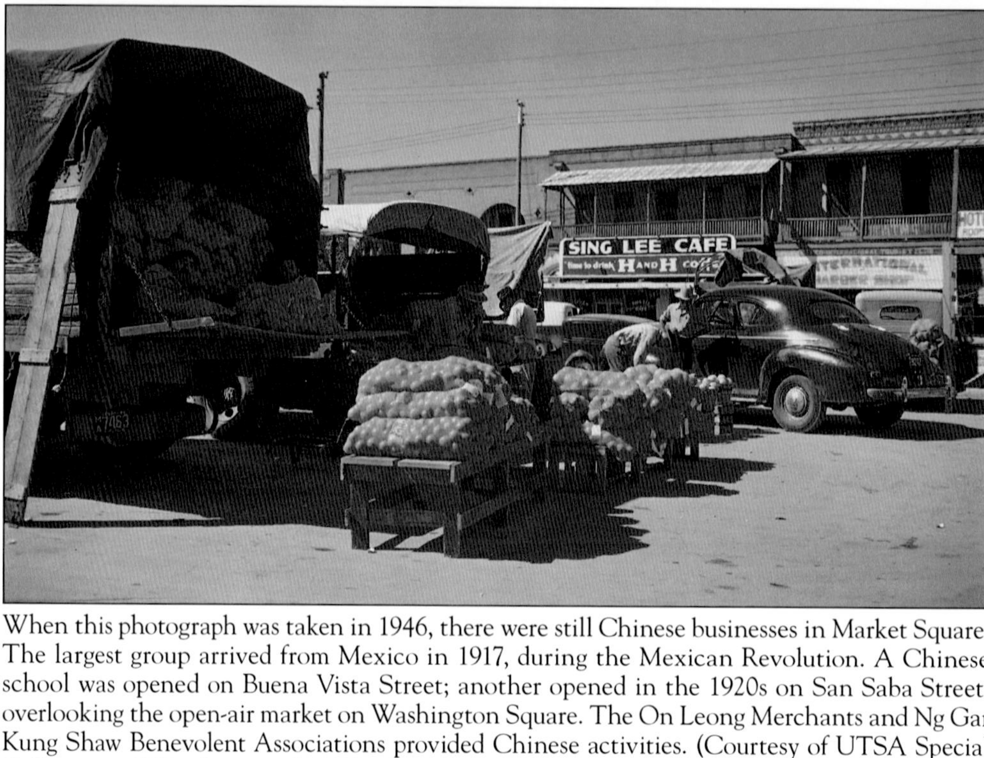

When this photograph was taken in 1946, there were still Chinese businesses in Market Square. The largest group arrived from Mexico in 1917, during the Mexican Revolution. A Chinese school was opened on Buena Vista Street; another opened in the 1920s on San Saba Street, overlooking the open-air market on Washington Square. The On Leong Merchants and Ng Gar Kung Shaw Benevolent Associations provided Chinese activities. (Courtesy of UTSA Special Collections–ITC, photograph MS389.)

Three

Market House Vicinity

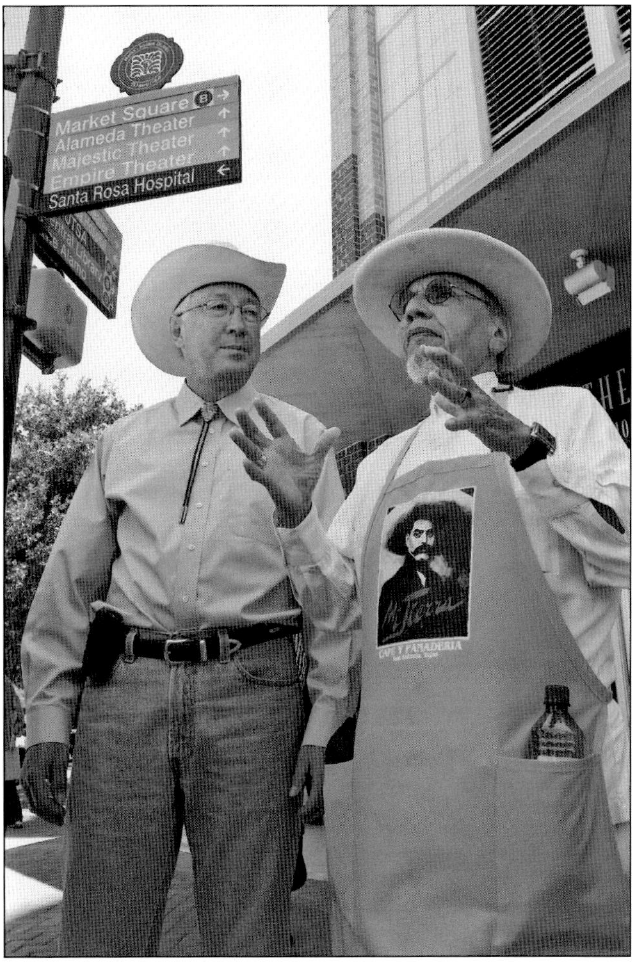

The area surrounding Market Square is filled with history. In this photograph, Jorge Cortez (right), of La Familia Cortez Restaurants, is discussing the decades of change in the vicinity of Market Square with Ken Salazar, the 50th US secretary of the interior. The sign above their heads points to other historical downtown locations and Santa Rosa Hospital across the street. (Photograph by Al Rendon; courtesy of La Familia Cortez Restaurants.)

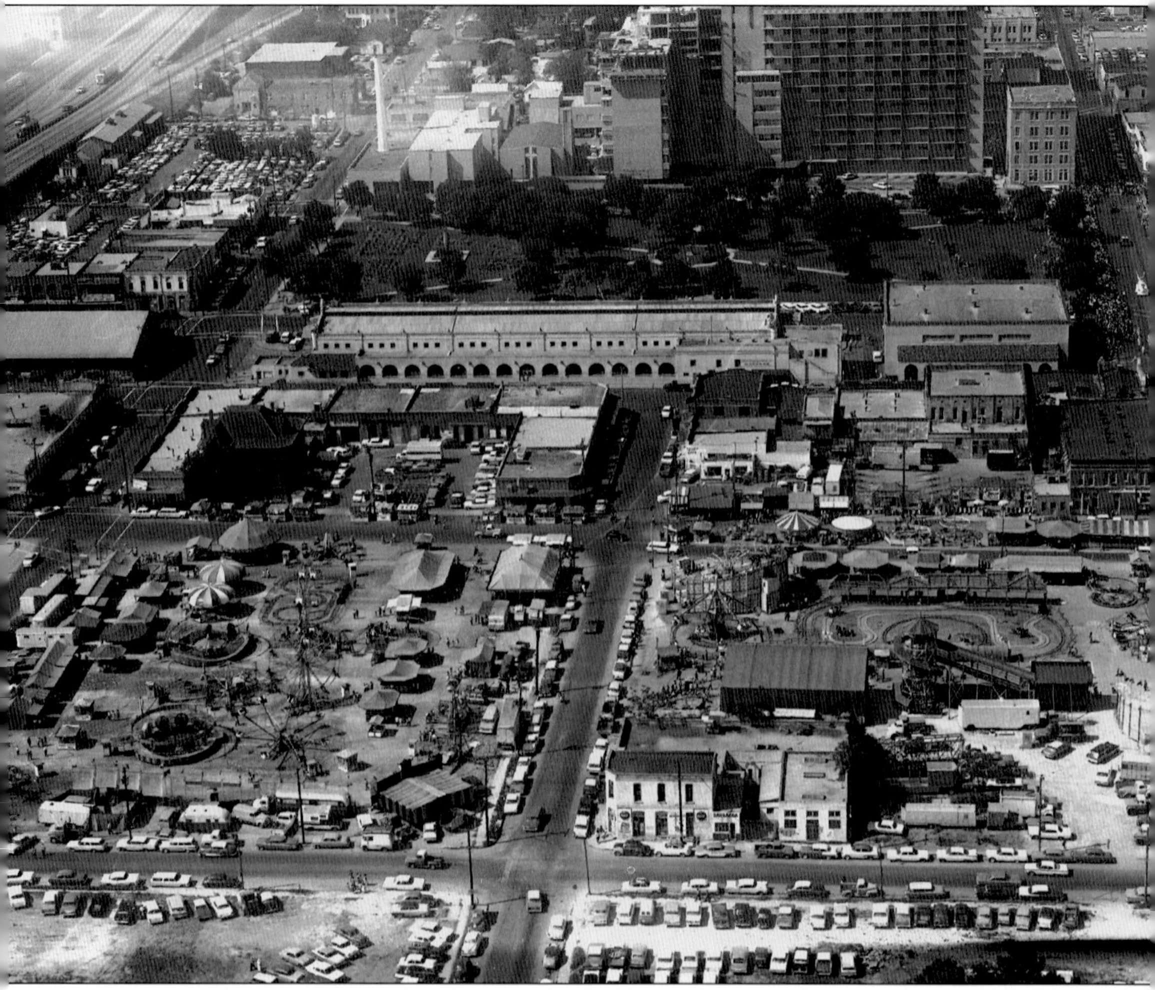

It is carnival time in Washington Square. This late 1950s photograph gives a glimpse of the block across the street from Market Square. The streets surrounding Washington Square were South San Saba, Monterey, South Concho, and Buena Vista Streets. In 1940, Lillie May Hagner described the square as an open-air market. Fruits and vegetables for sale came from local farmers, other states, and Mexico. The maguey plant, used in making tequila, could also be found here. The Municipal Market House, now El Mercado, is the building with arches. Directly to the left of the market building and across San Saba Street was the hay market. Currently, it is the Farmers Market Plaza. Today, the only reminder of Washington Square is a sign at 800 Dolorosa Street, the Washington Square Office Building. La Familia Cortez Restaurants corporate offices are in this building. (Courtesy of UTSA Special Collections–ITC; photograph B-21-A-01.)

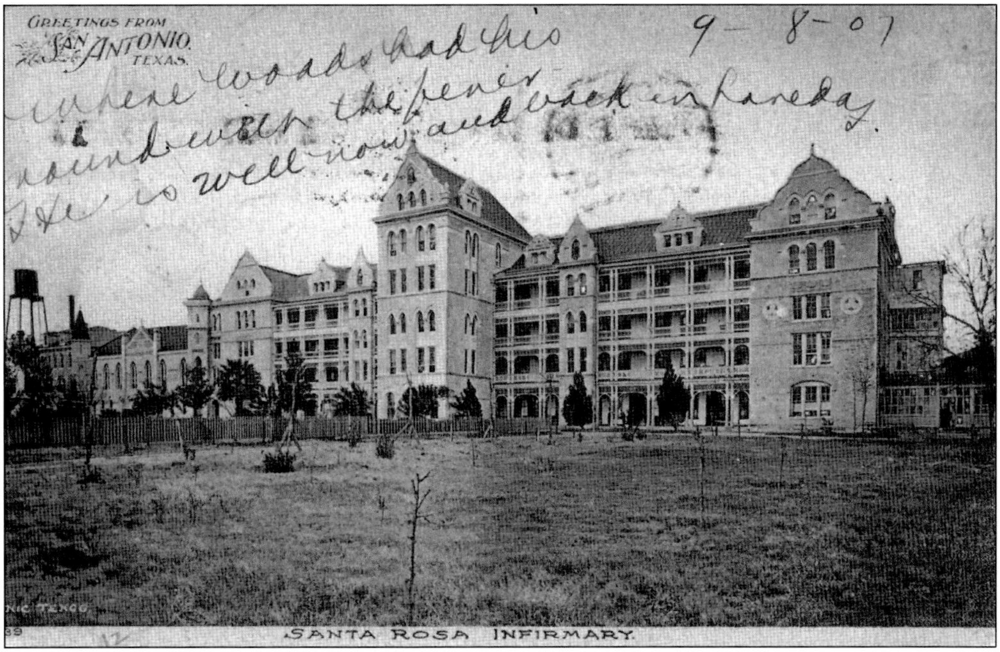

Santa Rosa Infirmary was founded in 1869 by the Sisters of Charity of the Incarnate Word as San Antonio's first private hospital. The nine-bed hospital opened on December 1, and eight patients were admitted that day. In 1910, three years after this postcard was mailed, a clinical pathology laboratory was added. In 1918, the hospital became the first in Texas to establish a separate unit for crippled children. (Author's collection.)

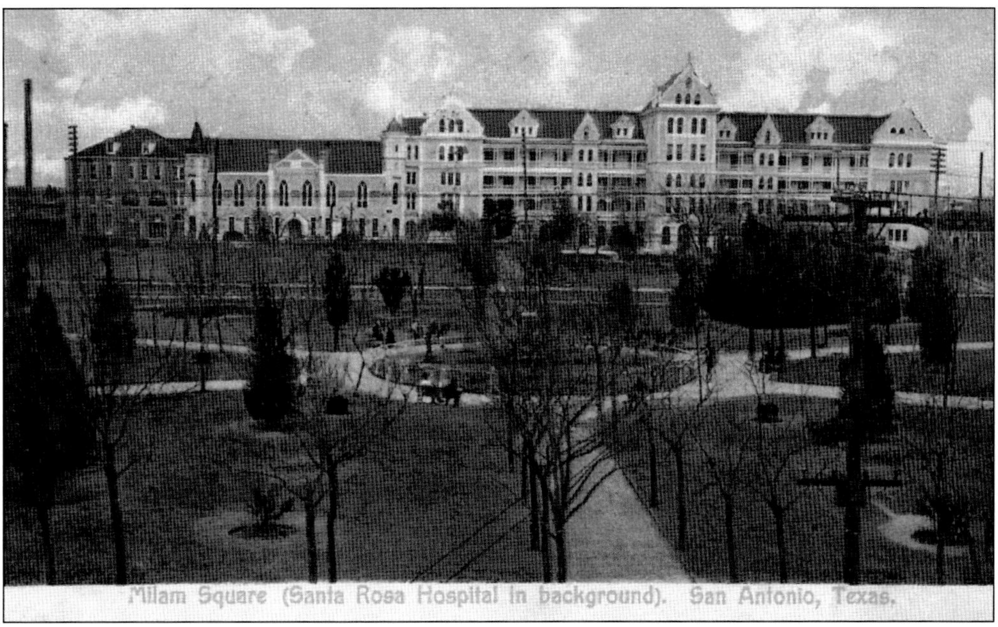

In 1930, Santa Rosa Infirmary changed its name to Santa Rosa Hospital. In 1935, it was the first hospital with air-conditioning in the state of Texas. In 1959, Santa Rosa was the first hospital in the state specifically dedicated to serve the needs of children. Today, the CHRISTUS Santa Rosa Health System serves San Antonio and South Central Texas residents. (Author's collection.)

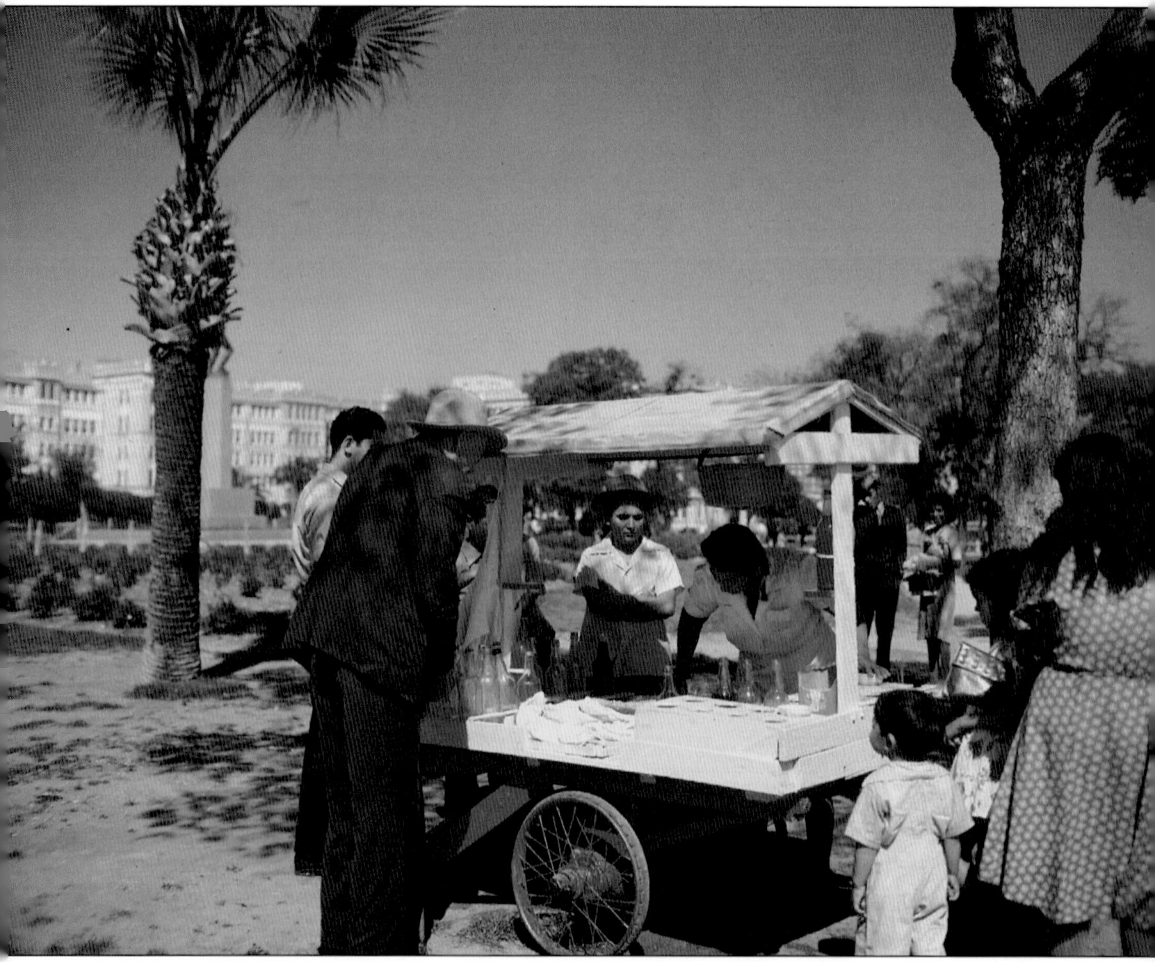

This type of portable vendor cart, photographed at Milam Park in 1946, could be found in the markets and throughout the city. In 1848, there were two cemeteries platted by the city council in San Antonio in the area that later became Santa Rosa Infirmary and Milam Park. The Catholic cemetery, Campo Santo, sat where Santa Rosa would be built in 1869, at the southeast corner. The City Cemetery would later become Milam Park. By the 1850s, the city was growing, and the cemeteries were too small. Most of the burials were moved to newer cemeteries on the east and west sides of the city. The grave of Ben Milam, who was killed by a sniper while defending San Antonio against the Mexican army in 1835, remained in the cemetery. In 1883, there was an offer to move Milam's remains; however, the city council turned it down and instead voted to build a park in Milam's honor. (Negative MS389-27; courtesy of UTSA Special Collections–ITC.)

The gazebo in Milam Park was designed by architect Salvador de Alba Martin and was a gift to San Antonio from a Mexican sister city. The nine-story tile mural *Spirit of Healing* at CHRISTUS Santa Rosa Hospital was created by Jesse Treviño and completed in 1997. Teviño was born in Monterrey, Mexico, and came to the city as a child. (Photograph by Al Rendon; courtesy of La Familia Cortez Restaurants.)

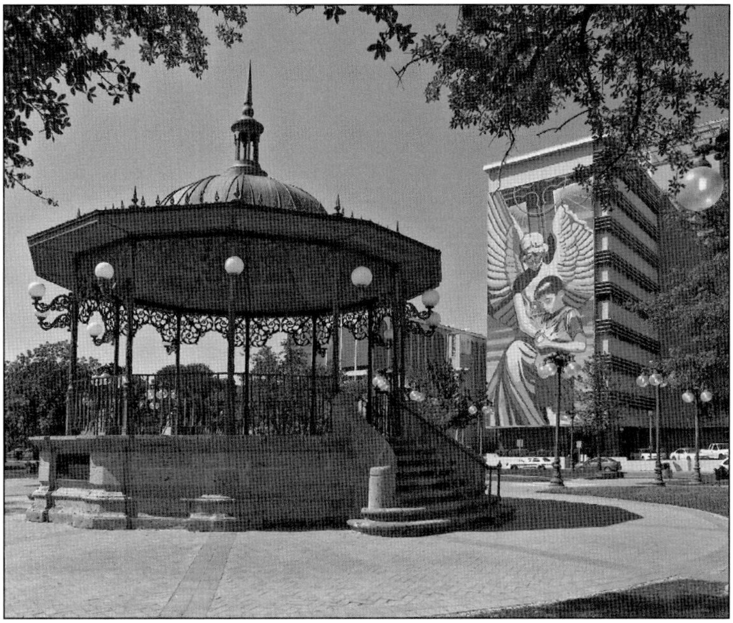

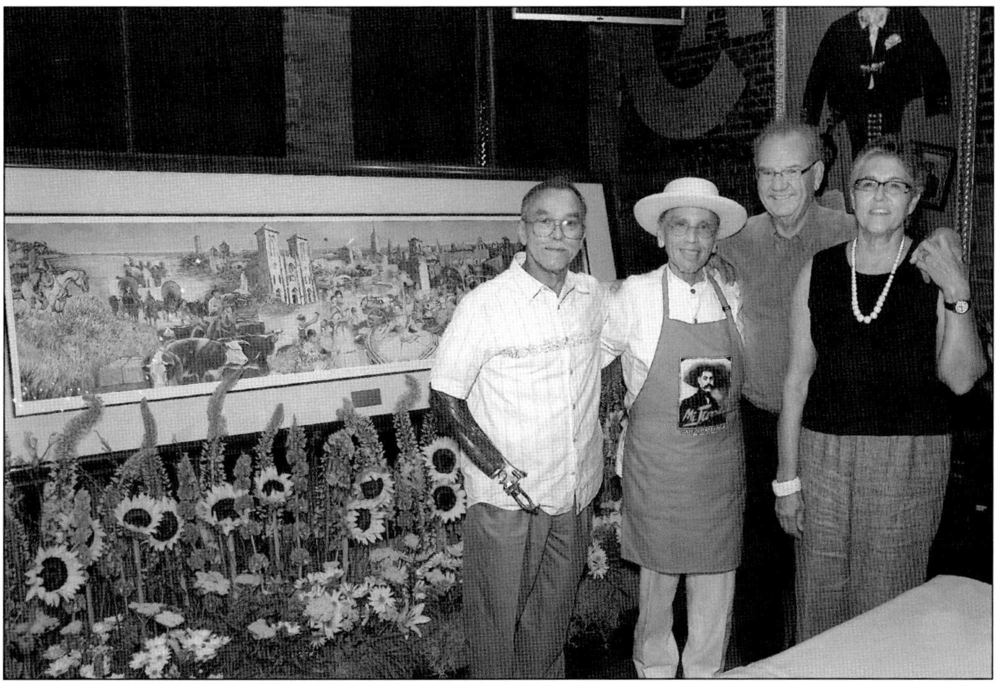

From left to right are Jesse Treviño, Jorge Cortez, former San Antonio mayor Phil Hardberger, and his wife, Linda, at the Mariachi Bar. In the mid-1960s, Treviño studied art in New York City. In 1967, he was injured in Vietnam and lost his right hand. He taught himself to paint with his left hand and went on to earn a master's degree. He became the first Mexican American to exhibit in the Smithsonian American Art Museum. (Photograph by Al Rendon; courtesy of La Familia Cortez Restaurants.)

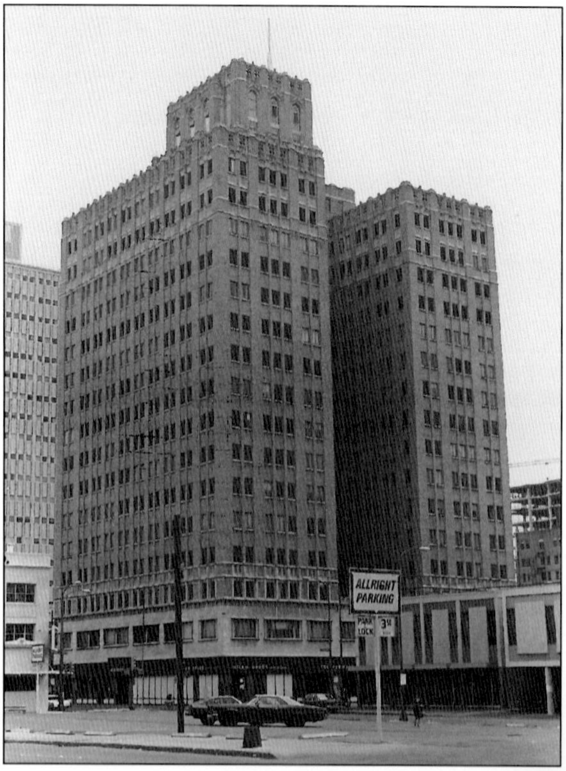

The Milam Building, pictured in 1981, opened in 1928. It was named in honor of Benjamin Milam, a historical figure in Texas. In the 1950s, tenants Mobil, Shell, Exxon, and the Railroad Commission of Texas had their Texas headquarters here. In 2014, the Milam Building was listed in the National Register of Historic Places. The building still flies only one flag, the Lone Star flag. (Courtesy of the San Antonio Conservation Society Foundation.)

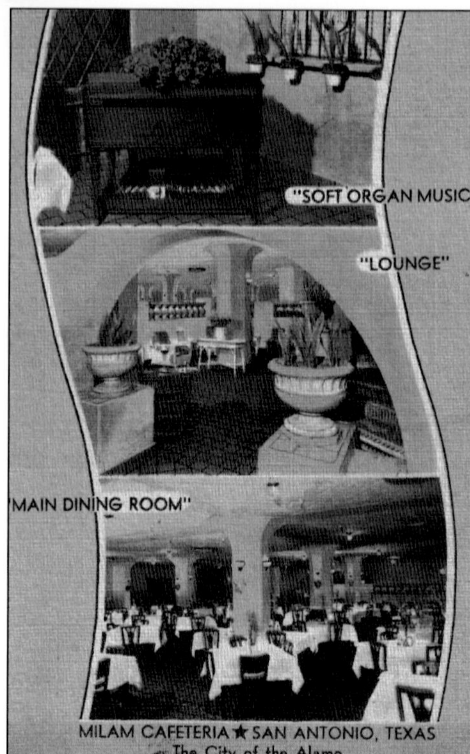

In 1930, there were two Milam Cafeterias. One was in the Milam Building, the other in the Central Building on East Houston. The cafeterias featured Southern cooking and music. The cafeteria in the Milam Building advertised that its lounge was open to guests, with seats for resting and reading. In the Central Building location, the mezzanine and first floor showcased murals of Texas and the San Antonio missions. (Author's collection.)

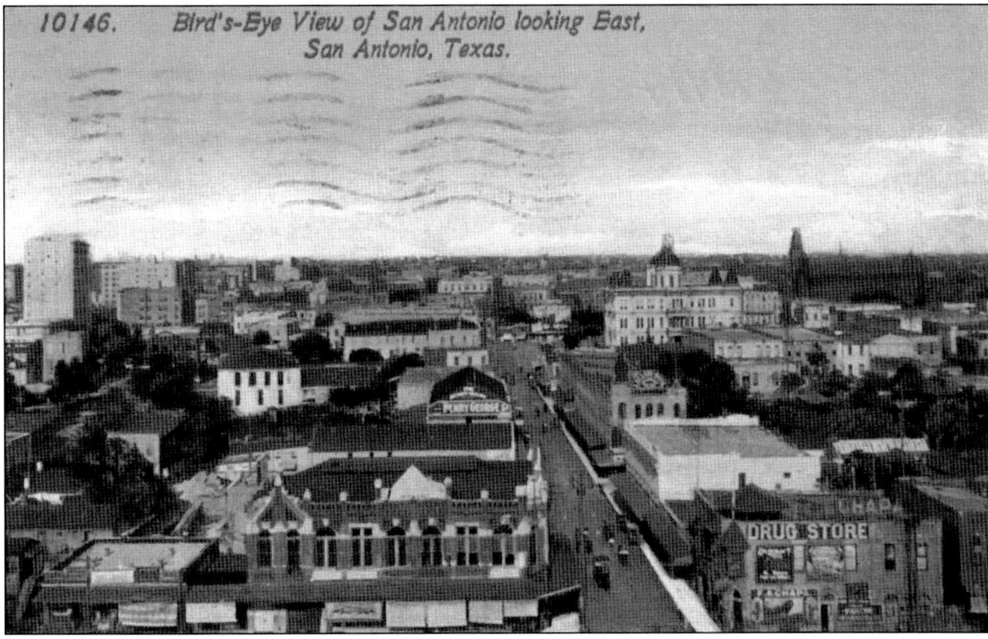

In this c. 1914 postcard, Francisco A. Chapa's drugstore stands at right. Chapa, born in Mexico, immigrated to New Orleans to study pharmacy at Tulane University. In 1890, he established Chapa's Drug Company in San Antonio. In 1894, he founded the Lion Drugstore. The University of Texas at San Antonio Libraries Special Collections houses the Francisco A. Chapa family papers, 1821–2011. (Courtesy of Texana Division, San Antonio Public Libraries, Postcard Collection.)

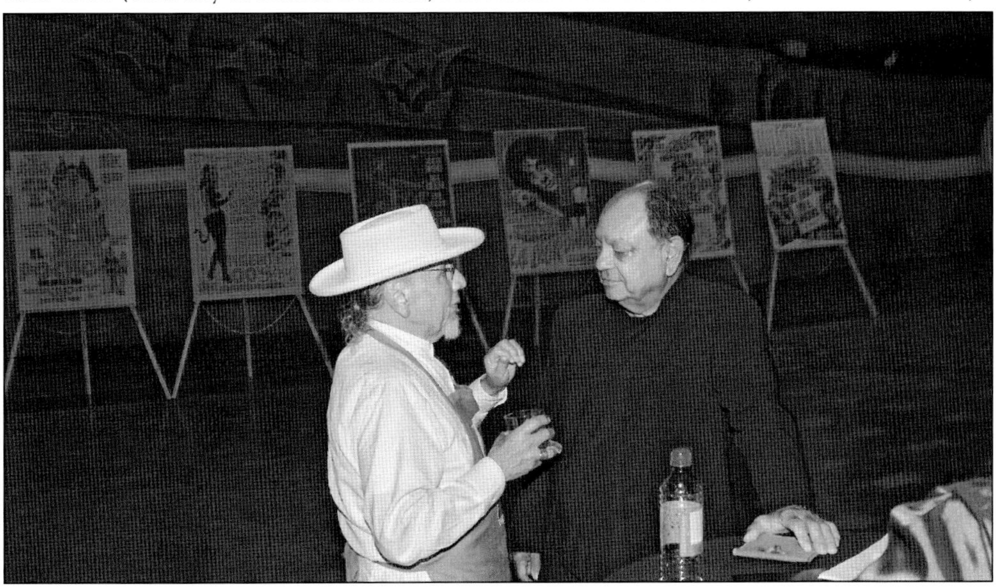

Jorge Cortez (left) and Cheech Marin are pictured at the Alameda Theater, designed in 1947 and completed in 1949. They are discussing what was once the largest Spanish-language movie and vaudeville theater in the country. Pedro Infante, Vicente Fernández, Maria Felix, and Cantinflas were among the Mexican artists who performed here. The front facade was restored in 2000, with further restorations following in 2014. (Photograph by Al Rendon; courtesy of La Familia Cortez Restaurants.)

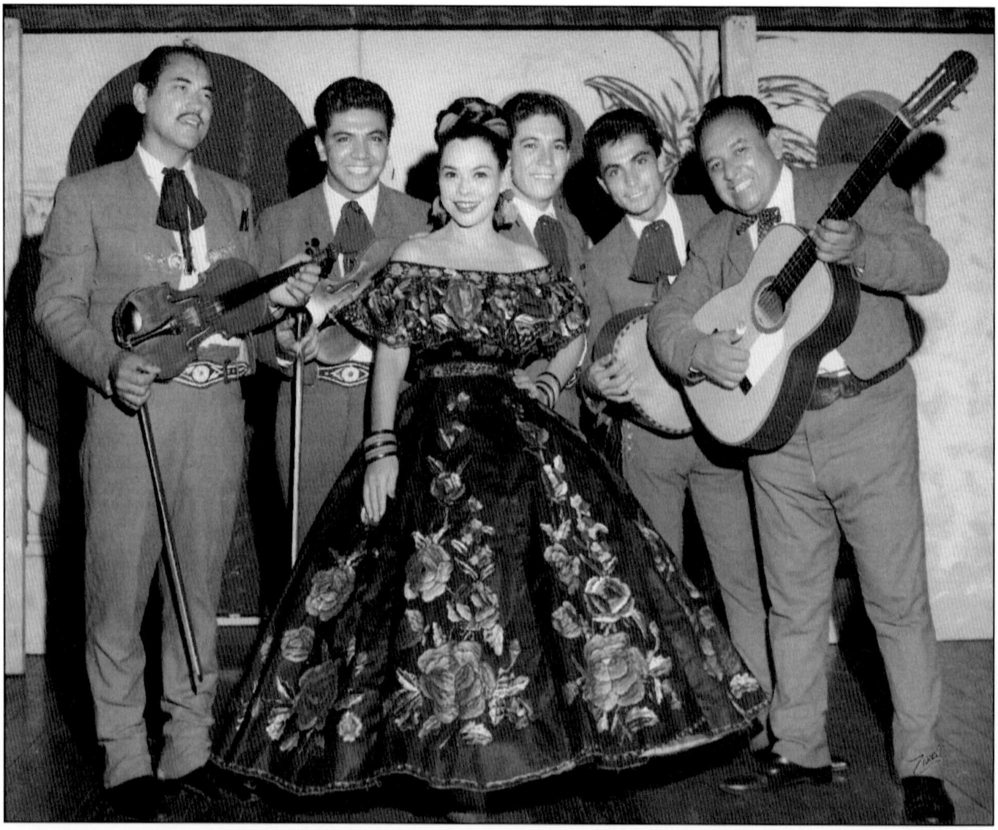

Actress and singer Rosita Fernández performed at the Alameda Theater. In this picture, taken in the late 1960s, Fernández is seen with Mariachis Chapultepec. The *mariachis* are, from left to right, Ben Valdez; brothers Alfonso, Arturo, and Alberto Lopez; and Jose Morate. In 1970, the Lopez brothers died in a fire in Chicago. When their bodies were flown to San Antonio, a crowd of 300 people greeted their widows. (Courtesy of Beatriz Llamas.)

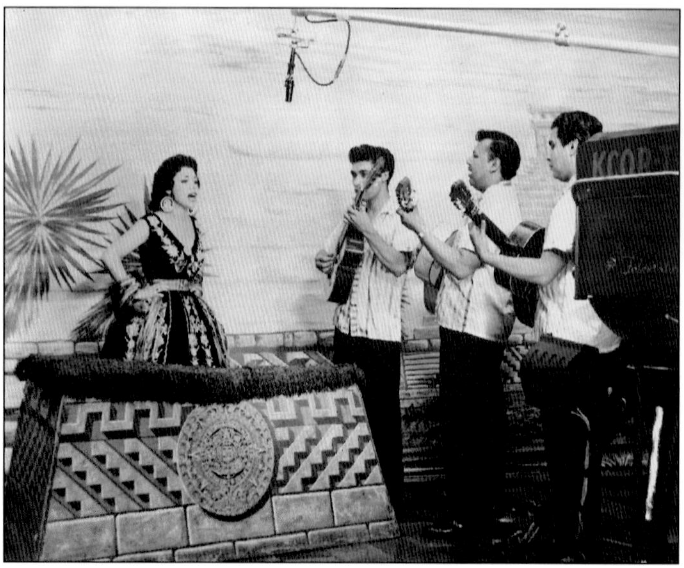

Beatriz Llamas, pictured in the 1960s, sings for the television-radio audiences of KCOR, which was located at the Alameda Theater. The musicians are, from left to right, Seferino Solis, Chicho Mireles, and unidentified. Llamas was married to Arturo Lopez of Mariachis Chapultepec. In 1969, they performed together at Hemisfair Plaza. Llamas, known as "La Paloma Del Norte," is still singing with Las Tesoros de San Antonio. (Courtesy of Beatriz Llamas.)

When the Majestic Theatre was built in 1929, it was the second largest theater in the country. The Majestic featured movies and vaudeville entertainment and closed in 1974. In the 1980s and 1990s, with funds raised by the nonprofit group Las Casas Foundation, the theater went through major renovations. Today, this performing arts facility is a national historic landmark with 2,264 seats. (Author's collection.)

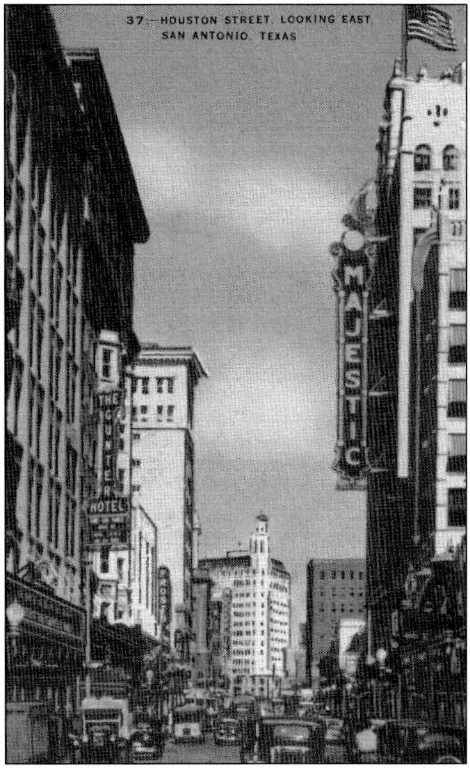

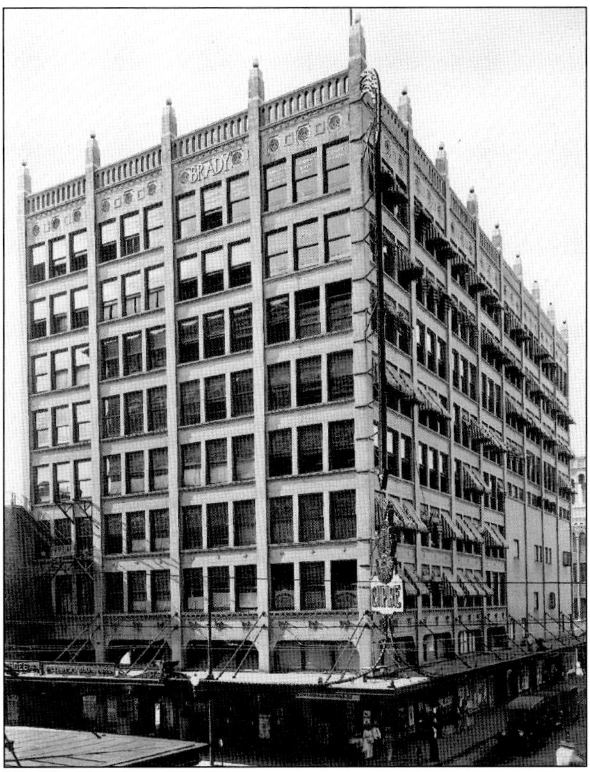

The Charline McCombs Empire Theatre was built in 1913 as a vaudeville house and movie theater. In the 1920s, the Empire showed silent movies featuring Lon Chaney and Charlie Chaplin. After years of decline, it closed in 1978. The theater reopened in 1998 after a major renovation made possible with funds raised by Las Casas Foundation. (Courtesy of Texana Division, San Antonio Public Libraries.)

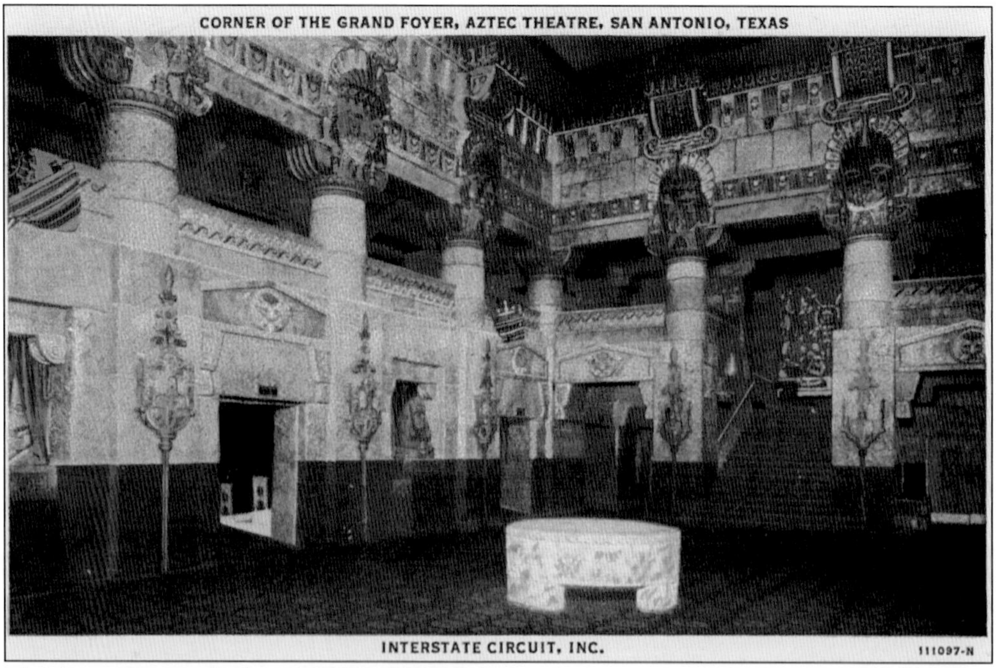

The Aztec Theatre, built in 1926, was designed from drawings of Mayan, Aztec, and Toltec ruins in Mexico. In the foyer, the Aztec moon goddess was replicated on columns, and a replica of the Aztec sacrificial stone sat in the center. In the 1930s, there was a restaurant in the theater known as The Old South Café. The San Antonio Conservation Society purchased the theater in 1988, and it was renovated in 2007. (Author's collection.)

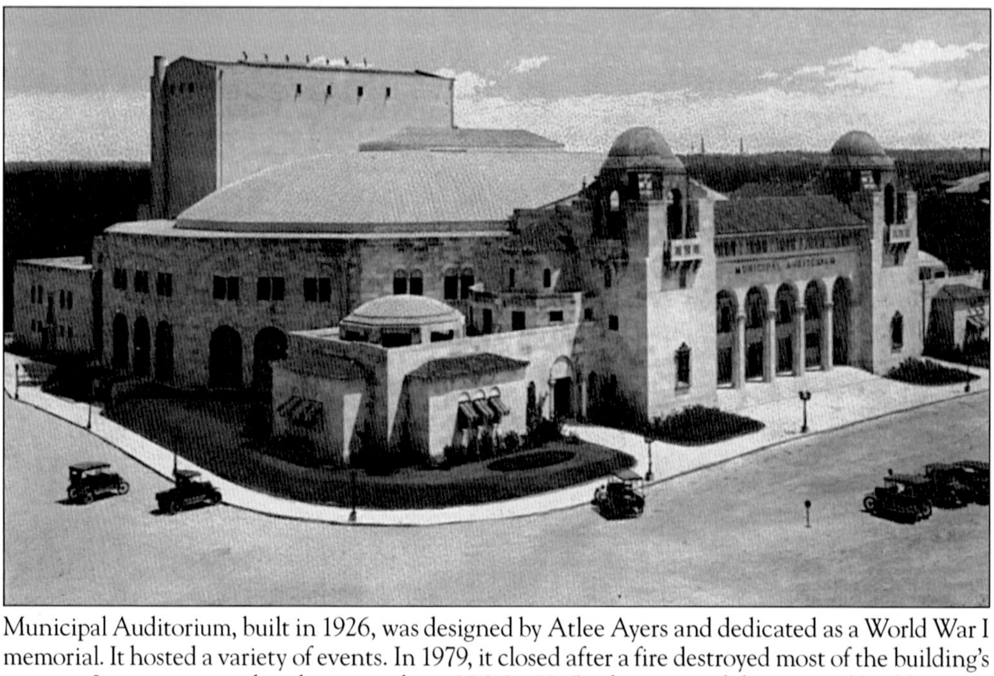

Municipal Auditorium, built in 1926, was designed by Atlee Ayers and dedicated as a World War I memorial. It hosted a variety of events. In 1979, it closed after a fire destroyed most of the building's interior. It was renovated and reopened in 1986. In 2015, after most of the original building was demolished, the Tobin Center for the Performing Arts opened its doors. (Author's collection.)

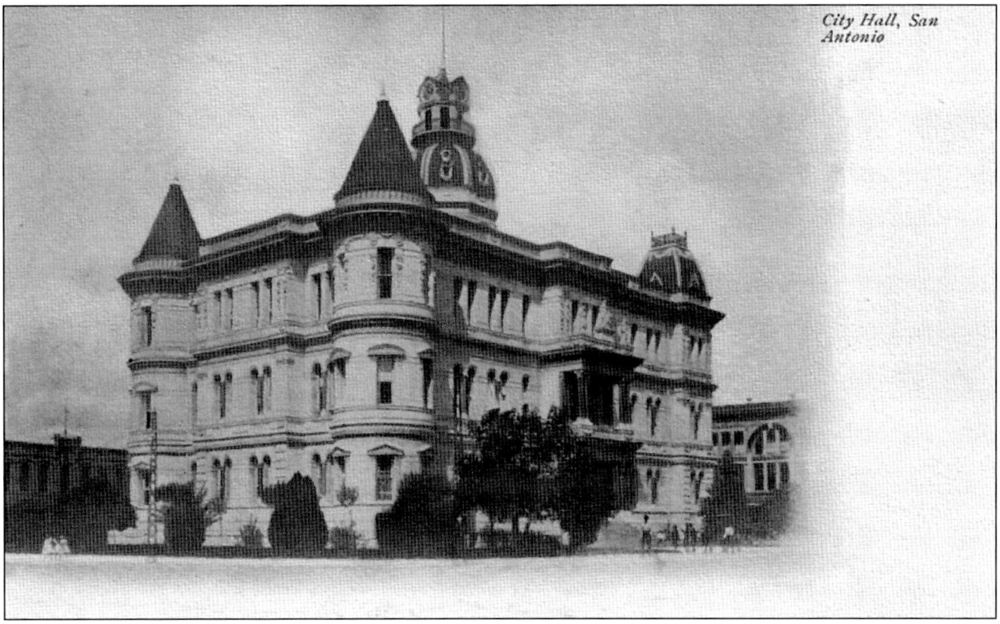

City hall in Military Plaza was completed in 1891. In 1927, the corner towers were removed and architectural details changed to accommodate the fourth floor. The clock on top of the cupola was damaged and had to be scrapped. As San Antonio grew, city departments relocated to other buildings. The offices of the mayor and city council are still housed in city hall. (Author's collection.)

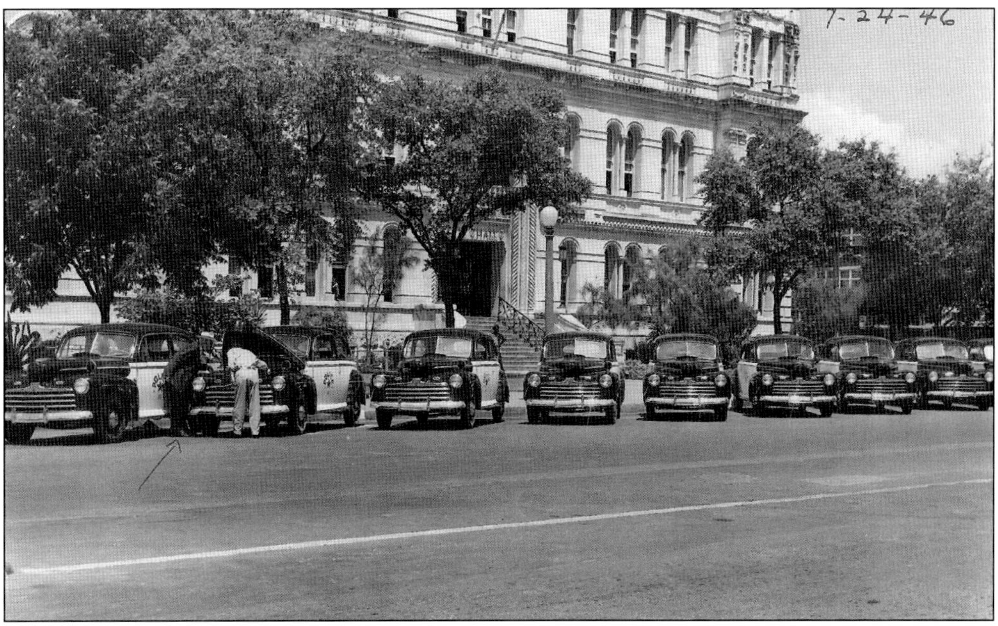

In the 1940s, the Parking Meters and Weights and Measures Departments were in the city hall basement. The first-floor offices all had to do with taxes. The mayor's office was on the second floor with other offices for city officials. Council chambers and the police and fire commissioners were on the third floor. The fourth-floor offices were used for construction departments. (Courtesy of the San Antonio Conservation Society Foundation.)

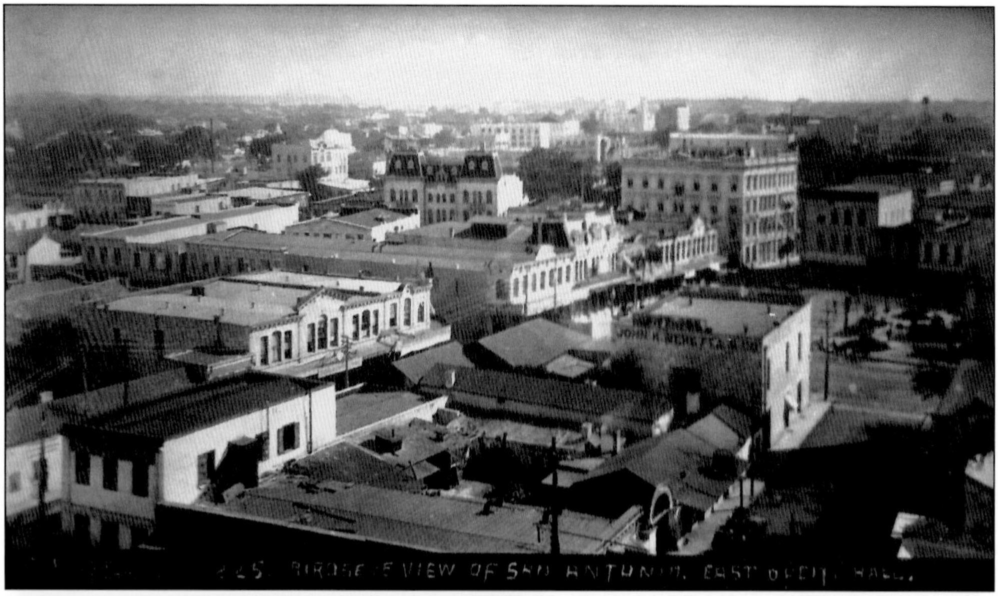

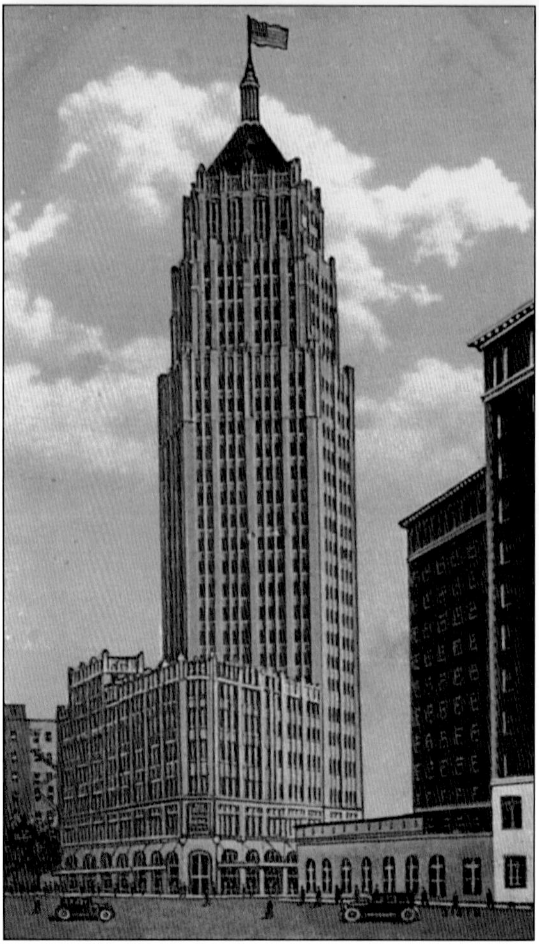

This photograph, taken between 1886 and 1893, gives a glimpse of the area surrounding Main Plaza, visible at far center right. In 1891, John K. Beretta & Company was located at 7–9 Main Plaza. Beretta's business partner was Thomas Claiborne Frost, the founder of Frost Bank. Beretta later became president of the National Bank of Commerce. (Courtesy of the San Antonio Conservation Society Foundation, Raba Collection.)

When the Smith-Young Tower opened in 1929, it was the only office building with an octagonal tower in the United States. The Tower Life Building, as it is known today, was designed by architects Atlee B. and Robert Ayers. There was a tunnel under St. Mary's Street connecting the building with the Plaza Hotel. A Sears, Roebuck & Company store occupied the first six floors. (Author's collection.)

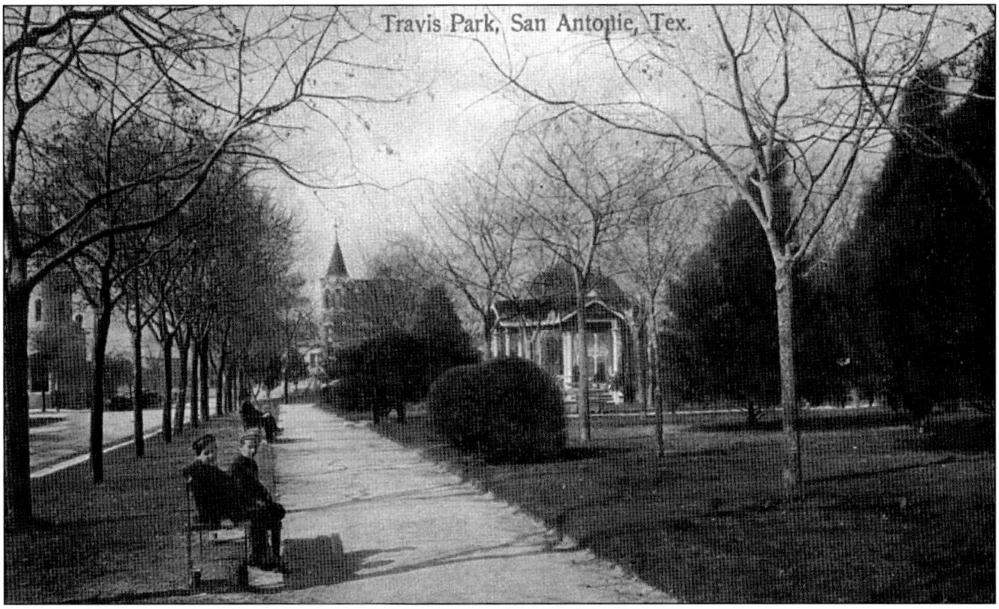

Travis Park was established in 1870 and is the second-oldest city park in the United States. Samuel Maverick donated what used to be his orchard for the park. This c. 1910 postcard was printed around the same time the St. Anthony Hotel opened across the street. The church at left is Travis Park United Methodist Church, completed in 1886. (Author's collection.)

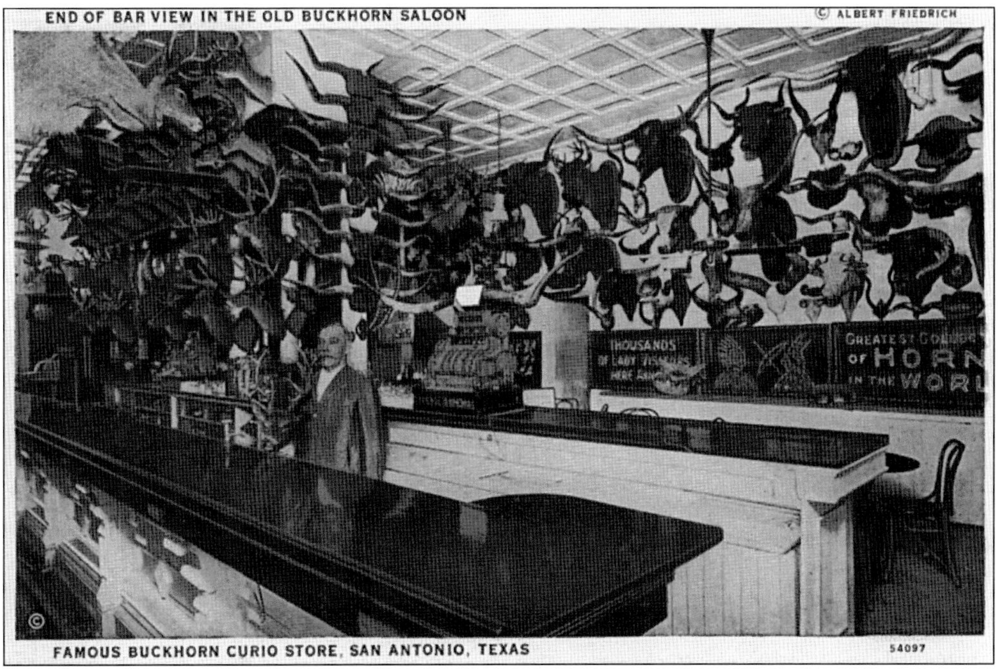

Albert Friedrich, pictured around 1910, was the founder of the Buckhorn Saloon and Curio Store. Friedrich opened his Buckhorn Saloon on Main Plaza in 1881 when he was 17 years old. He had been working across the street at the Southern Hotel as a bartender and bellhop. Friedrich soon realized travelers did not have much money, so he began accepting horns and antlers as payment for beer and whiskey. (Author's collection.)

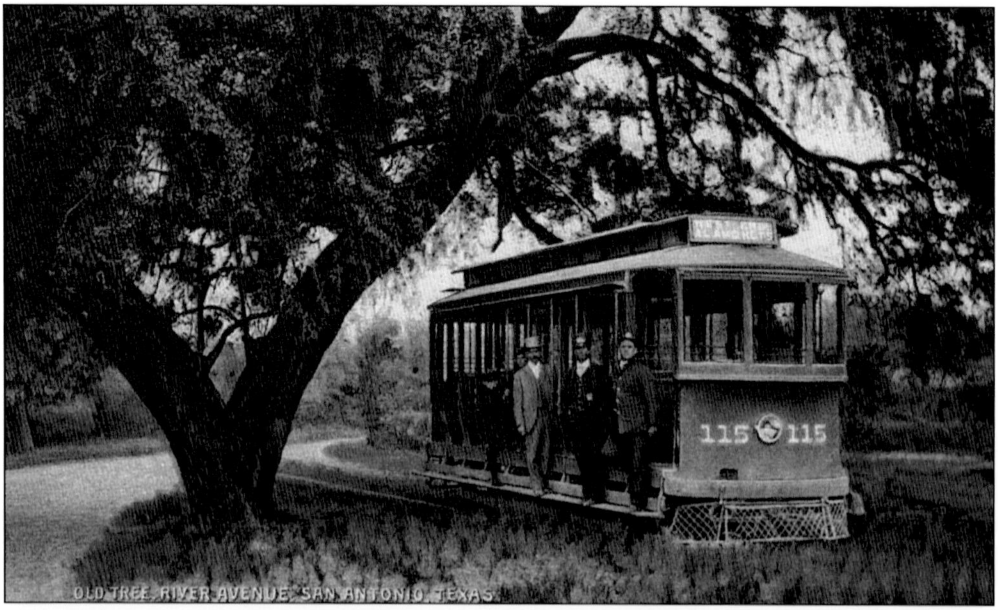

This trolley postcard, mailed in 1909 from San Antonio to New York, reads, "River Avenue is the gateway to Brackenridge Park." It goes on to say that the location is at the head of the San Antonio River, near Brackenridge Villa and the country club. The oak tree was estimated to be 150–200 years old. (Author's collection.)

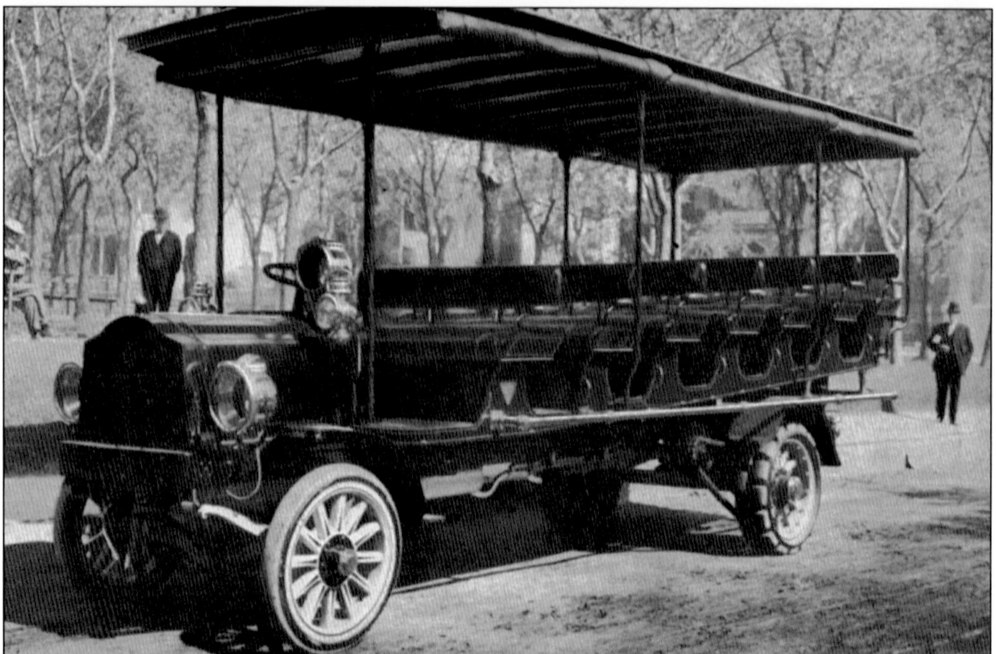
The Texas Tally Ho Company used Packard touring cars to take visitors to places of interest, including the Spanish missions, a pear orchard and pecan grove, White Horse Tavern, a Mexican village, Berg's Wool Mill, an insane asylum, Schuermeyer's Garden, Hot Sulphur Wells, and an ostrich farm. An advertisement in the September 4, 1910, *San Antonio Daily News* listed the company's location as 922–924 San Pedro Avenue. (Author's collection.)

Four

El Mercado

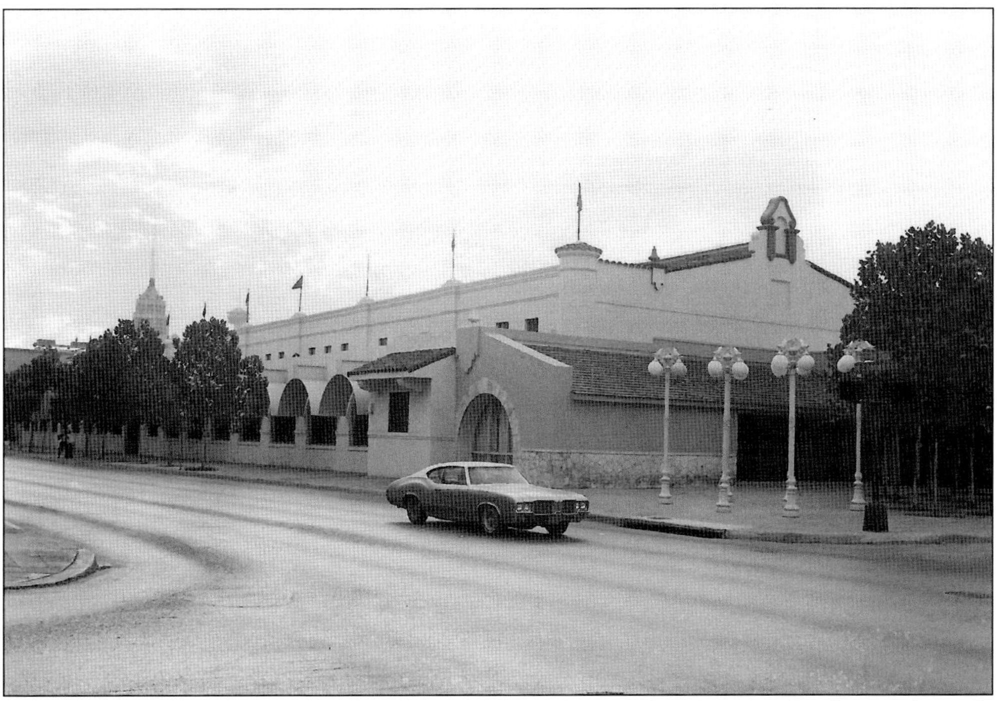

El Mercado is the former Municipal Market House building. This photograph taken in the early 1980s was part of the San Antonio downtown resources survey. Before the 1976 renovation, vendors could drive their trucks into the building at the San Saba Street entrance and sell produce directly from them. The fruits and vegetables were replaced by curios attractive to tourists. (Courtesy of the San Antonio Conservation Society Foundation.)

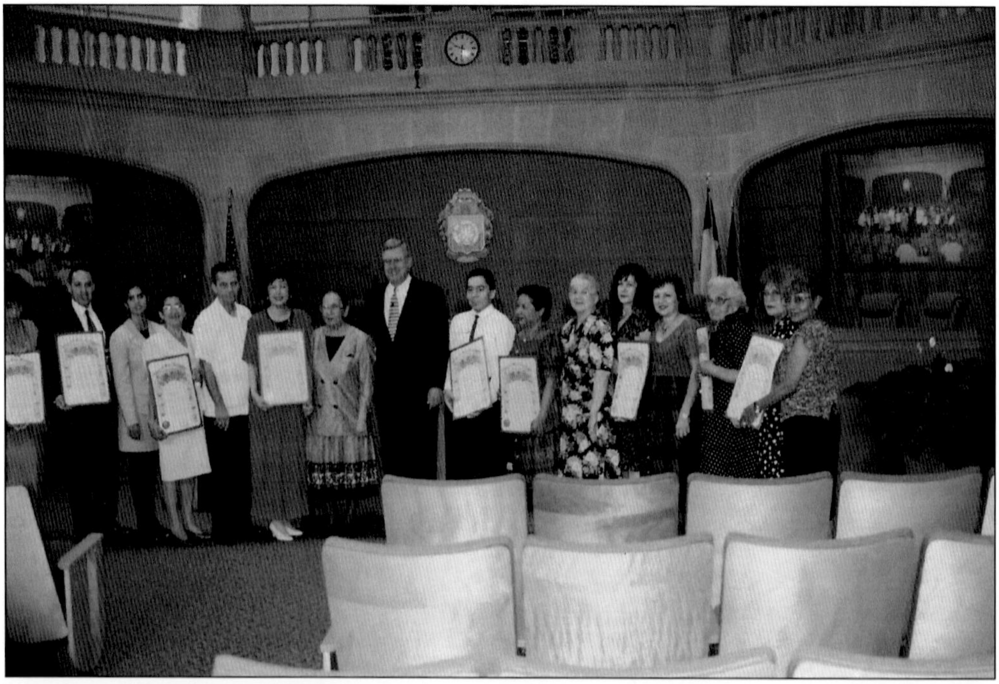

The City of San Antonio issued a proclamation designating August 30–September 30, 1996, as El Mercado Month, marking the 20th anniversary of the redevelopment of Market Square/ El Mercado. Mayor William E. Thornton honored the families with businesses dating to 1976 and earlier. Families honored were Cortez, Douglas, Garza, Herrejon, Larios, Mares, Perales, San Miguel, Reyes, Valdivia, and Villarreal. (Courtesy of Mary Perales Valdez.)

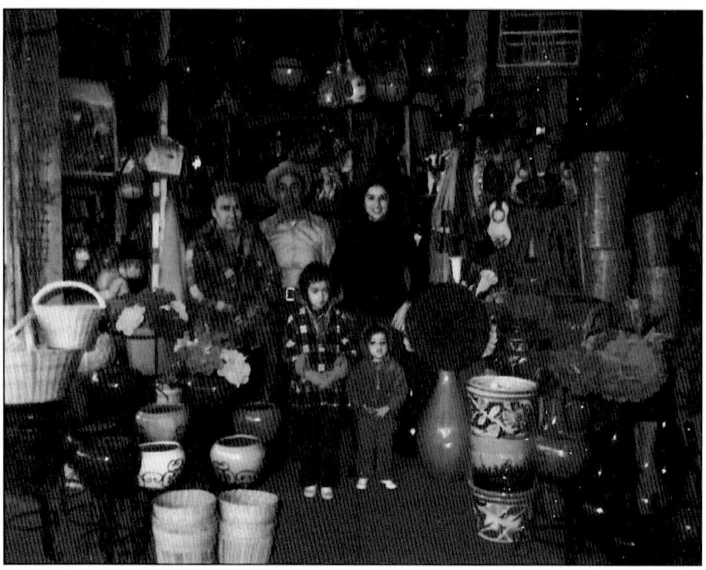

In 1917, at the age of 14, Felipe Perales immigrated to the United States from Mexico. He settled in Pharr, Texas. In October 1951, he moved his wife and three daughters to San Antonio and went straight to work selling watermelons and vegetables at the Washington Square Market. Felipe and Elena Perales (at left) moved their wares to Hay Market Plaza in 1969. (Courtesy of Mary Perales Valdez.)

In 1976, with renovations completed, Felipe and Elena Perales moved Perales Mexican Imports to Plaza del Mercado. The remodeling of the El Mercado building included heating and air-conditioning, a welcome improvement from the open-air market they had started their business in, in 1952. Elena passed away in 2001 at 87 years old. Felipe died the next year, at the age of 96. (Courtesy of Mary Perales Valdez.)

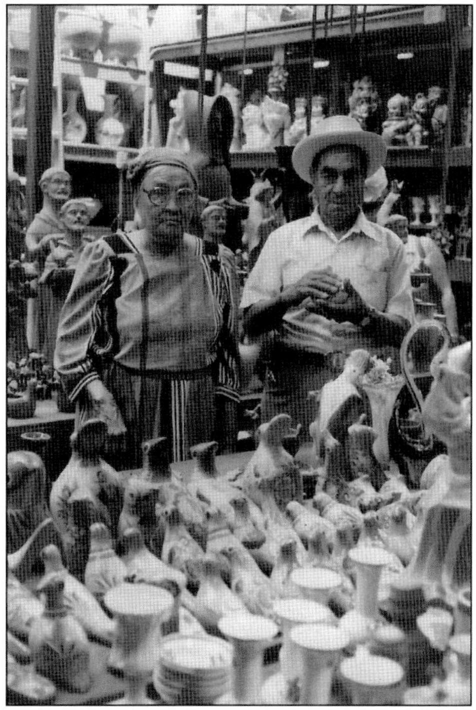

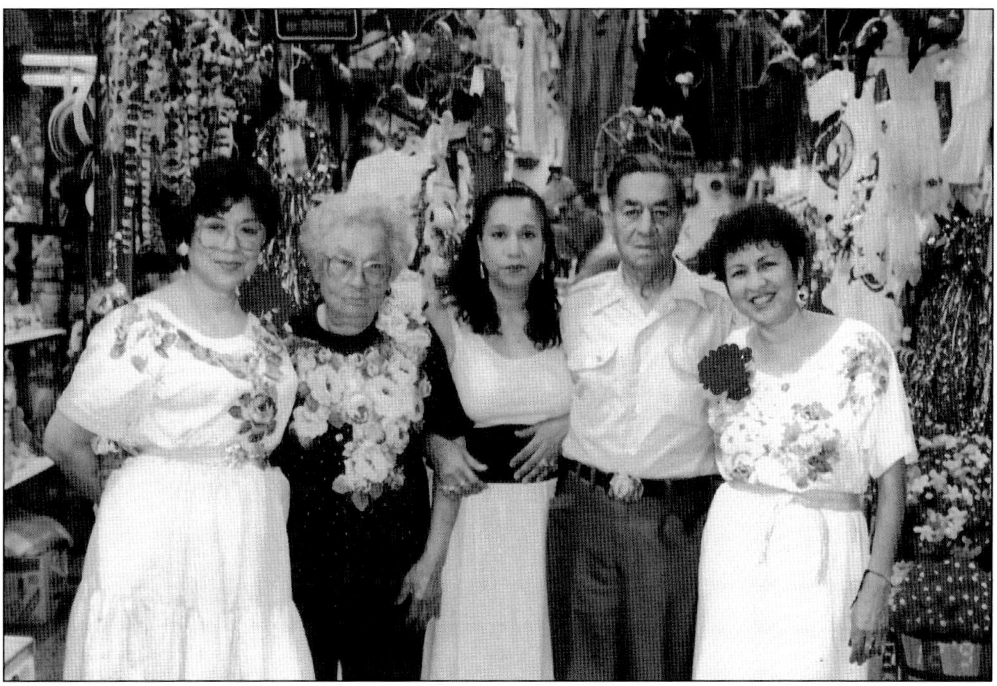

Felipe and Elena Perales and their daughters are pictured in the shop. From left to right are Flavia Galvan, Elena Perales, Elva Anthony, Felipe Perales, and Mary Valdez. The clothes and souvenirs hanging on racks in the background give an indication of how the business had evolved. Originally a fruit stand, the business is currently run by Mary Valdez and her husband, Rudy. (Courtesy of Mary Perales Valdez.)

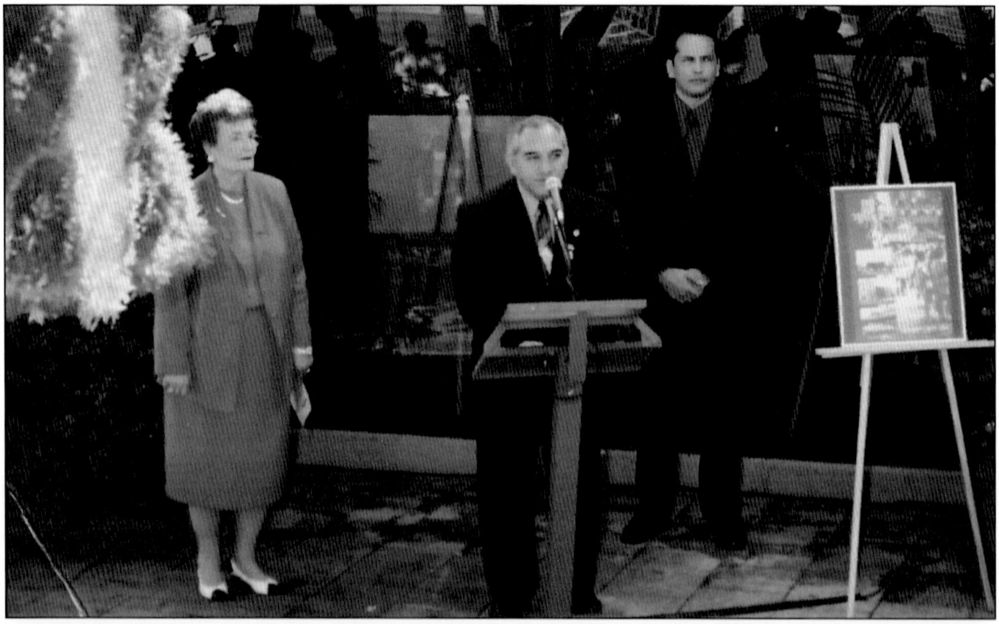

Market Square celebrated the 25th anniversary of its renovation in 2001. In this photograph, Jaime Herrejon addresses the audience. Lila Corkrell, former mayor of San Antonio, is at left, and at right is Mayor Edward D. Garza. In 1996, the Herrejon family, of Little Mexico Imports, had been honored in a city proclamation celebrating the 20th anniversary of the renovation of Market Square. (Courtesy of the Herrejon family.)

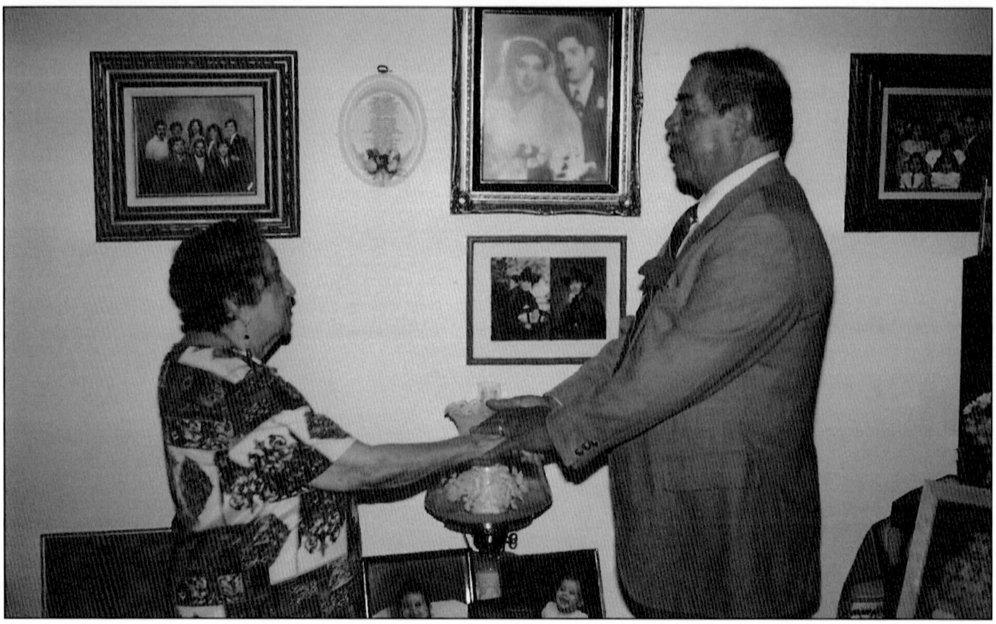

Raquel and Faustino Herrejon, of Old Mexico Imports, celebrate a wedding anniversary in the 1980s. Family friend Johnny Ramirez remembers helping the Herrejons with the business as early as 1965. As a teenager, Ramirez felt all grown-up—he had a job and credit at Penners Men's Clothing Store. He still helps Connie and Jaime Herrejon when they need an extra hand at their shop, Little Mexico Imports. (Courtesy of the Herrejon family.)

Faustino Herrejon discusses Mexican *piñatas* at Old Mexico Imports in 1975. Raquel and Faustino would eventually run the business together, but it was Raquel who officially started it in 1962, selling produce at the old Hay Market Plaza. While Faustino was working at Kelly Air Force Base, his wife applied for and got permission to set up shop. Raquel passed away in 2001 and Faustino in 2005. (Courtesy of the Herrejon family.)

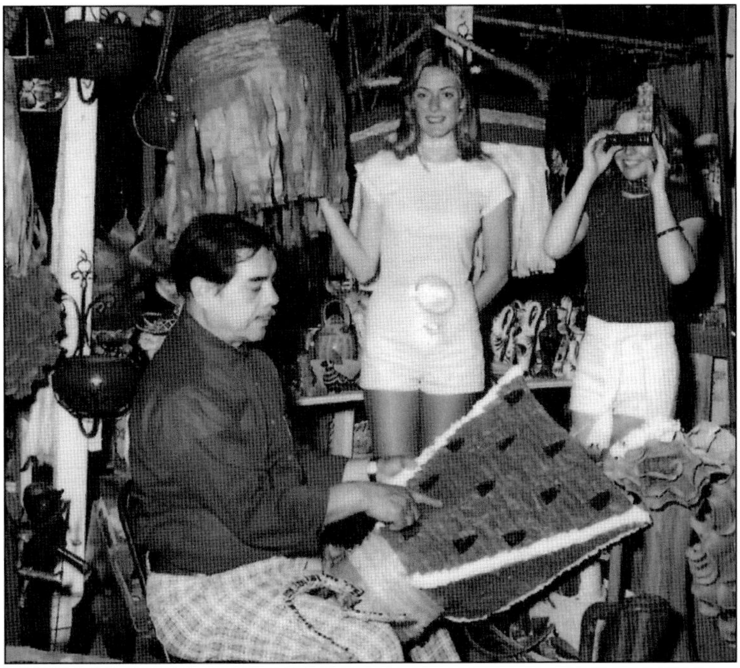

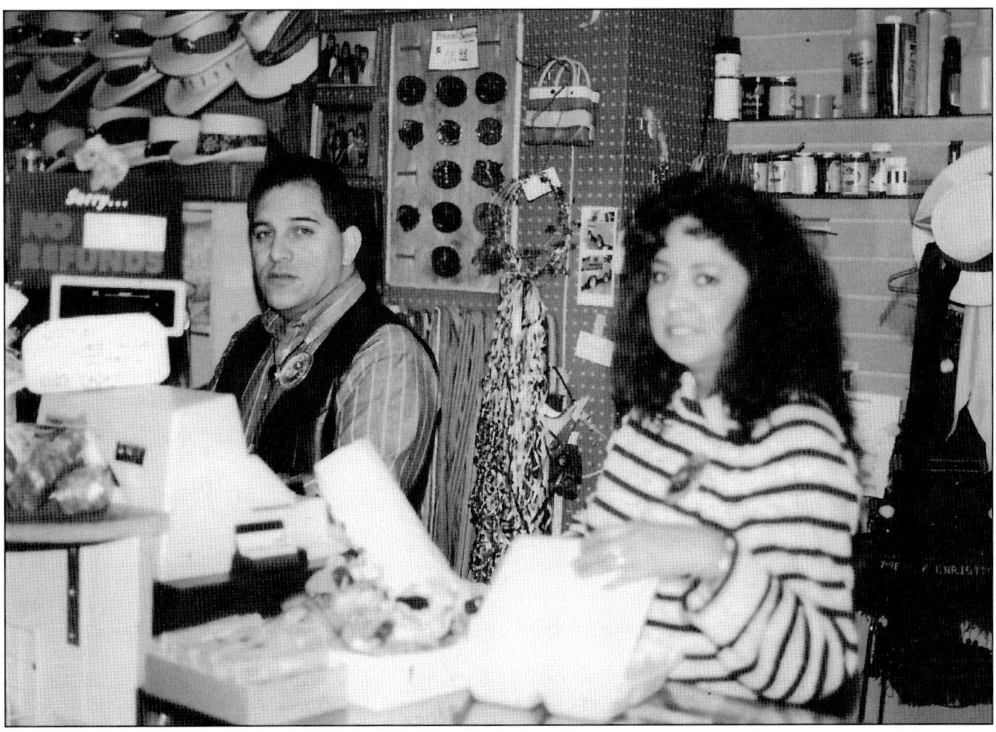

The second generation of Old Mexico Imports evolved into two separate businesses, both located in El Mercado. Pictured are Jaime and Connie Herrejon, owners of Little Mexico Imports. Jaime's brother Michael Herrejon owns Old Mexico Imports. Another brother and his wife, Carlos and Rhonda, were former partners of Little Mexico Imports. Many of the businesses in Market Square are managed by second- and third-generation family members. (Courtesy of the Herrejon family.)

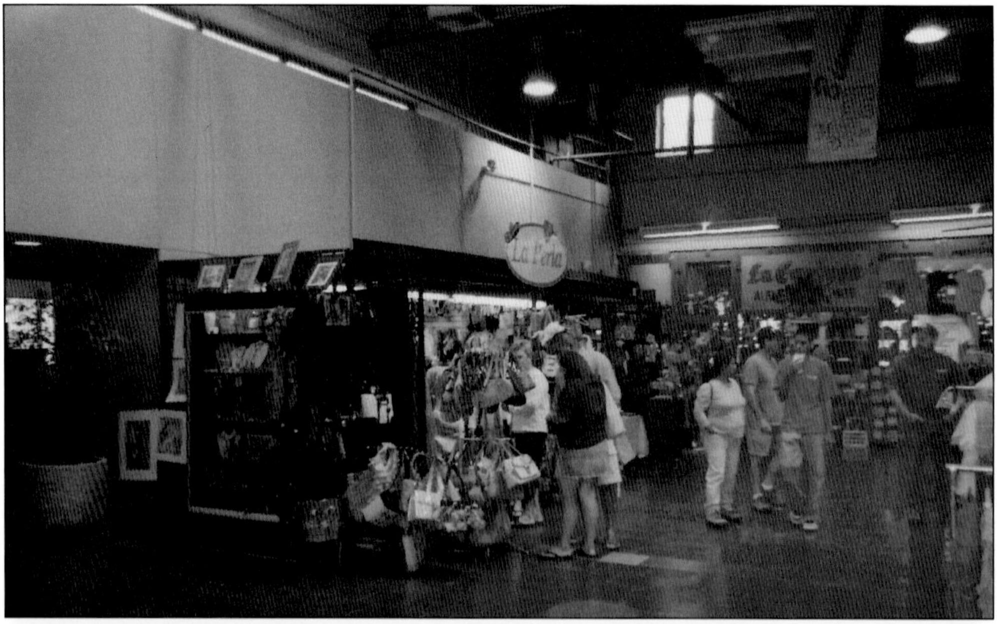

At the time this photograph was taken in the 1990s, La Condesa Alfareria Imports was owned by the Valdivia family. The Valdivias were honored in 1996 as one of original businesses since before the 1976 renovation of Market Square. In 2015, a spokesperson for the family, Randy Gallegos, announced that the shop was for sale. In 2017, new owner Roberto Delgado changed the name to Maya Imports. (Courtesy of Alice and Phillip Leon.)

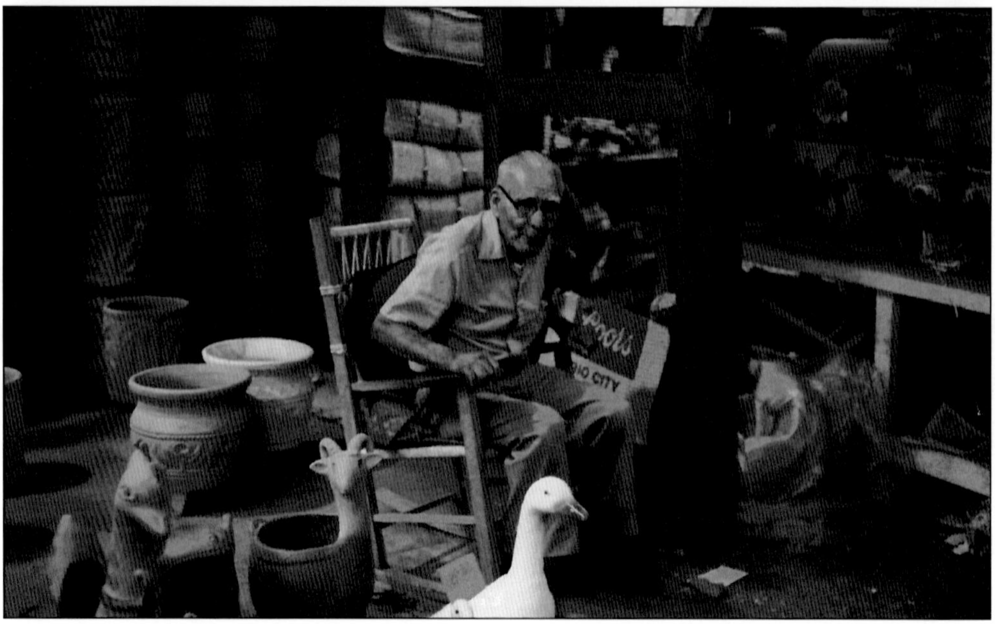

Ruperto Valdivia founded La Condesa Alfareria Imports in 1934. Valdivia had deep roots in the area; in 1922, his residence was listed at rear 400 South Laredo Street. At the same address were Crescencio, Jesus, and Jesusa Valdivia. In the 1977 city directory, Ruperto was listed as a produce dealer. He continued to run the shop until his death, when the fourth generation continued the business. (Courtesy of Mary Perales Valdez.)

Alvaro and Carmen Munevar of La Boutique International are at a Market Square Christmas party in the 1990s. Alvaro Munevar is one of the original merchants of El Mercado. Their daughter Gabriella Albright grew up in the business and helped her parents buy and sell while still in middle school. Today, with the help of her father, Gabriella runs the business. (Courtesy of the Munevar family.)

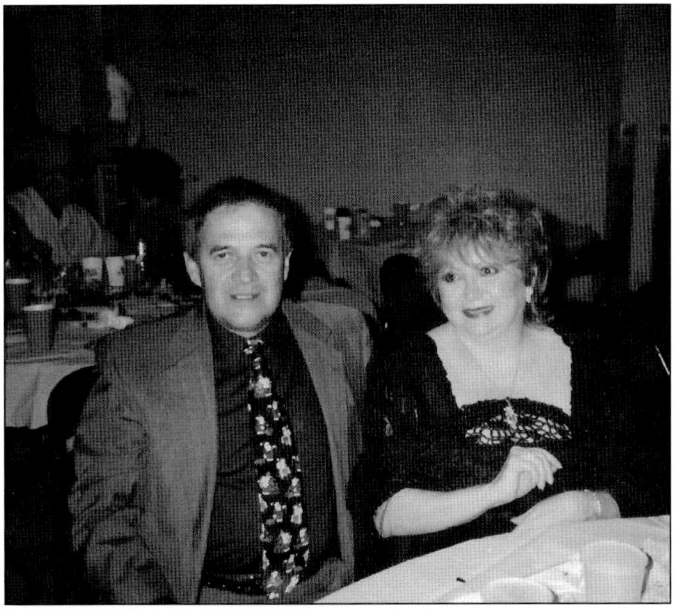

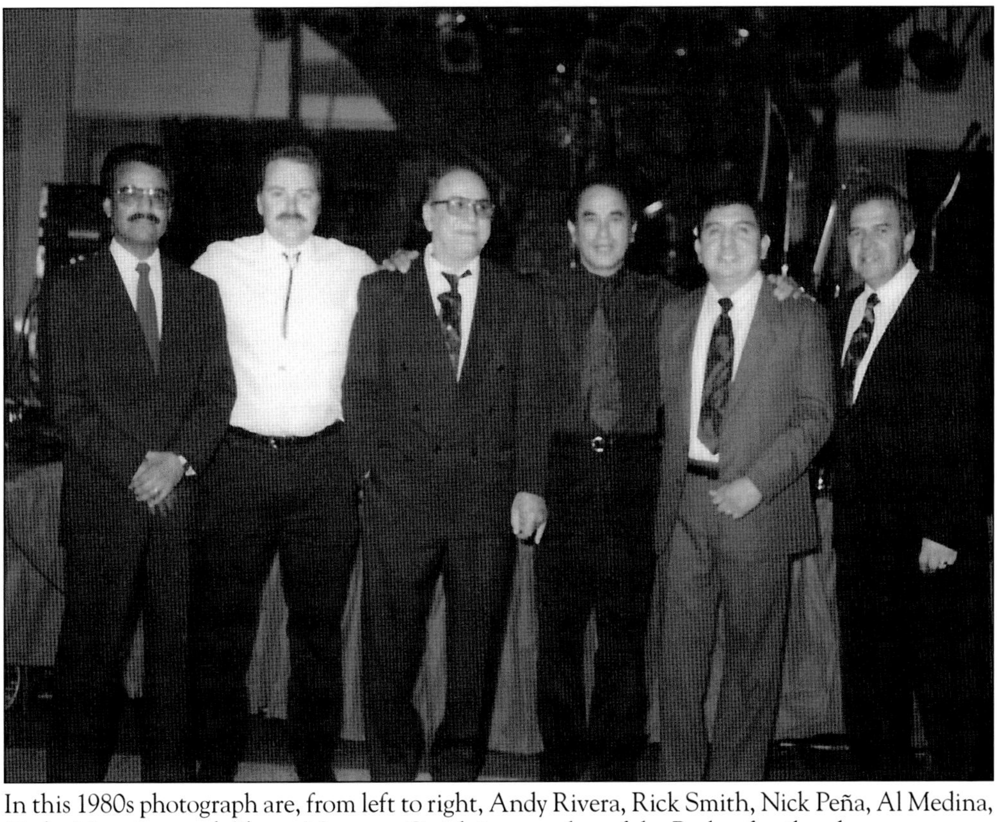

In this 1980s photograph are, from left to right, Andy Rivera, Rick Smith, Nick Peña, Al Medina, Carlos Herrejon, and Alvaro Munevar. Smith is a member of the Barker family, who were owners of Barker's Collectables, El Sol Gift Shop, Wooden Indian, Billie's Restaurant, and Marie's. Peña is the second generation of the Don Roman and Naturaleza Celestial family. Medina was the owner of The Candy Man. (Courtesy of the Munevar family.)

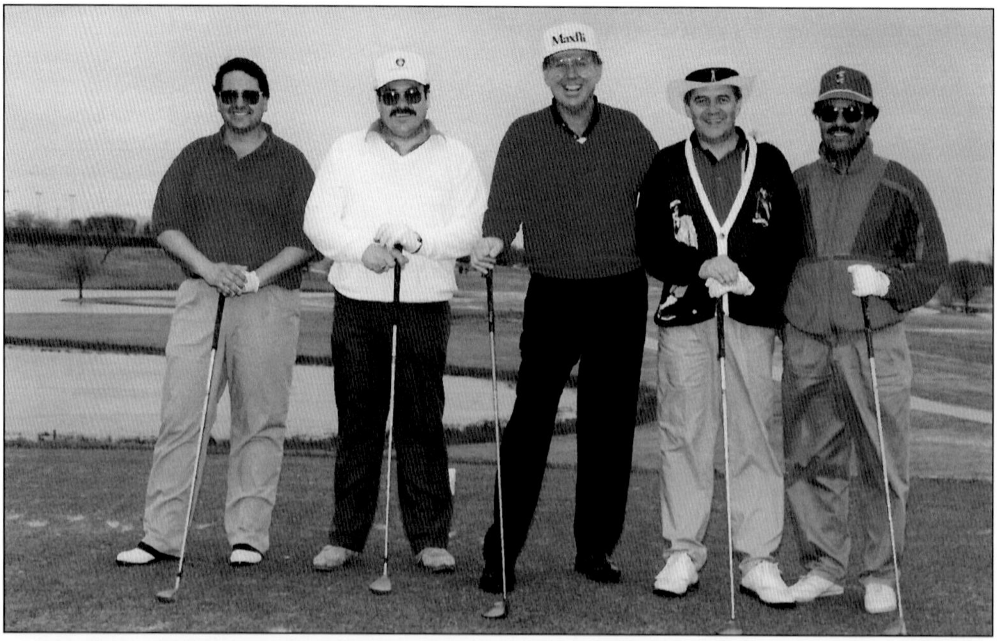

On March 15, 1993, two Market Square merchants, Alvaro Munevar and Andy Rivera, played in the Chi Chi Rodriguez & Toyota Children's Classic. The tournament was held at Woodlake Country Club. From left to right are two unidentified, Chi Chi Rodriguez, Munevar, and Rivera. Rodriguez was inducted into the PGA World Golf Hall of Fame in 1992. (Courtesy of the Munevar family.)

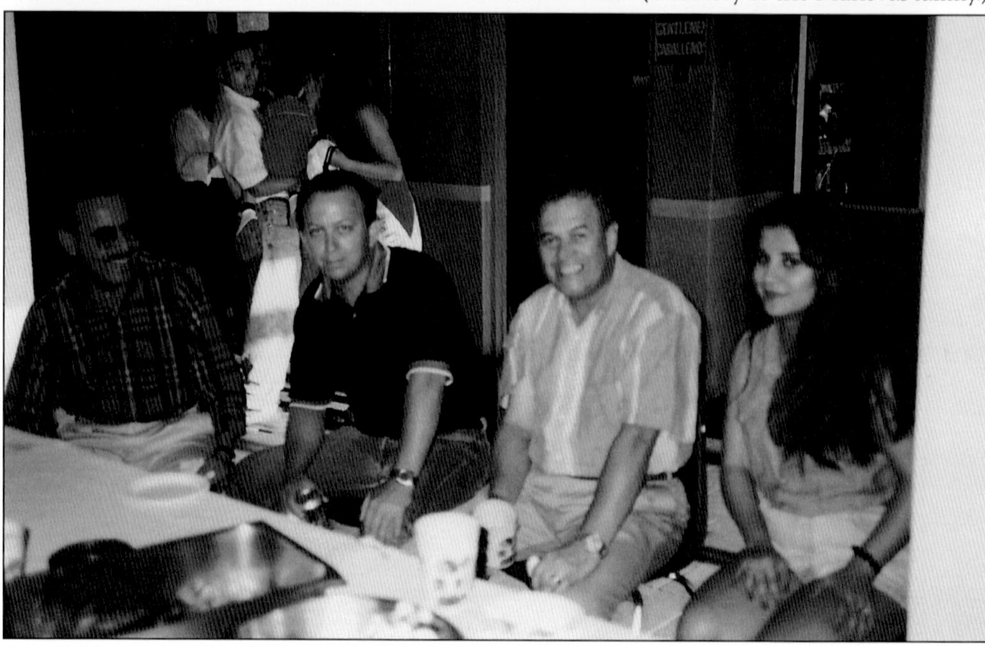

At a 1980s vendors' luncheon are, from left to right, Andy Rivera, Mark Barker, Alvaro Munevar, and unidentified. Andy and Mary Lou Rivera owned Rivera's Trading Post, Market Square T-shirt Shop, and The Chili Shop. Barker, former owner of El Sol Gift Shop, currently owns De La Luz Imports. Mark Baker Jr. owns Artes Metalicas, and Aaron Barker helps manage the shop. Munevar owns La Boutique International. (Courtesy of the Munevar family.)

Gathering for conversation outside Karlos Imports are, from left to right, Alvaro Munevar, Don Panchito, Felipe Perales, and Andy Rivera. Esperanza Ferreyro founded the business with the quartz floors in 1977. She and her husband, Carlos, managed the shop until her death in 2010. In 2016, Carlos decided to retire and sold the business to Trini Traylor, owner of Little Bit of Texas. (Courtesy of Mary Perales Valdez.)

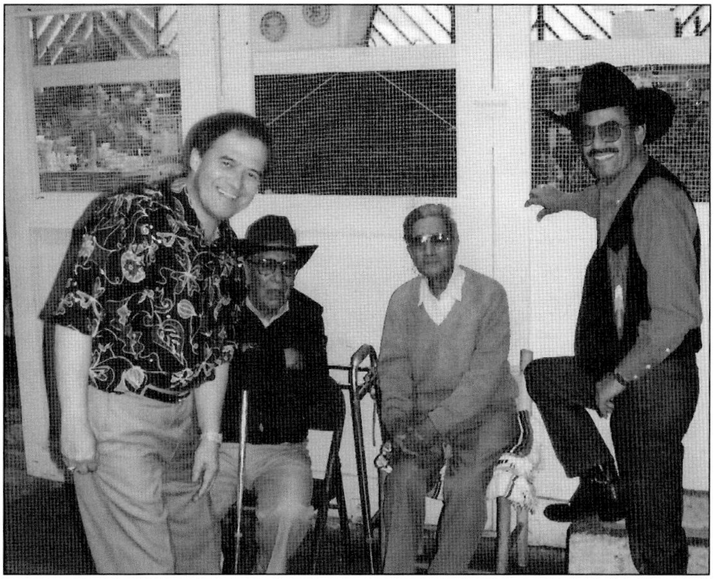

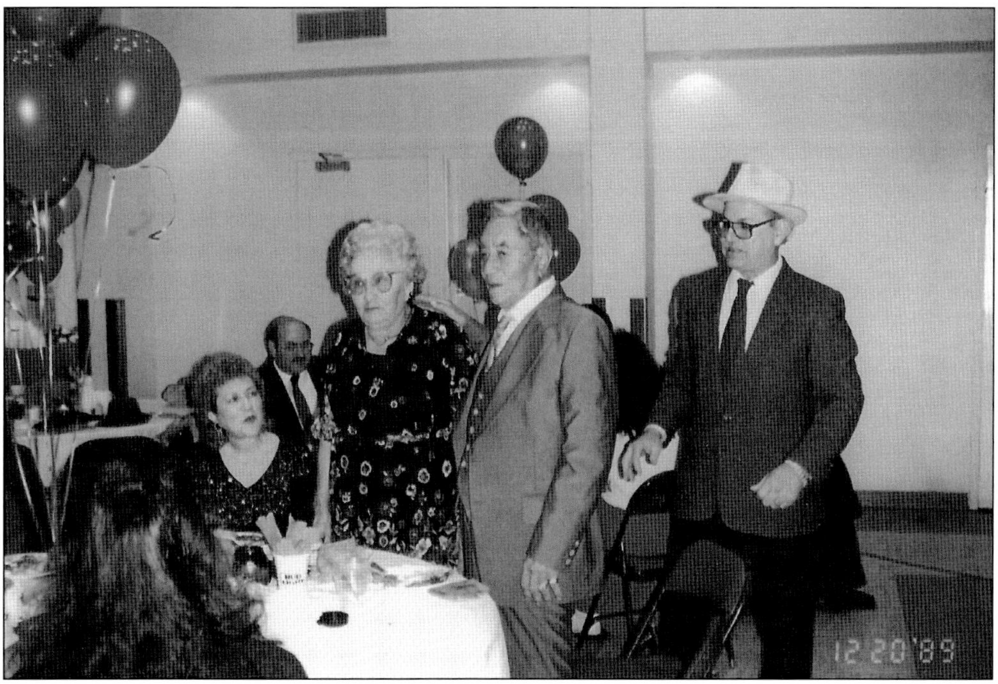

At the Merchants' Christmas Party in 1989 are, from left to right, Mary Perales; her parents, Elena and Felipe Perales, of Perales Mexican Imports; Nick Peña, of Don Roman; and Naturaleza Celestial. The Perales and Peña families continue to run their businesses in El Mercado. The second generation, Mary Perales, runs Perales Imports. The third generation of Peñas—Lucinda, Greg, and Gabriel—help their father operate the shops. (Courtesy of Mary Perales Valdez.)

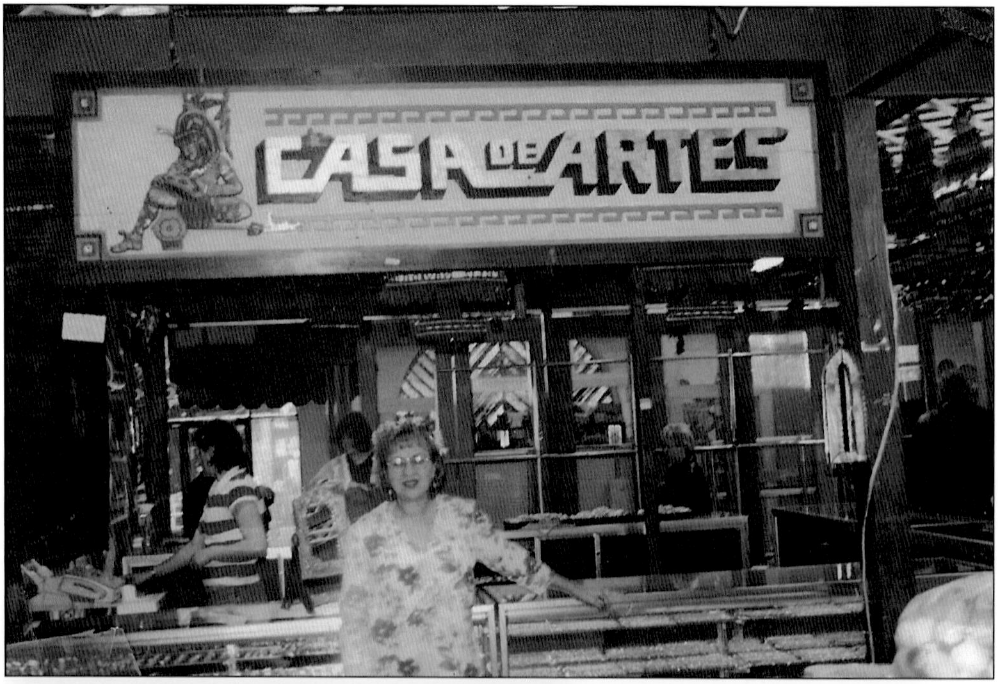

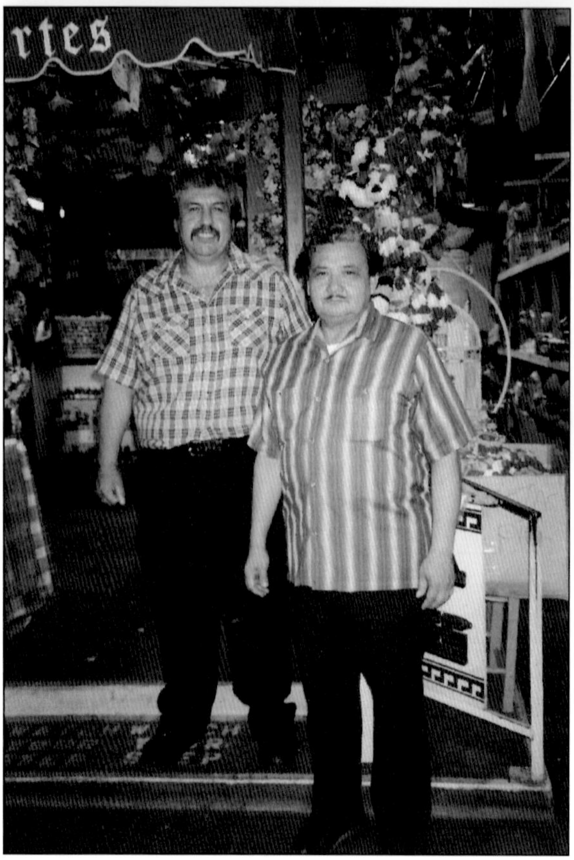

Casa de Artes was established by Alejandro and Alicia Reyes in the late 1970s. The Reyes family has been part of the market since the early 1950s, when Alex's parents, Hilario and Elvira, opened a fruit stand. The fruit stand was later expanded, and offered trinkets, pottery, and Mexican art. Mary Perales, of Perales Imports, poses for this photograph taken in the early 1980s. (Courtesy of Alicia Reyes.)

In 1978, the Casa de Artes employees were Raul Lopez and Pedro Rios. The success of this business helped create the wholesale corporation of A.R. Trade and Manufacturing. During this time, the Reyes family also owned The Pepper Tree. The shop started out with two employees, had a deli, and sold a variety of products. When fruit baskets were in high demand, the shop employed 12 people. (Courtesy of Mary Perales Valdez.)

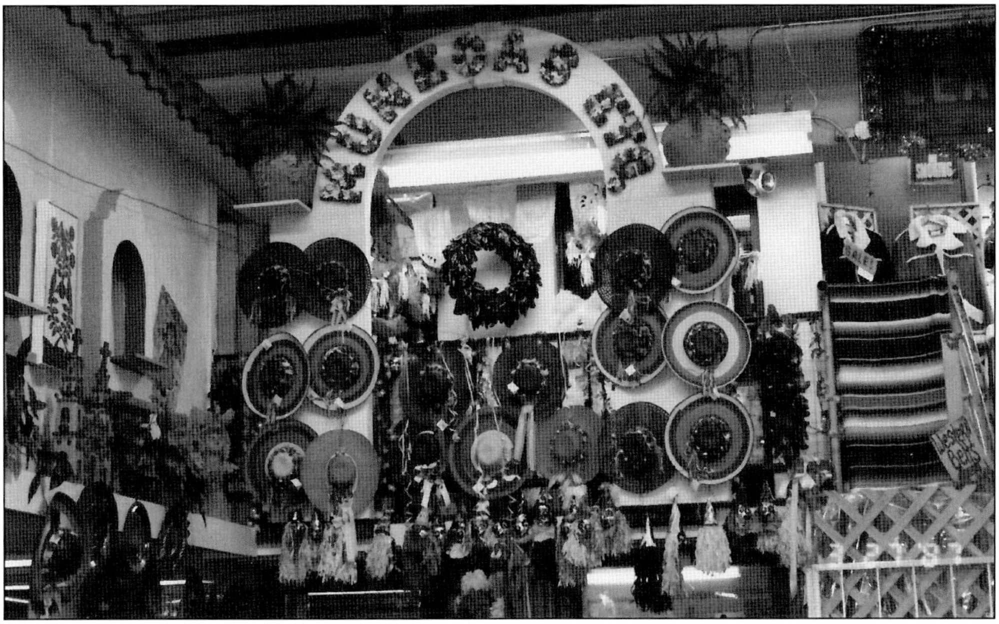

Muñecas Etc., established in 1986, is owned by artist Yolix Luna. Luna's mission in her art is to preserve Mexican traditions. In 2016, she teamed up with Bobe D'león for her Day of the Dead exhibits honoring entertainers Juan Gabriel and Celia Cruz. Luna is a great storyteller and proud of her heritage. She shares her knowledge to insure that traditions carry on for generations. (Courtesy of Yolix Luna.)

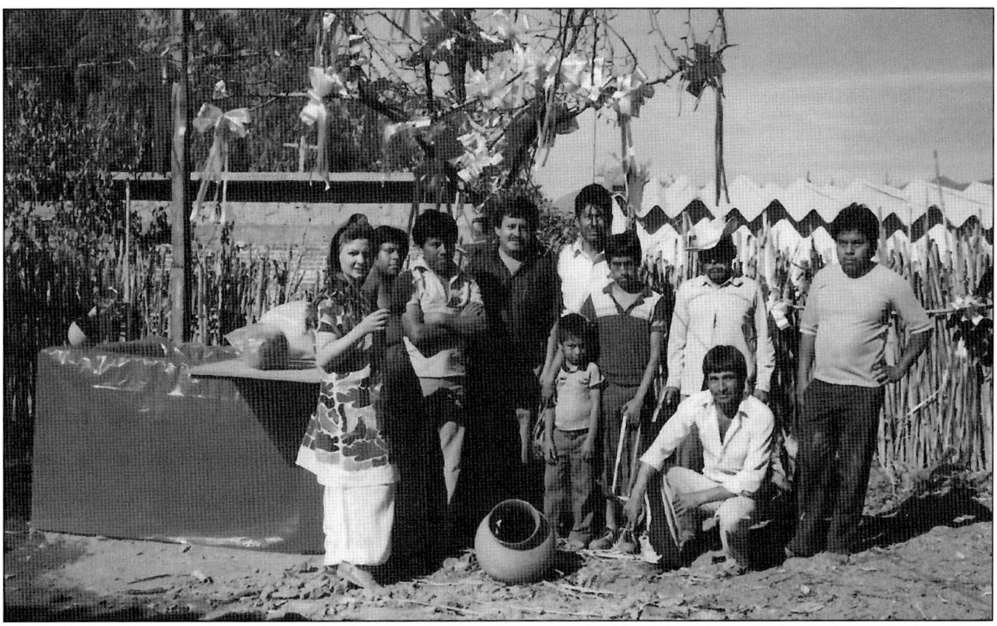

This photograph of potters who supplied Muñecas Etc. with merchandise was taken in 1987 in Oaxaca, Mexico. Atzompa pottery comes from the town of Santa Maria Atzompa. The pottery has a jade green color from the application of a lead monoxide glaze. Lead-free glazes were introduced in the 1990s after concerns in the United States. Potter Dolores Porras has introduced other colors while promoting lead-free glazes. (Courtesy of Yolix Luna.)

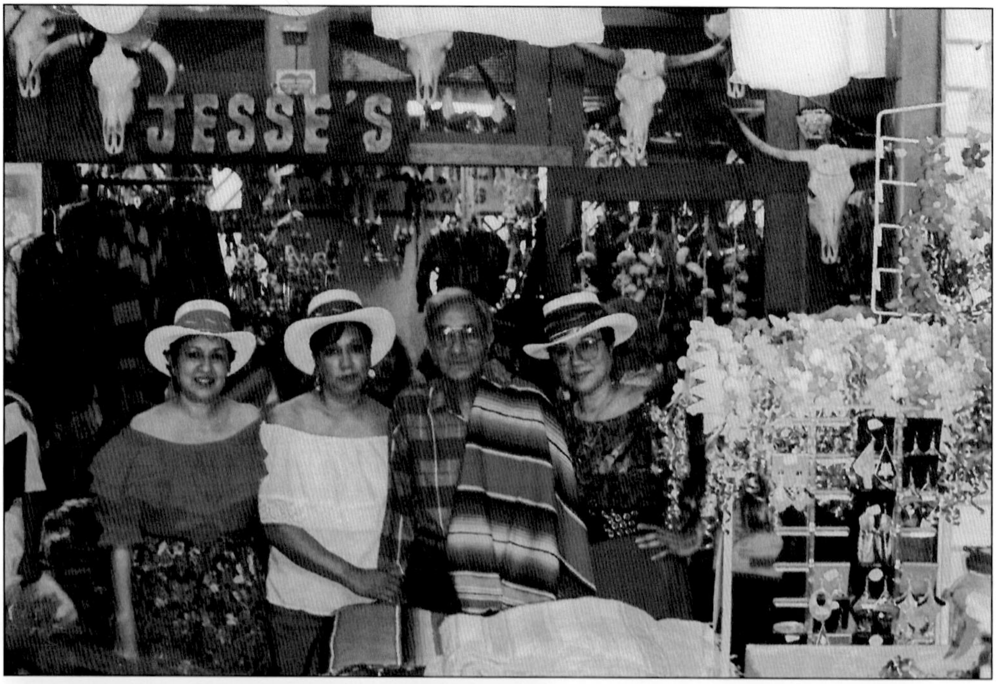

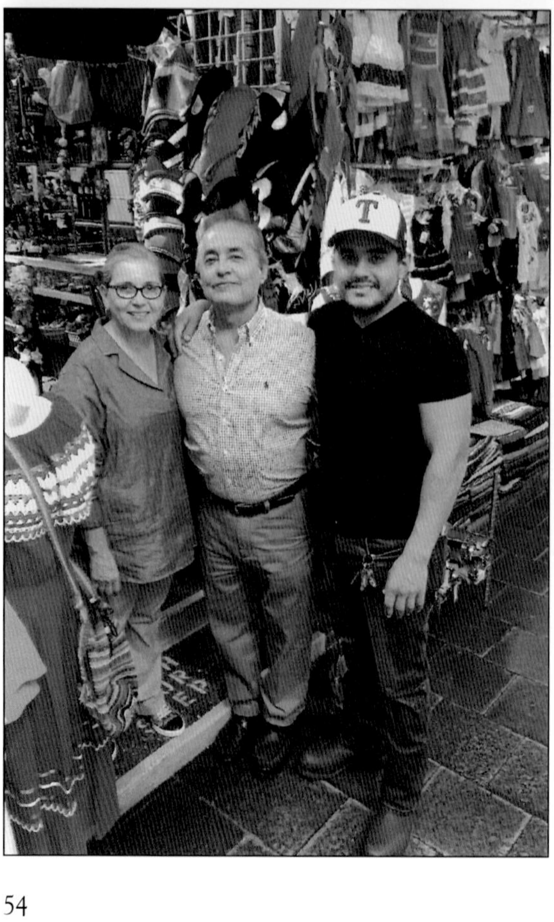

In 1989, the Perales sisters Mary Perales, Elva Anthony, and Flavia Galvan pose with their father, Felipe Perales, in front of Jesse's Jewelry and Leather. Jesse's was owned by Eduardo and Maria Ramirez and Anita Moreno. Jesse's is still in El Mercado. Across the aisle, Perales Imports continues the family's entrepreneurial spirit with Mary Perales and her husband, Rudy Valdez, running the business. (Courtesy of Mary Perales Valdez.)

Victor and Sandra Dominguez founded their Mexican imports wholesale business in 1990. They sell clothing and accessories and supply restaurant employees with traditional Mexican garments required for their line of work. In 2009, they established La Morenita Imports. Now they sell both retail and wholesale. Omar, owner of House of Mexico Imports in Farmers Market Plaza, joins his parents in front of La Morenita. (Courtesy of Victor and Sandra Dominguez.)

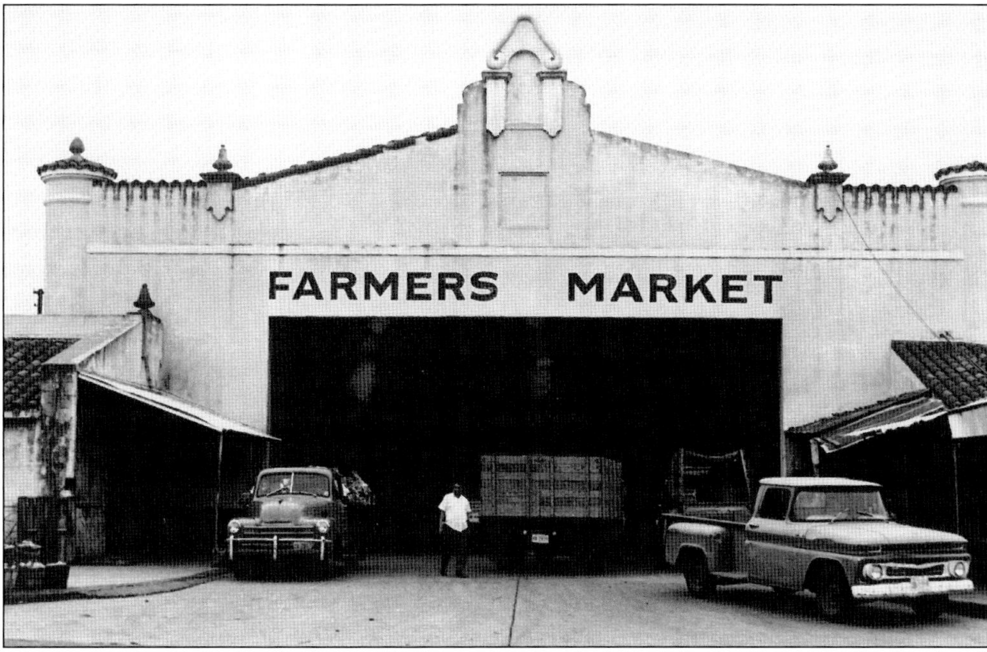

In 1970, trucks could drive in and out of the market. This entrance to the Farmers Market, now El Mercado, looks very different today. Prior to the 1976 renovations, there was no heating or air-conditioning. The Perales and Reyes families started their businesses in Hay Market Plaza, then moved to El Mercado. They remember the harsh conditions at the market. (Courtesy of UTSA Special Collections–ITC, photograph 82-539.)

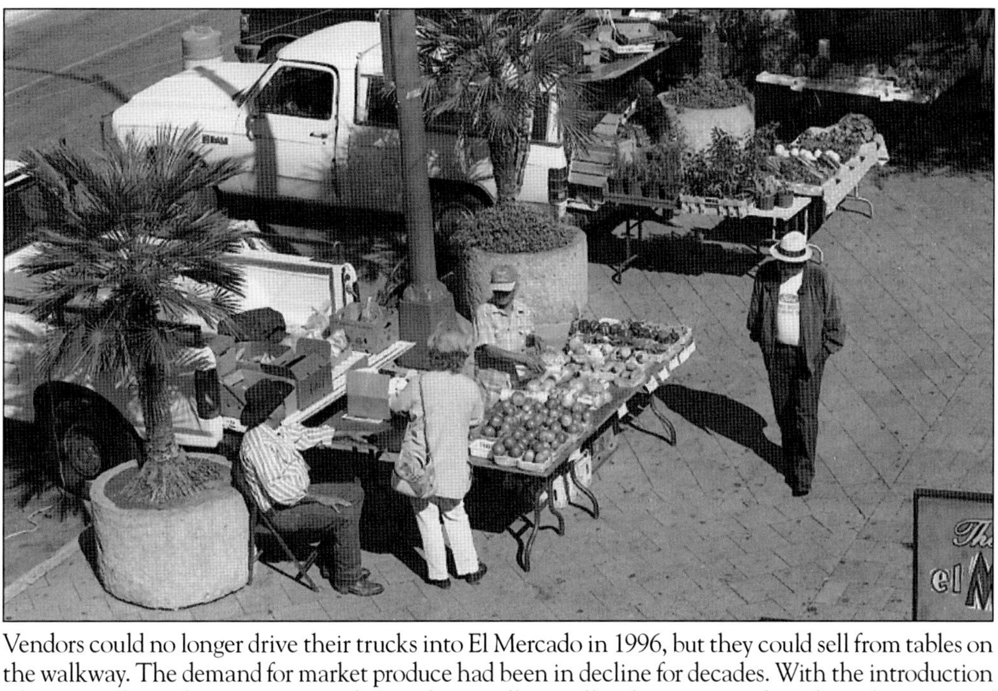

Vendors could no longer drive their trucks into El Mercado in 1996, but they could sell from tables on the walkway. The demand for market produce had been in decline for decades. With the introduction of supermarkets, there was no need to go from stall to stall to buy meat and produce. (Courtesy of the City of San Antonio, Office of the City Clerk Municipal Archives & Records.)

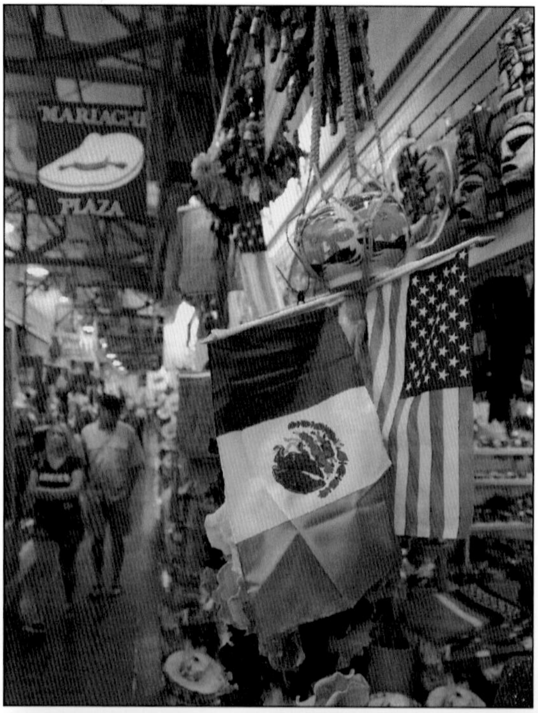

The Mexican and American flags in El Mercado are representative of San Antonio and its people. According to the San Antonio City, Texas, Statistics and Demographics report, which is based on the 2000 US Census, 58.66 percent of the population is Hispanic or Latino (of any race) and 41.36 percent is Mexican. The city and state's multiple ethnicities are celebrated during Texas Folklife Festival at the Institute of Texan Cultures. (Photograph by Al Rendon; courtesy of La Familia Cortez Restaurants.)

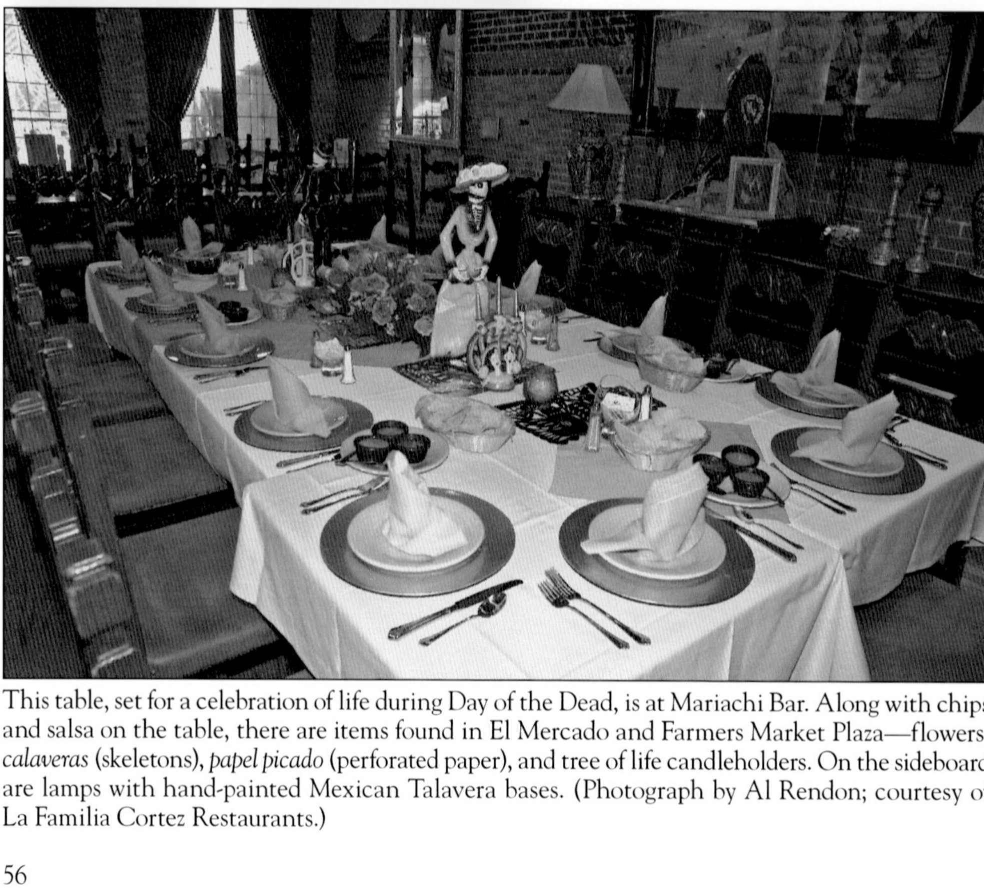

This table, set for a celebration of life during Day of the Dead, is at Mariachi Bar. Along with chips and salsa on the table, there are items found in El Mercado and Farmers Market Plaza—flowers, *calaveras* (skeletons), *papel picado* (perforated paper), and tree of life candleholders. On the sideboard are lamps with hand-painted Mexican Talavera bases. (Photograph by Al Rendon; courtesy of La Familia Cortez Restaurants.)

Five

FARMERS MARKET PLAZA

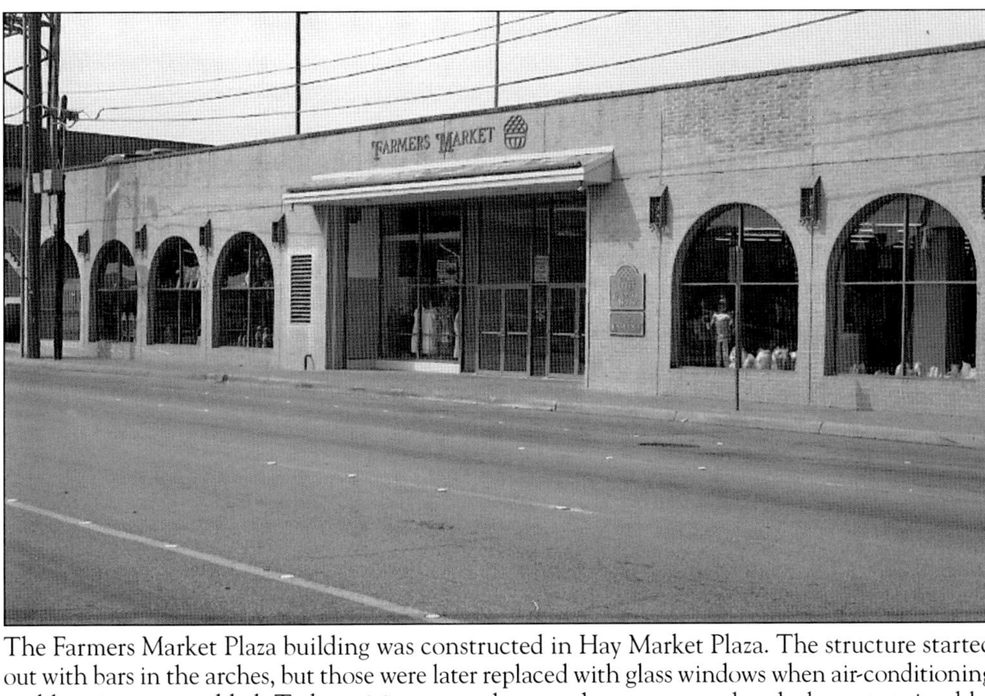

The Farmers Market Plaza building was constructed in Hay Market Plaza. The structure started out with bars in the arches, but those were later replaced with glass windows when air-conditioning and heating were added. Today, visitors can shop, and on most weekends, be entertained by Mexican music and traditional folk dances preformed at center stage. (Courtesy of the City of San Antonio, Office of the City Clerk Municipal Archives & Records.)

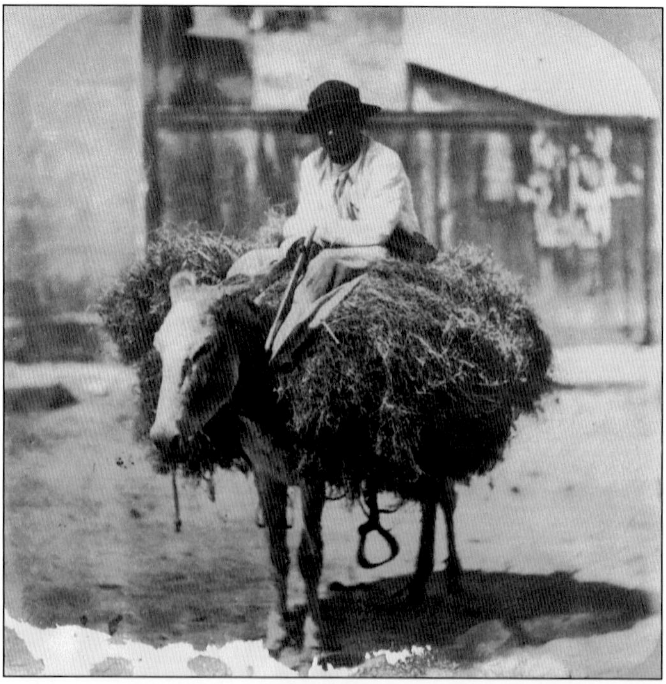

Hay, wood, and drinking water peddlers were a common site in the early days of Hay Market Plaza. Most vendors brought their wares to market in wagons or on donkeys; others carried their products on their backs. Some peddlers sold their products door-to-door to people who were too far from the central market. (Courtesy of the San Antonio Conservation Society Foundation.)

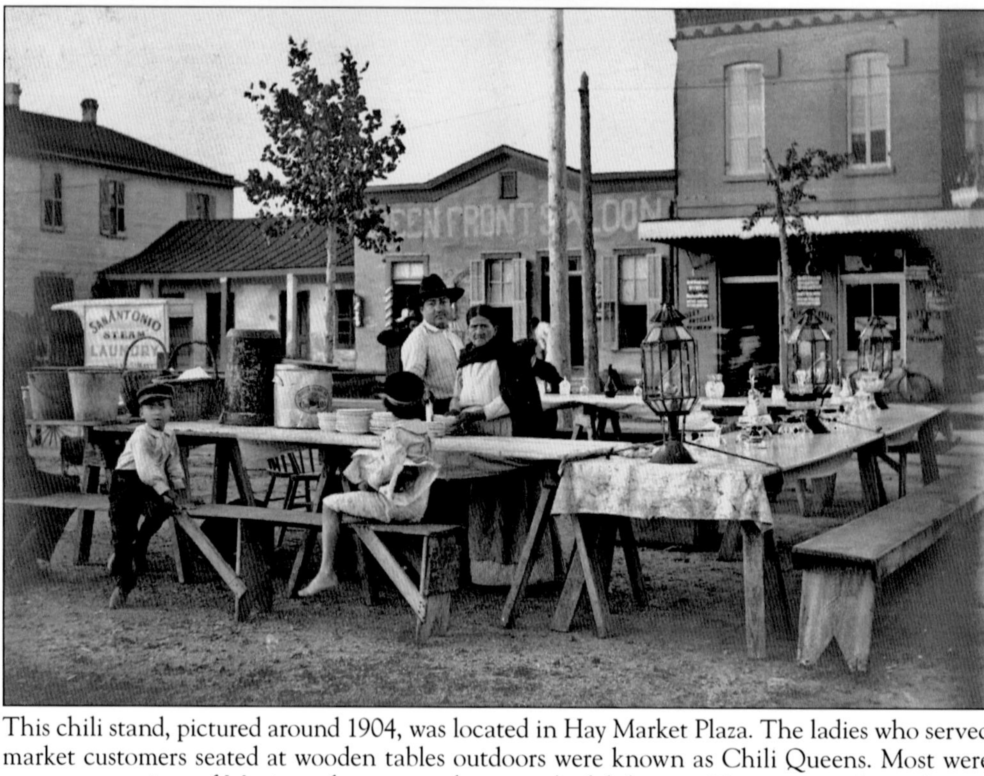

This chili stand, pictured around 1904, was located in Hay Market Plaza. The ladies who served market customers seated at wooden tables outdoors were known as Chili Queens. Most were young, attractive, of Mexican descent, and wore colorful dresses. This attracted travelers to sample the Mexican food served in the plazas. (Courtesy of UTSA Special Collections–ITC, photograph 101-84.)

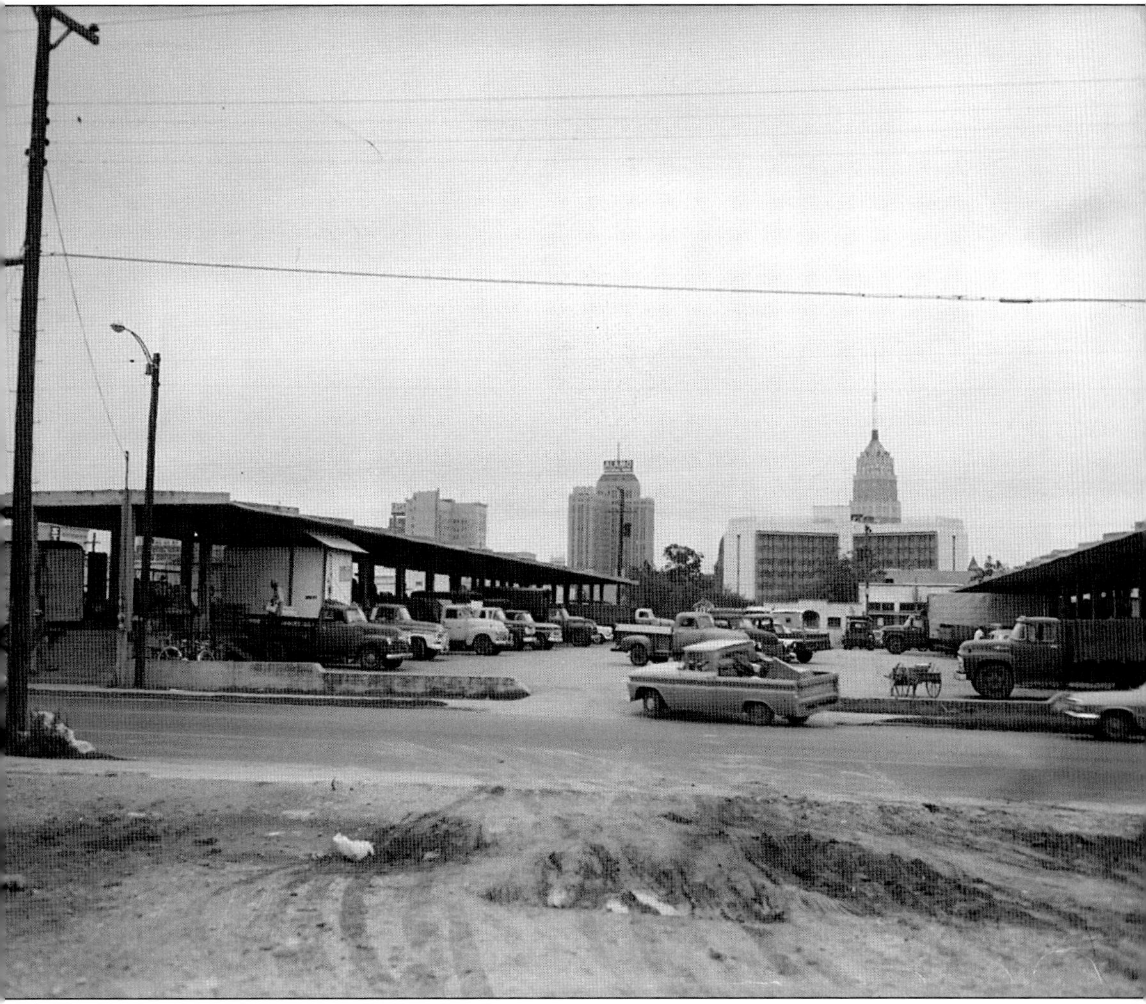

Washington Square Market, pictured here in the early 1960s, was continuing to do business, even though it was difficult for the produce vendors selling from the backs of their trucks to compete with supermarkets. The end was near. According to an 1896 Sanborn map, Washington Square took up a city block, bounded by Buena Vista, South San Saba, Monterey, and South Concho Streets. The open-air market offered fruits and vegetables grown by farmers in the area, other states, and Mexico. In 1951, the wholesale companies had outgrown their spaces in the Municipal Market House, Produce Row, and Washington Square, and moved their business to a 36-acre tract on Zarzamora Street. This location, with a railroad terminal, provided distribution throughout the United States. The San Antonio Produce Terminal is located at 1500 South Zarzamora Street. The market fell victim to an urban renewal project during the late 1960s and disappeared. (Courtesy of UTSA Special Collections–ITC, photograph B-21-A-06.)

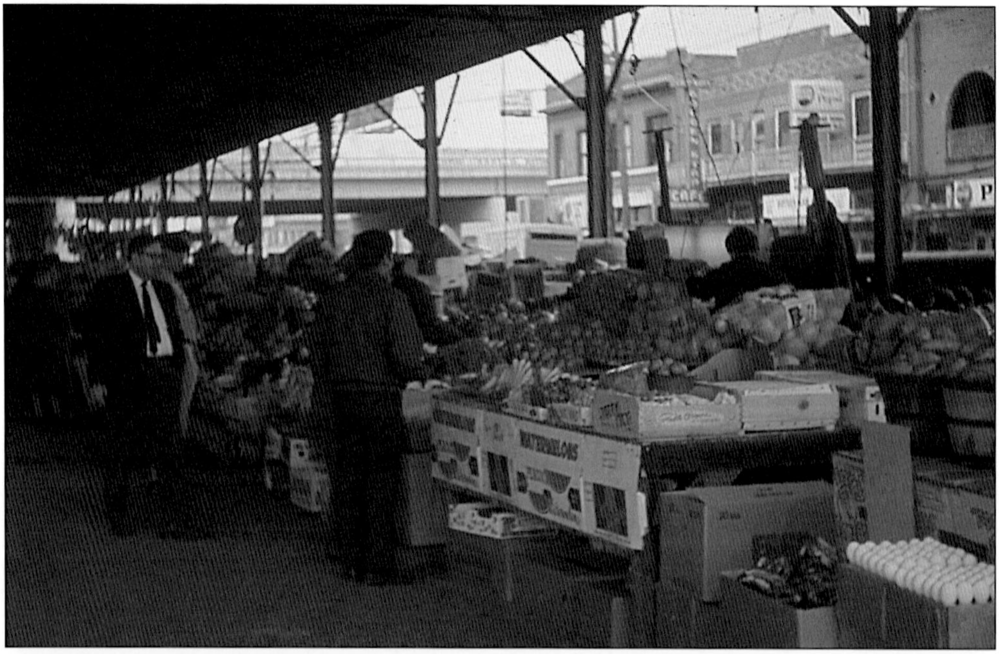

These stalls in Hay Market Plaza were photographed in 1966. Looking at the mounds of fruit, vegetables, and eggs, the market was busy. But these outdoor markets would soon be a thing of the past, as supermarkets like Handy Andy expanded throughout the city. The first Handy Andy opened on Broadway Street in 1926. (Courtesy of the City of San Antonio, Office of the City Clerk Municipal Archives & Records.)

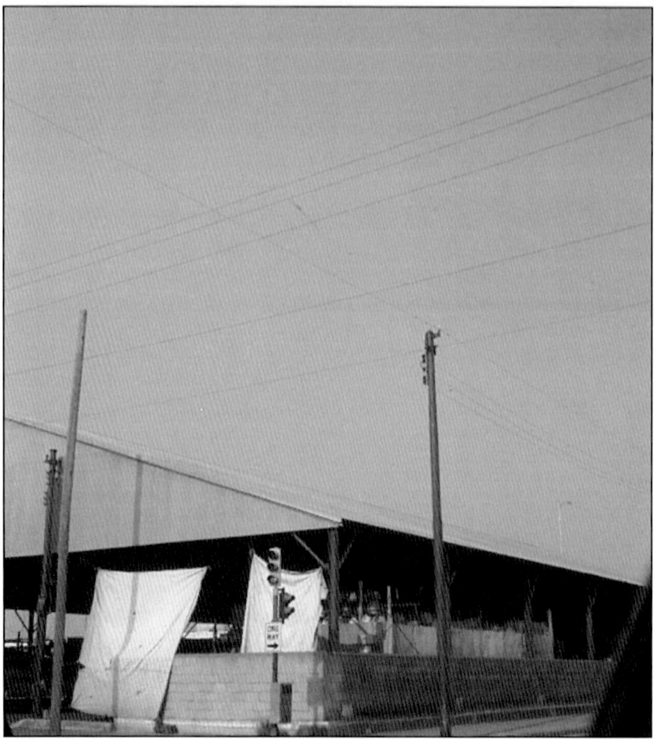

In 1966, the market in Hay Market Plaza was in dire need of renovations. An article in the September 5, 1966, *San Antonio Express and News* discussed the urban uplift for Rosa Verde project, the west section of the central business district: "An additional attraction will be the expansion and beautification of the Municipal Farmers' Market." (Courtesy of the City of San Antonio, Office of the City Clerk Municipal Archives & Records.)

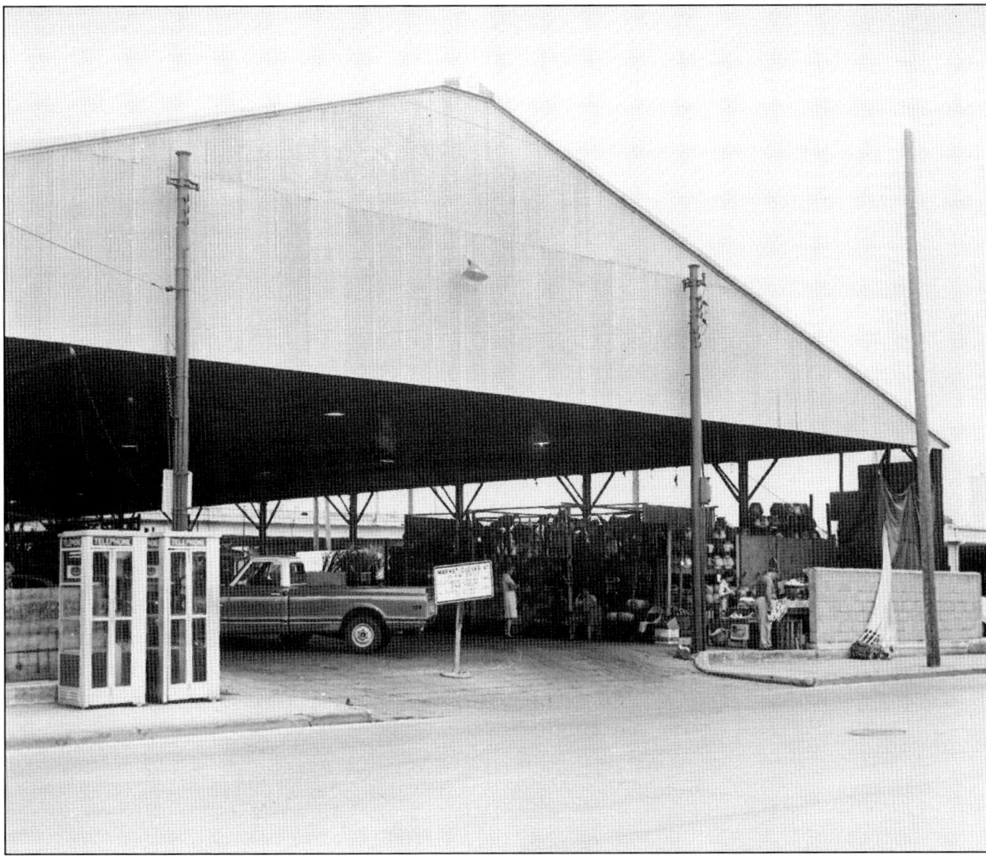

When this c. 1970 photograph was taken, the renovations to the market had not begun. In 1971, the redevelopment of the market was still in the planning and funding stage. An article in the *San Antonio Express and News* on October 29, 1972, opened with, "Whatever high hopes there are for a revitalized Farmers Market are in the deep freeze." (Courtesy of UTSA Special Collections–ITC, photograph 82-538.)

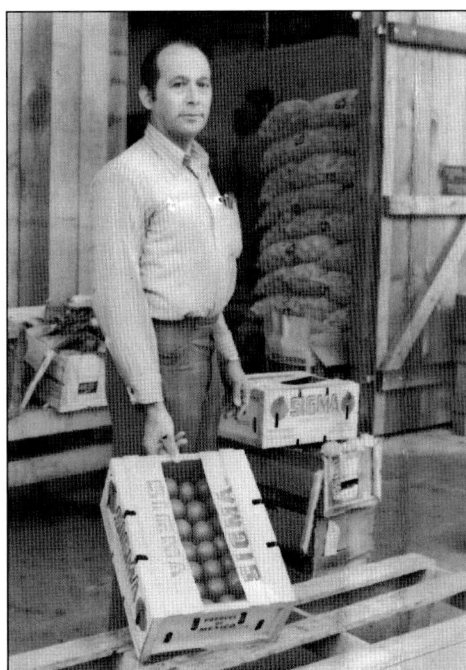

Martin Edward Douglas unloads produce for the day's business sometime in the 1970s. In 1996, Douglas family members were recognized as merchants who had been in business since before the market renovation in 1976. Douglas's sister, Pauline, accepted the proclamation for Martin's Produce at a ceremony hosted by Mayor Bill Thornton. Currently, Martin's Curios is operated by Martin's son, Michael Anthony Douglas. (Courtesy of the Douglas family.)

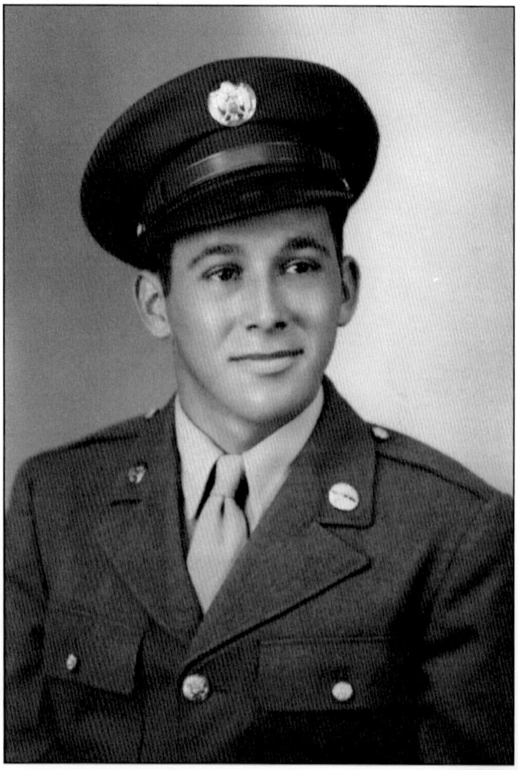

Martin Douglas was drafted into the US Army during World War II while he was attending Central Catholic High School. He went into the military right after graduation. While his son was at war, Daniel Douglas ran the family farm in Poteet. After the war, Martin set up his produce business. Later, Pauline Douglas joined her brother to help him manage the business. (Courtesy of the Douglas family.)

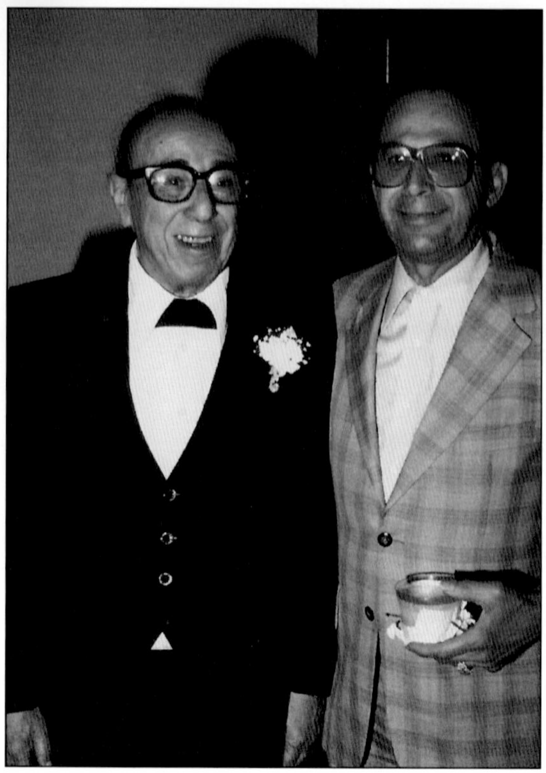

Henry B. González (left) and Martin Douglas are pictured together in 1985. González, a Democratic politician, represented the 20th Congressional District of Texas from 1961 to 1999. Both men had immigrant parents: González's parents emigrated from Mexico during the Mexican Revolution, and Douglas's father emigrated in 1890. San Antonio's Henry B. González Convention Center is named in González's honor. González died in 2000, and Douglas died in 2008. (Courtesy of the Douglas family.)

Joe Gonzales started working in produce as a kid. When this photograph was taken in 1947, he was 16. Gonzales married Mary, who had a dream of owning her own business. In the early 1970s, Mary established her produce business with $40. Mary's Produce grew into Marie's Creations & Imports. Her father, Celestino Contreras, and her daughter Joanne helped operate the business. (Courtesy of Joanne Gonzales.)

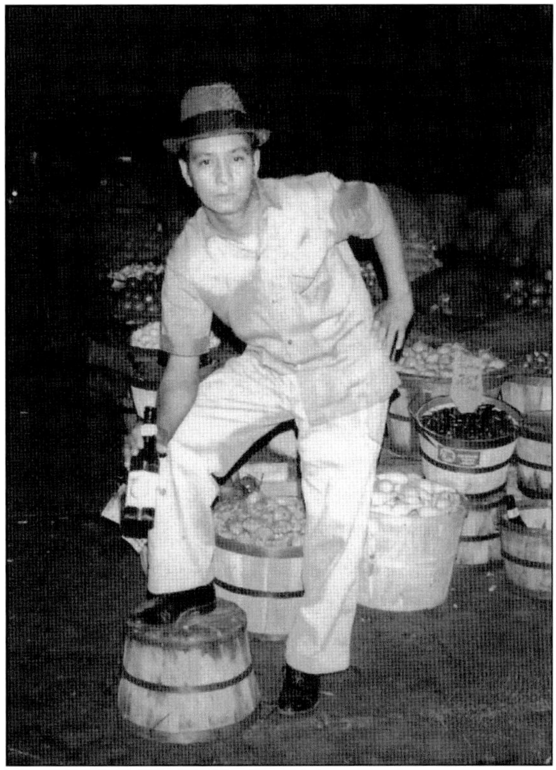

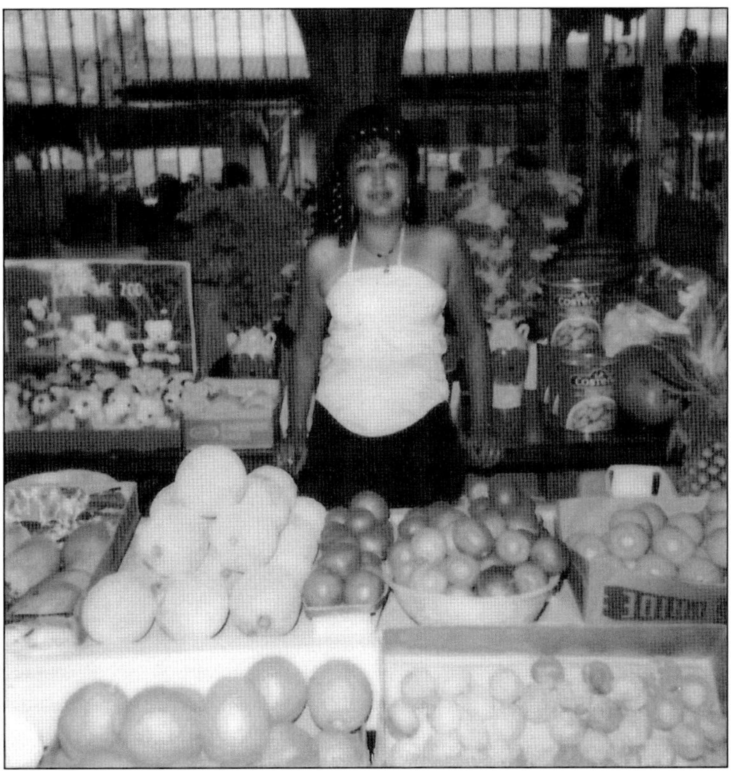

In the early 1970s, there were few female produce vendors at the Farmers Market. Mary Gonzales was one of the first women to set up shop there. She continued to do business at the market until her death in 2007. Her daughter Joanne took over, but it was emotionally draining to continue without her mother. Joanne sold Marie's Creations & Imports to a family friend. (Courtesy of Joanne Gonzales.)

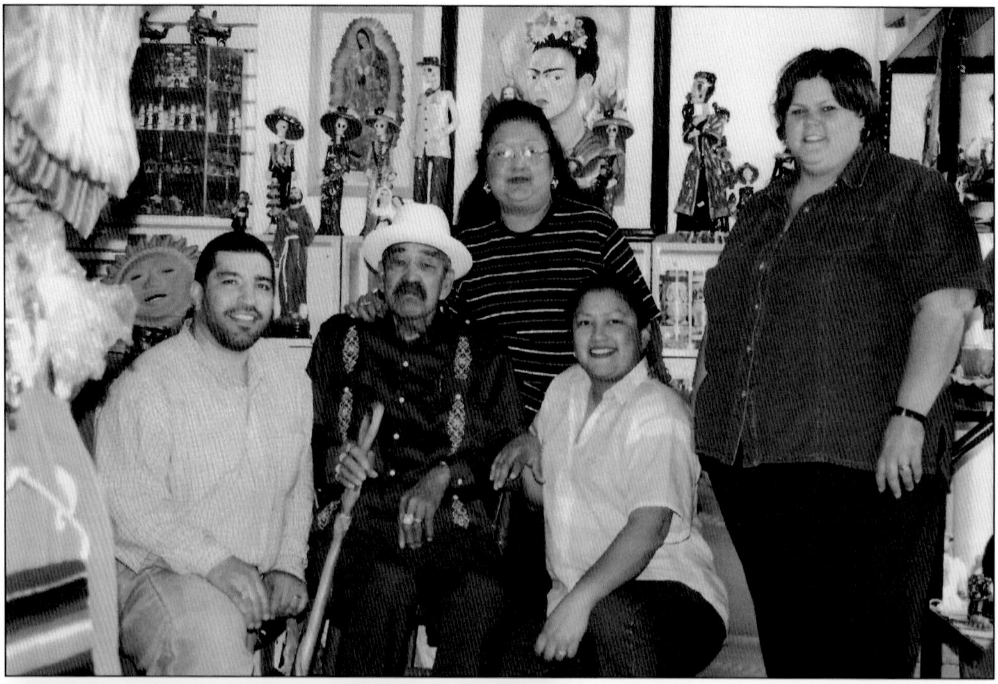

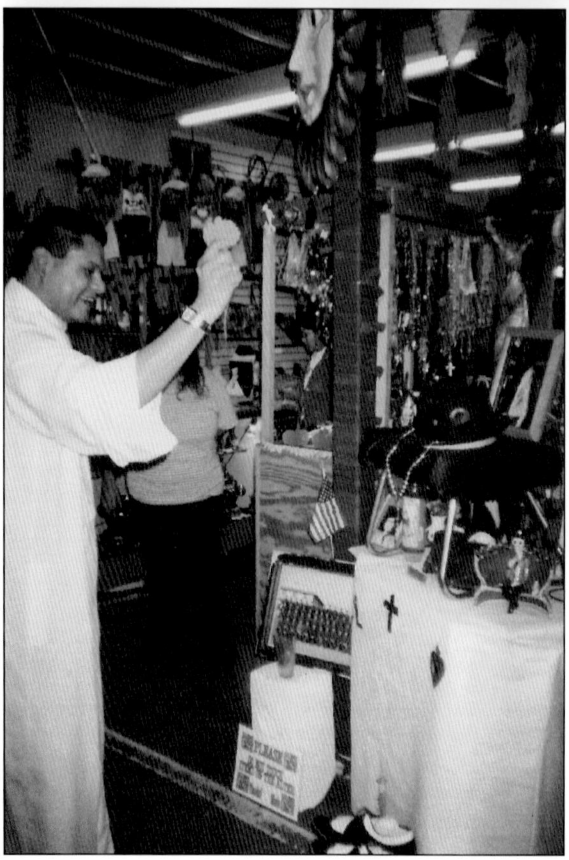

At Marie's Creations & Imports in 1998 are, from left to right, Daniel Gonzalez, Celestino Contreras, Mary Gonzales, Joanne Gonzales, and Tracy Morones. Mary and the business are gone, but her entrepreneurial spirit lives on in her daughter. In 2009, Joanne Gonzales and Margie Hernandez established Queen Bee Pest Control. These ladies are proud to be two of the few women in their industry, not as employees but as owners. (Courtesy of Joanne Gonzales.)

In 2003, a priest blessed the altar honoring Celestino Contreras during the Day of the Dead festivities. Contreras was a sharp dresser who liked to accent his wardrobe with a hat and Stacy Adams shoes; he also walked with a cane. His cane and his favorite shoes were placed at the foot of the altar, along with other cherished items and traditional decorations. (Courtesy of Joanne Gonzales.)

Rene L. Gonzalez is selling sausage tacos at Little Bits of Nature during the week of Fiesta San Antonio in 1988. The business was owned by his daughter Thelma Gonzalez. She later changed the name of the business to G's Gonzalez Gift Shop. Thelma Gonzalez is active in the San Antonio Farmers Market Plaza Association and has served as president, vice president, secretary, and treasurer. (Courtesy of Thelma Gonzalez.)

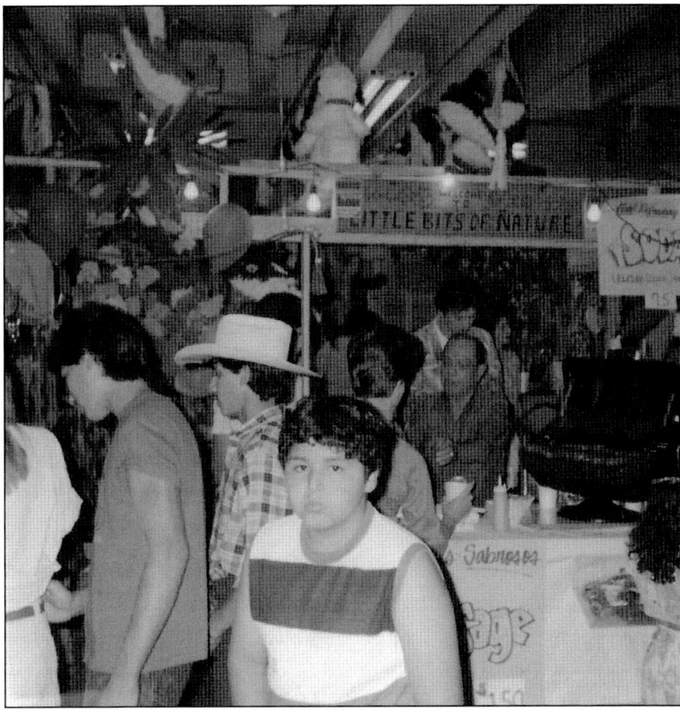

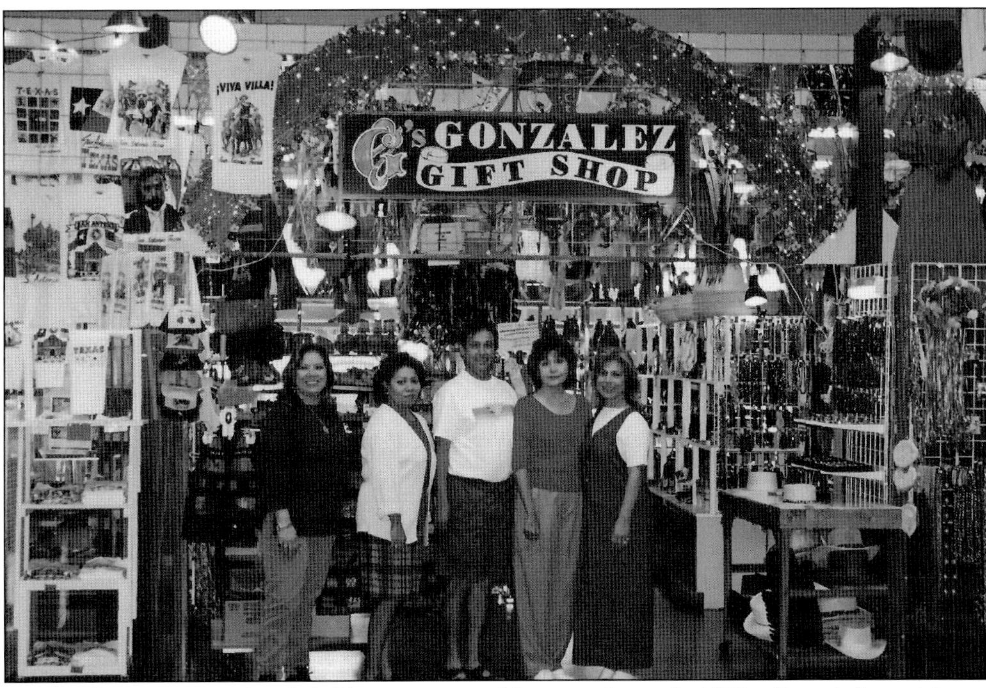

The staff at G's Gonzalez Gift Shop is pictured here in the early 1990s. From left to right are Maria Blanca Caballero, Cathy Martinez, Richard Diaz, Molly Gonzalez, and Thelma Gonzalez. During the 1990s, T-shirts and decorated hats were big business, so Thelma taught herself and her employees how to decorate the hats. During Fiesta San Antonio, the hats were a hot item at parties, festivals, and parades. (Courtesy of Thelma Gonzalez.)

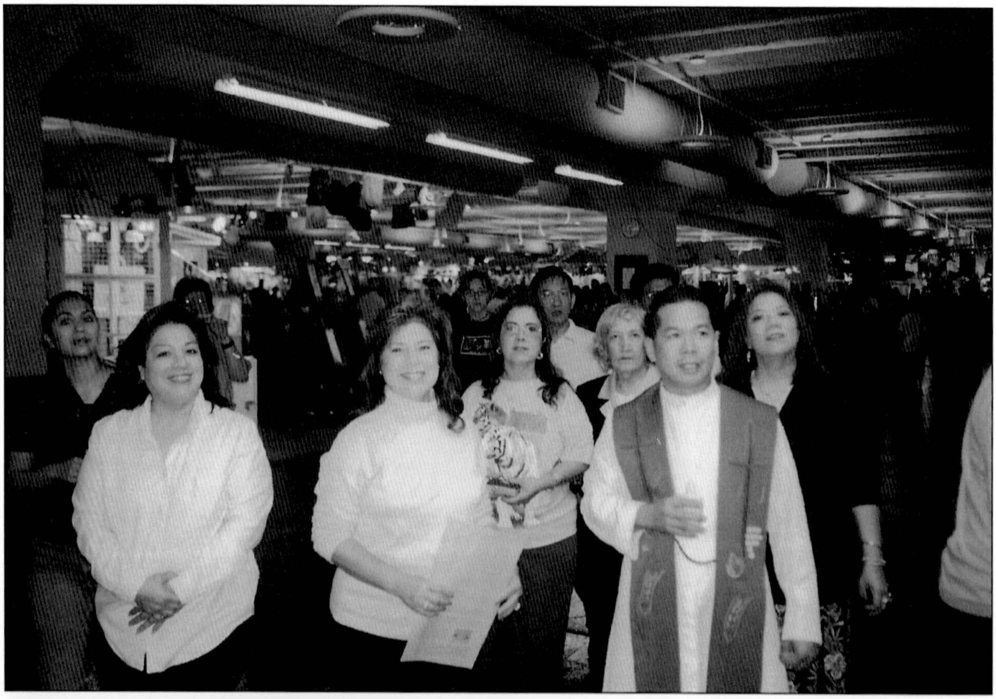

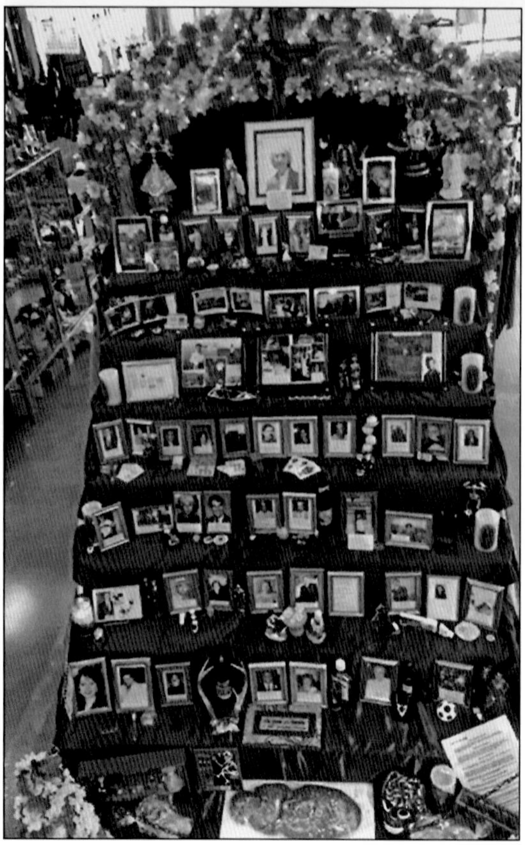

Gonzalez family members and friends celebrate the Day of the Dead in 2002. The altar honoring Thelma's father, Rene L. Gonzalez Sr., was set up in the shop and blessed by Father Martin from Santo Niño Catholic Church. Gathered at the blessing ceremony are, from left to right, Felicia Alanis, Rita Alanis, Thelma Gonzalez, Adela Rivera, Susan Gonzalez (Thelma's mother), and Maria Blanca Caballero. (Courtesy of Thelma Gonzalez.)

Thelma Gonzalez, her family, and staff set up an altar in the shop every year. In 2015, the altar was in honor of her mother, Susan Montes Gonzalez. Every tier showcases photographs of family members and friends who have passed on. The last tier holds items traditional to the Day of the Dead and a loaf of Mexican bread of the dead. (Courtesy of Thelma Gonzalez.)

In 1966, the opened-sided building located at the old hay market was uncomfortable most of the year. The city had plans for a new building, but it would not be constructed until the 1970s. For years, there would be conflict between the market and the San Antonio Development Agency, formerly called Urban Renewal Agency. (Courtesy of the City of San Antonio, Office of the City Clerk Municipal Archives & Records.)

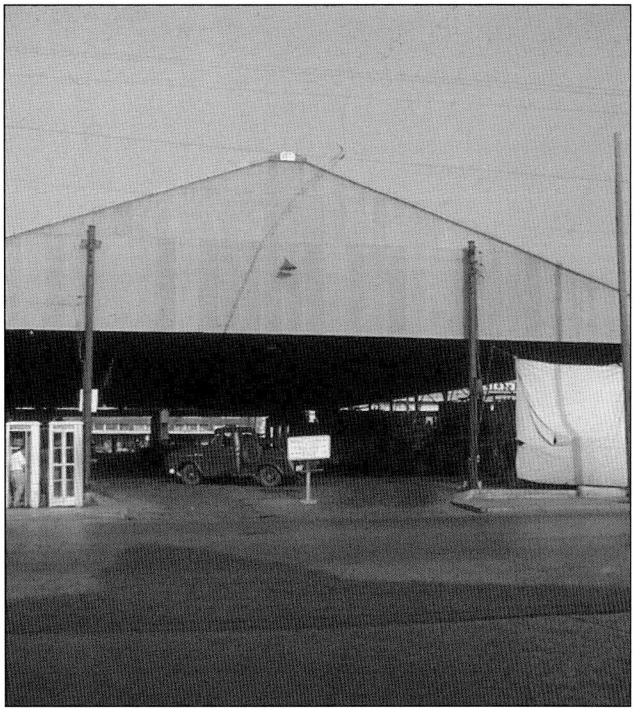

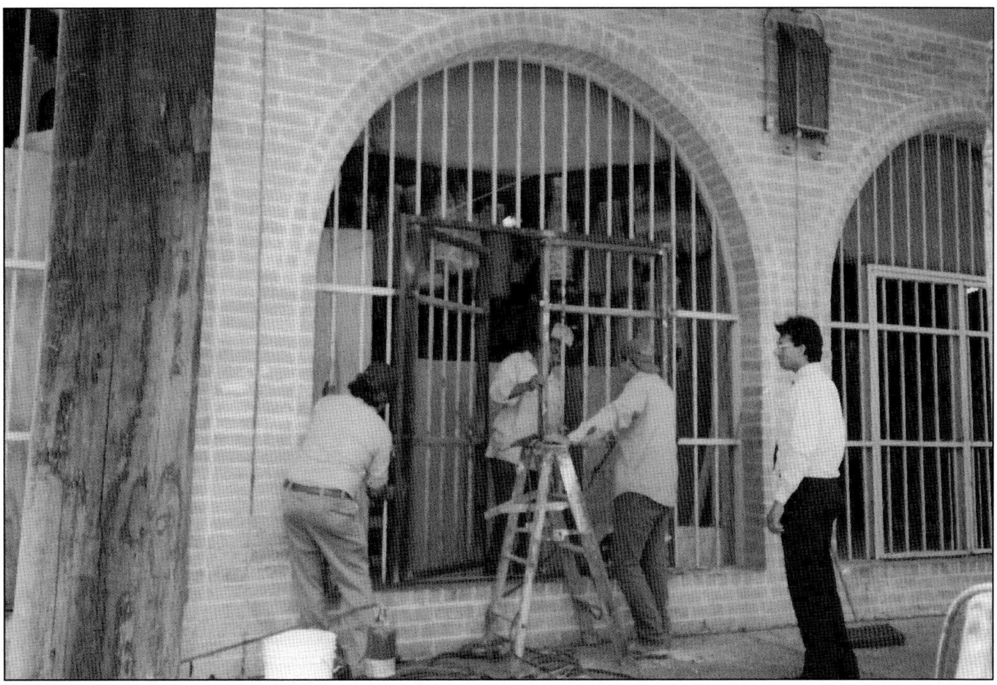

In 1993, Robert Tagle, manager of Market Square, looks on while men work on a shop gate. These gates were used by vendors to bring in their merchandise, and the bars worked well to display merchandise during business hours. Vendors were also allowed to stack their wares outside and keep their doors open until 1:00 a.m. to take advantage of party traffic. (Courtesy of Thelma Gonzalez.)

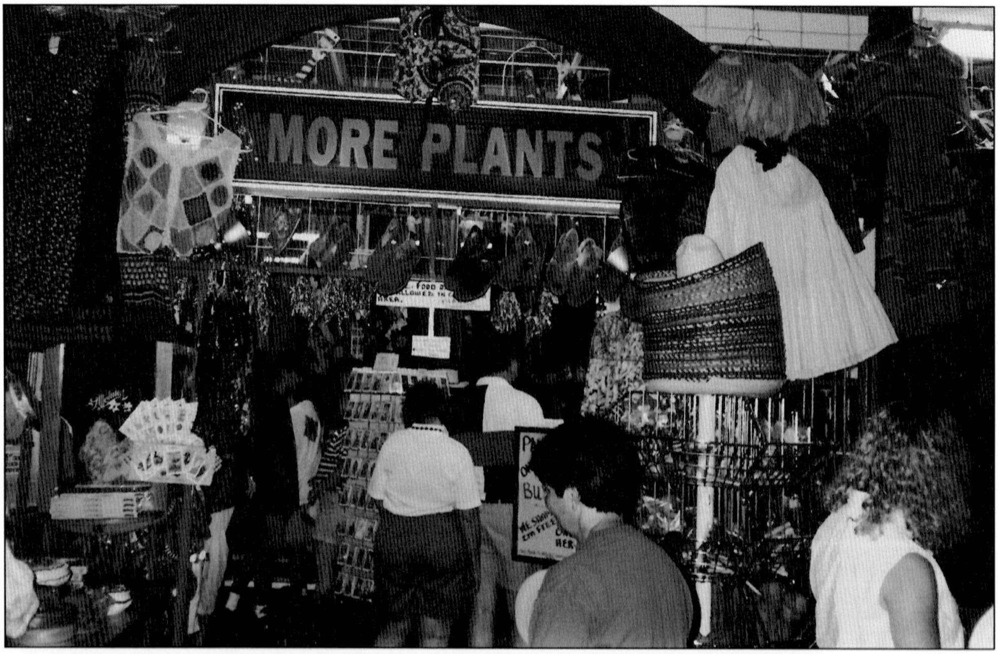

More Plants was established in the Farmers Market Plaza in 1985 by Phillip John and Alice Leon. Shortly after the business opened, the Leons decided they would no longer sell plants. In the late 1980s, they bought Olmec Imports. Phillip managed More Plants, while Alice managed Olmec Imports. Their children Phillip Jr. and Marie Evelyn Wilson helped out during busy seasons. (Courtesy of Phillip and Alice Leon.)

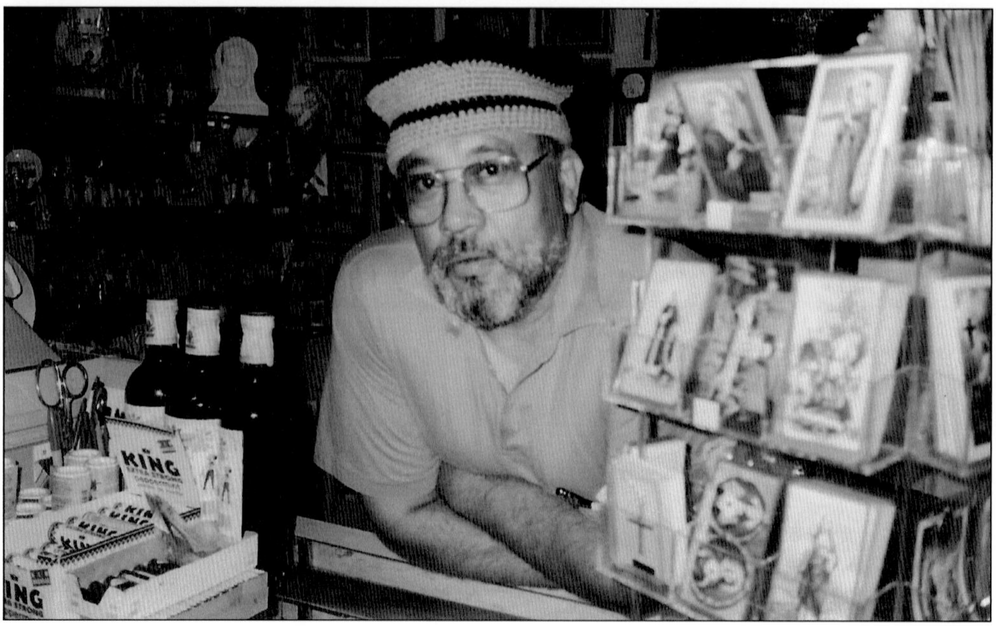

Phillip John Leon leans on the counter of More Plants. He was born on October 11, 1943, and served in the US Army in the 1960s. Leon was very helpful with photographs and information during work on this book. His death on November 22, 2016, was unexpected. For now, Phillip Jr. is running the business. (Courtesy of Phillip and Alice Leon.)

Owners Phillip and Alice Leon are pictured in their shop, More Plants. The Leons started their business from their home in 1983. They sold plants in a parking lot off Highway 90. In the 1980s, potted plants were very popular and used as indoor air purifiers. By 1985, they needed a permanent space, and relocated to Farmers Market Plaza. (Courtesy of Phillip and Alice Leon.)

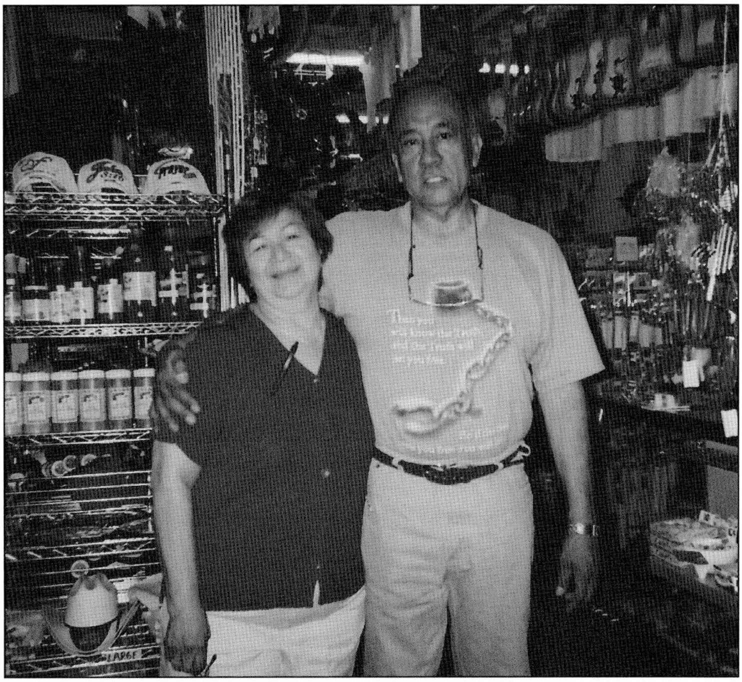

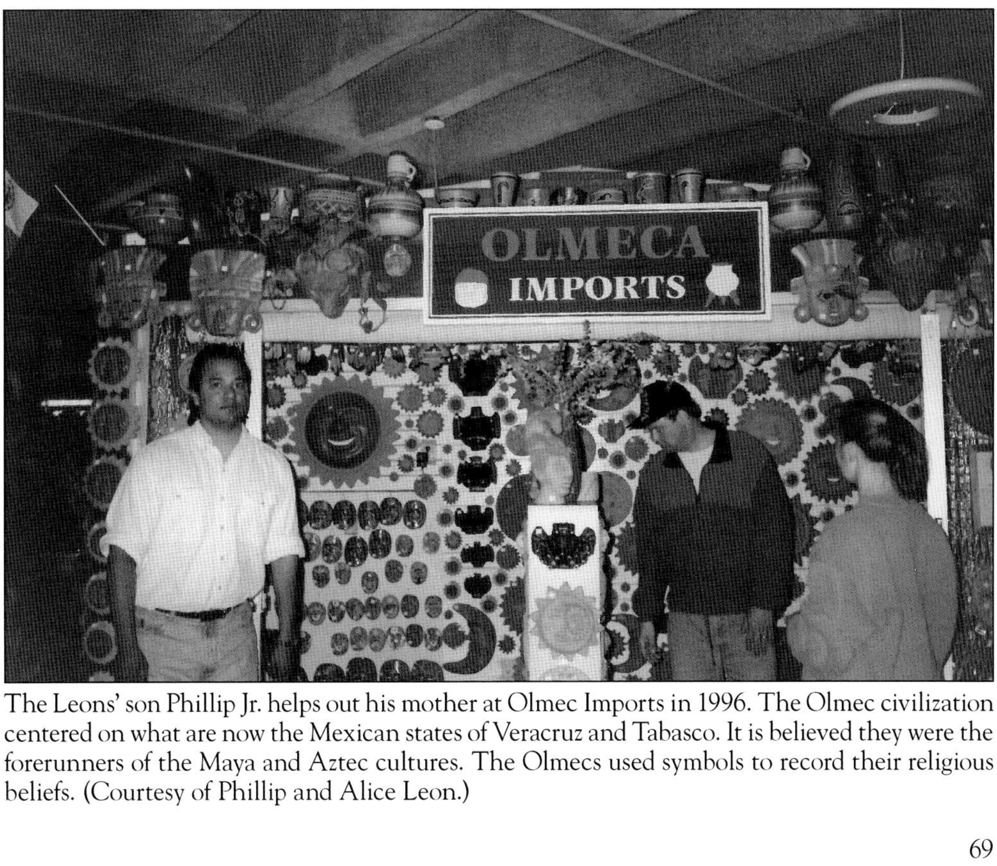

The Leons' son Phillip Jr. helps out his mother at Olmec Imports in 1996. The Olmec civilization centered on what are now the Mexican states of Veracruz and Tabasco. It is believed they were the forerunners of the Maya and Aztec cultures. The Olmecs used symbols to record their religious beliefs. (Courtesy of Phillip and Alice Leon.)

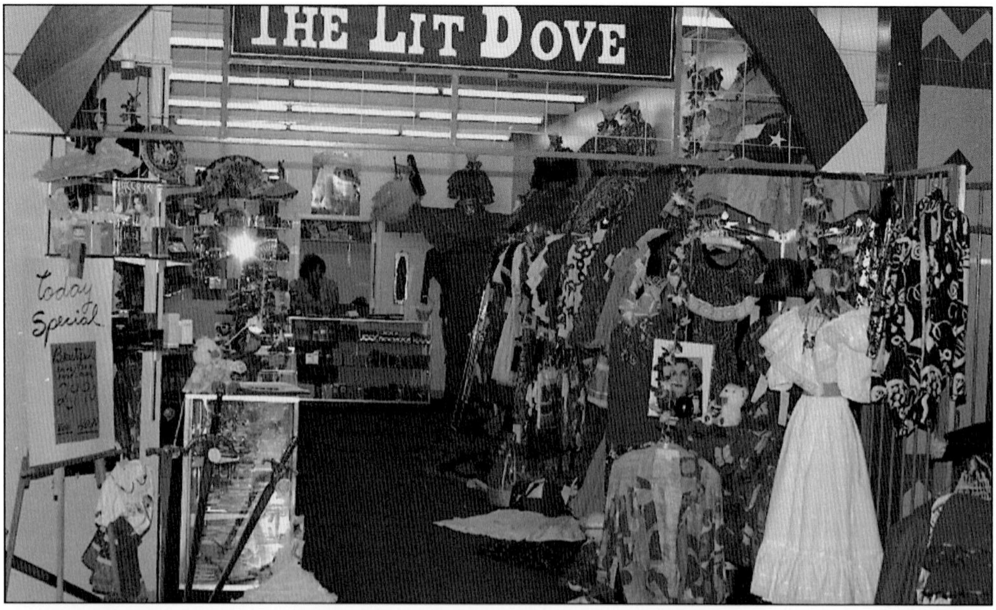

The Lit Dove, pictured in 1994, was owned by Emeterio and Rosa Maria de Miguel. There is currently a business in the Farmers Market Plaza called Yesi's the Lit Dove. This business sells dresses, hats, accessories, and children's mariachi outfits. (Courtesy of the City of San Antonio, Office of the City Clerk Municipal Archives & Records.)

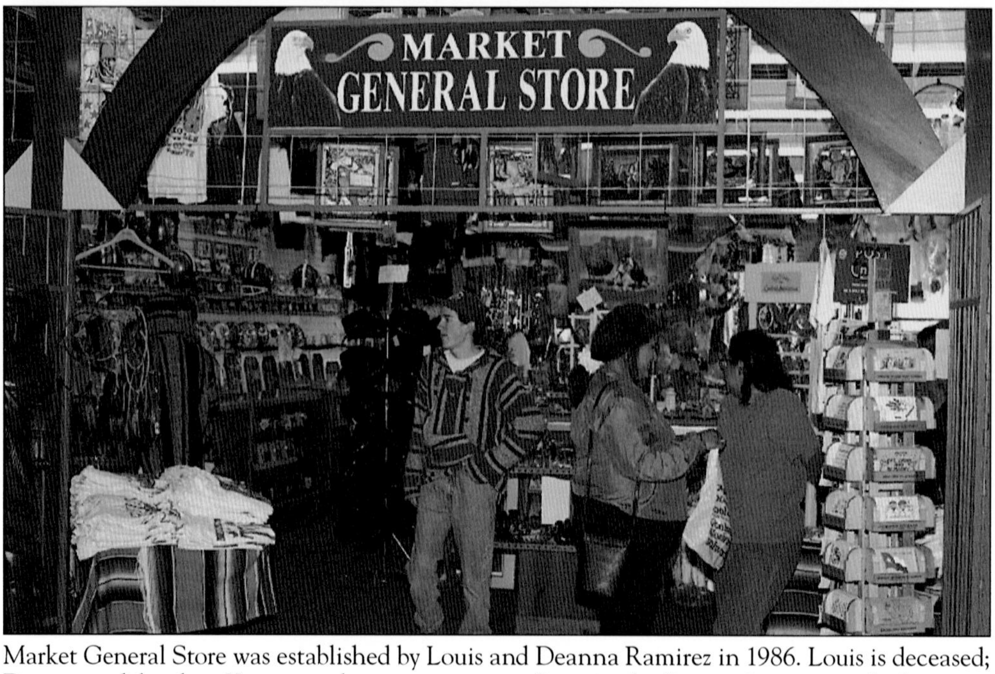

Market General Store was established by Louis and Deanna Ramirez in 1986. Louis is deceased; Deanna and daughter Yvette are the current owners. Ronnie, the Ramirez's son, runs the business. Yvette bought Tejano Lou's in 2013. The Ramirez family has a long history at the market; their grandfather, Salvador Martell, bought produce for resale. (Courtesy of the City of San Antonio, Office of the City Clerk Municipal Archives & Records.)

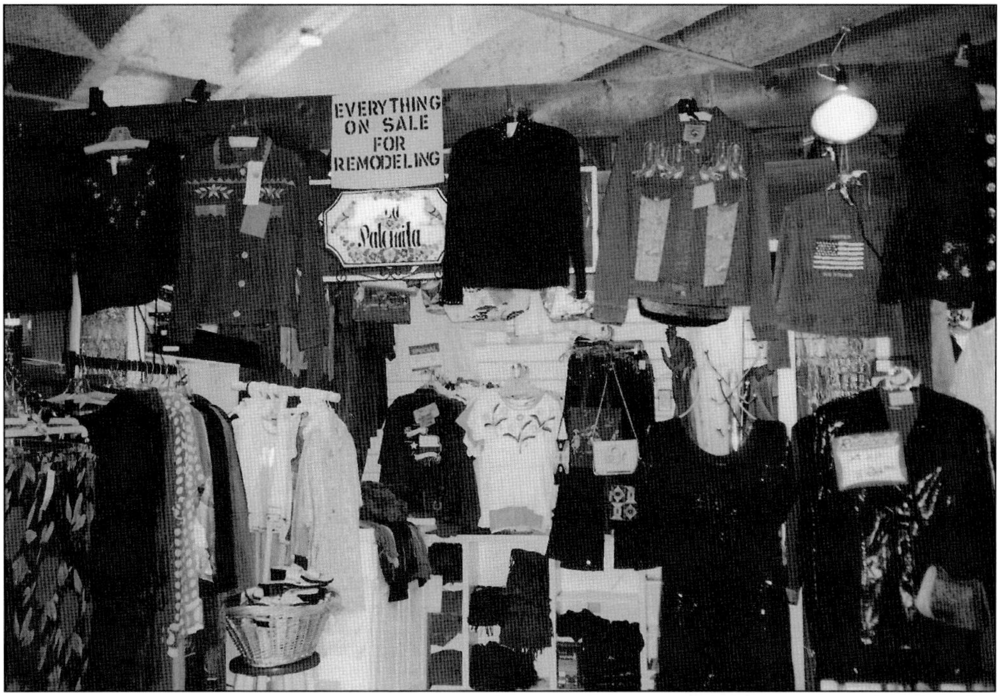

In 1993, the Farmers Market Plaza was remodeled to create the shops in the building today. La Palomita and the other shops needed to reduce their inventory for remodeling. While the building was under construction, the 12 original businesses moved to Centro de Artes. When the project was finished, the shops were larger and the kiosks and carts in the center of the building were gone. (Courtesy of Thelma Gonzalez.)

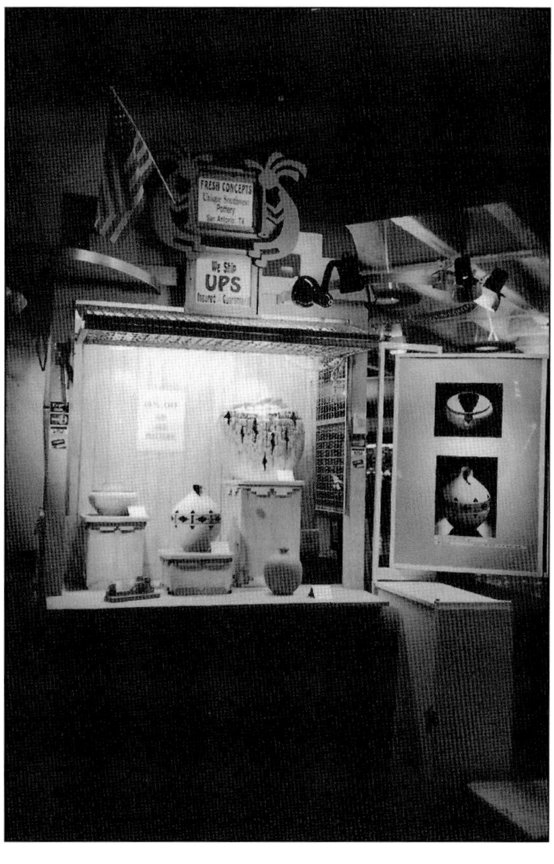

Fresh Concepts was established by artist David Kirby, who specialized in Southwestern pottery. According to a lease agreement with the city dated February 19, 2015, Aurora Lomas Sandoval took over the business in 2009. The lease identifies the business as Mexican Imports. In 2015, the lease was transferred to Bertha Mayte De La Rosa. (Courtesy of Thelma Gonzalez.)

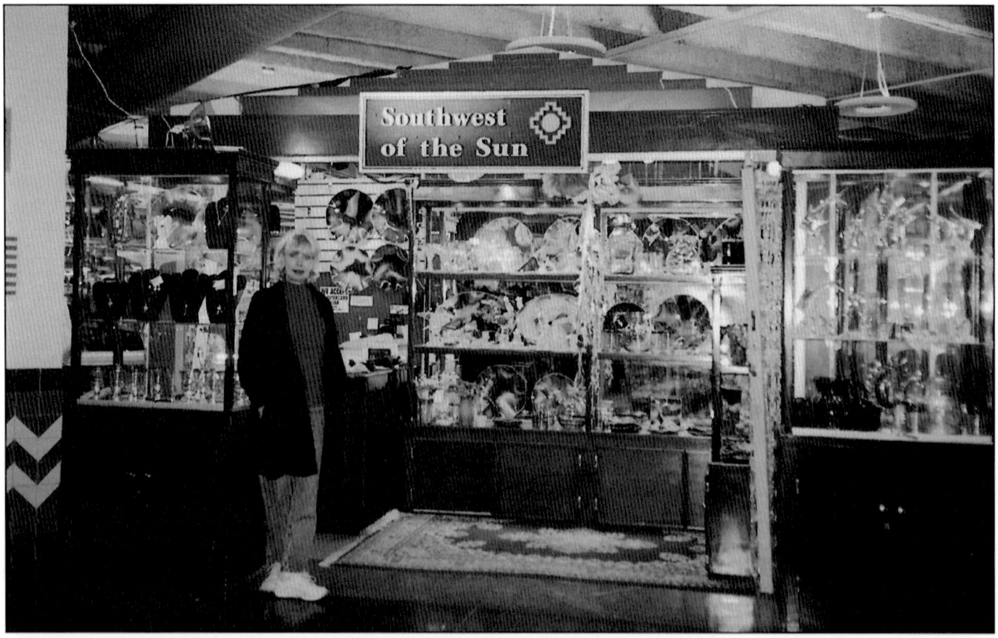

Southwest of the Sun was owned by glass artist Bobbi Wolfe. The shop is no longer in Farmers Market Plaza, and according to other business owners, it has been a few years since Wolfe passed away. Visitors in the market for glass art can check out Garcia Art Glass, owned by Gini Garcia. Her glassblowing studio is located at 715 South Alamo Street. (Courtesy of Thelma Gonzalez.)

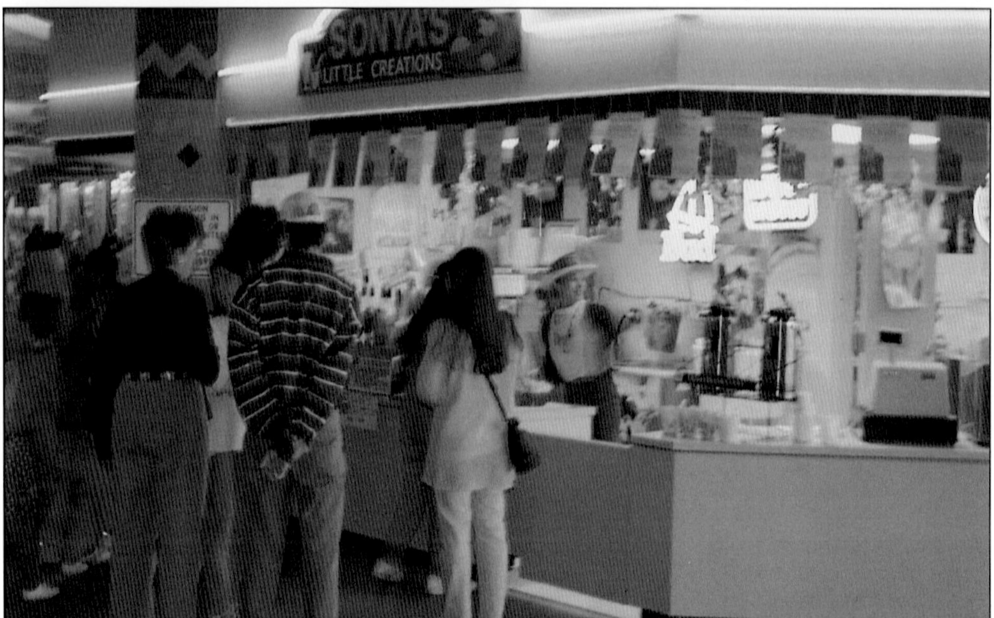

Sonya's Little Creations was established by third-generation vendor Sonya Zamora in the late 1970s. In the 1920s, her grandfather, Antonio Garcia, sold wood he brought to market in a wagon from the Rio Grande Valley. When Zamora's father, Patricio Garcia, was 19, he started helping his father. Later, Patricio had his own business selling produce. (Courtesy of the City of San Antonio, Office of the City Clerk Municipal Archives & Records.)

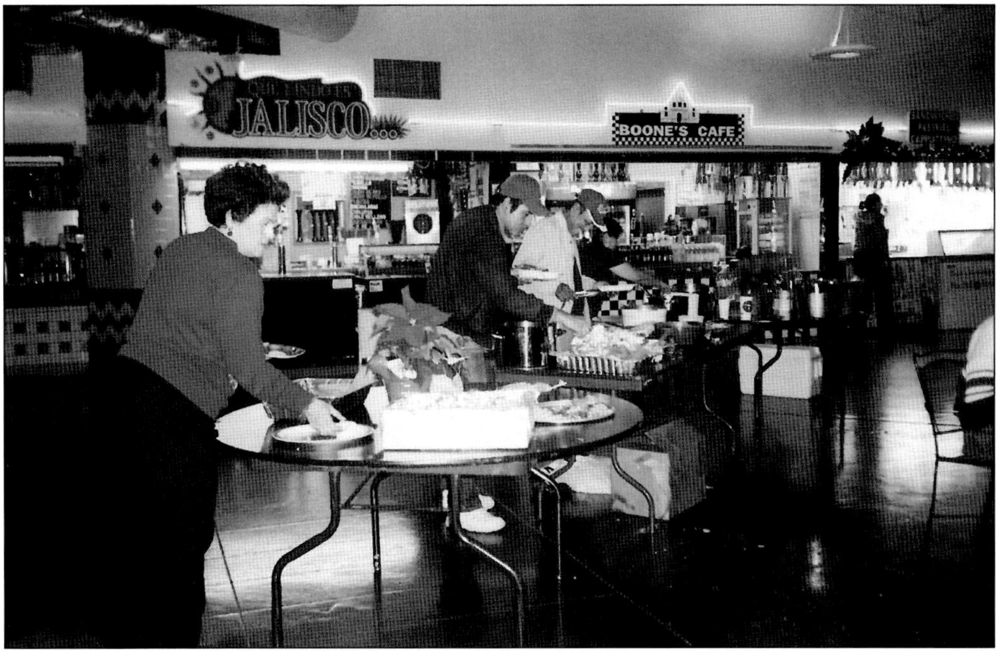

Farmers Market Plaza business owners enjoy a Christmas meal in 1994 after business hours. In the background is the restaurant Que Lindo Es Jalisco and Boone's Café, owned by Boone Brinson. Boone opened his café in 1994, the same year he opened Boone's Fine Prints. The fine print business did not make it, but Boone's Café is still in business. (Courtesy of Thelma Gonzalez.)

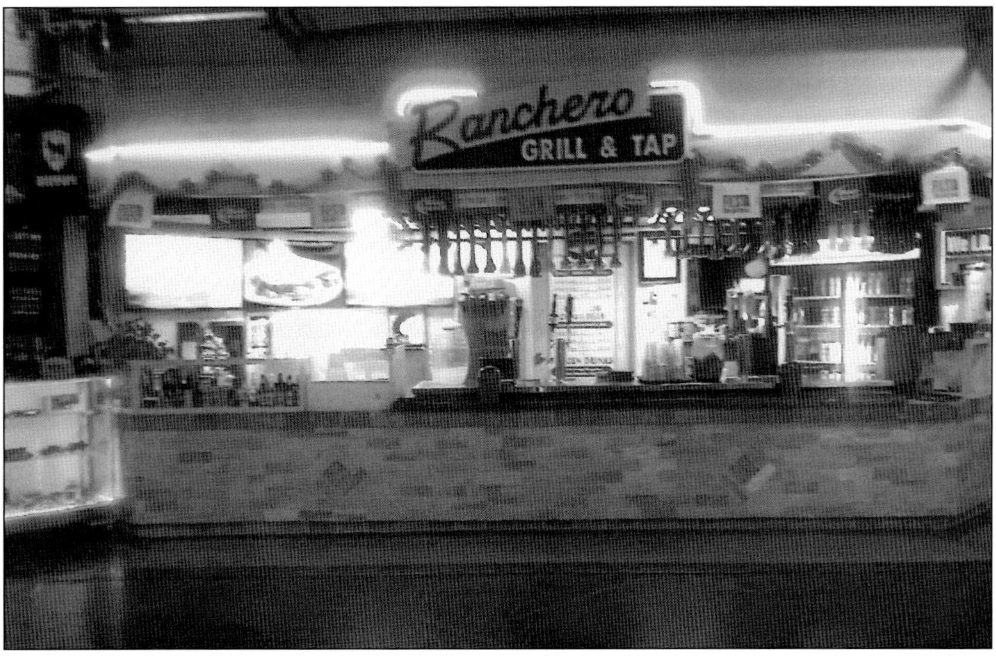

Ranchero Grill & Tap is owned by Alicia Reyes and her son James. They run a brisk and clean business. Three times, the grill has had a perfect score of 100 points in health inspections. Spring is a busy time for them; March brings a large number of tourists to the city, and Fiesta San Antonio in April brings crowds of tourists and locals to the market. (Courtesy of Alicia Reyes.)

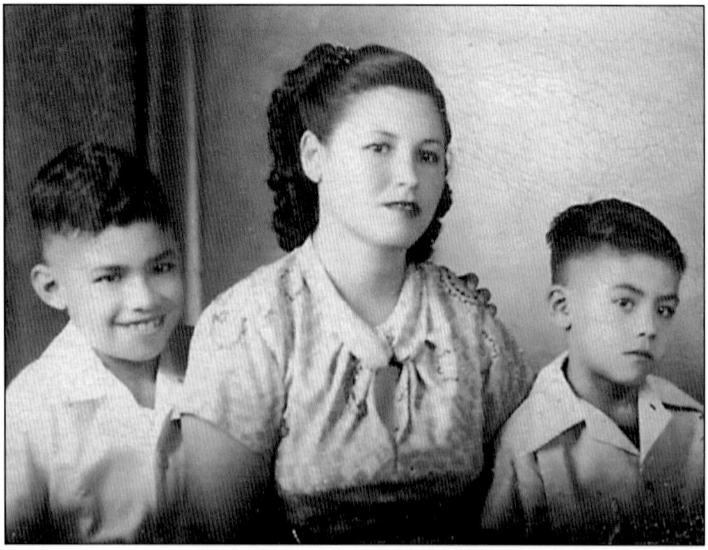

Elvira Reyes is seen here on May 19, 1951, with her sons Hilario (left) and Alejandro (Alex). The photograph was taken at The Modern Studio, located at 118 South Laredo Street. When Alex was around seven years old, he started helping his mother and his brother sell produce at the Hay Market Plaza. In 1969, Alex founded The Pepper Tree. (Courtesy of Alicia Reyes.)

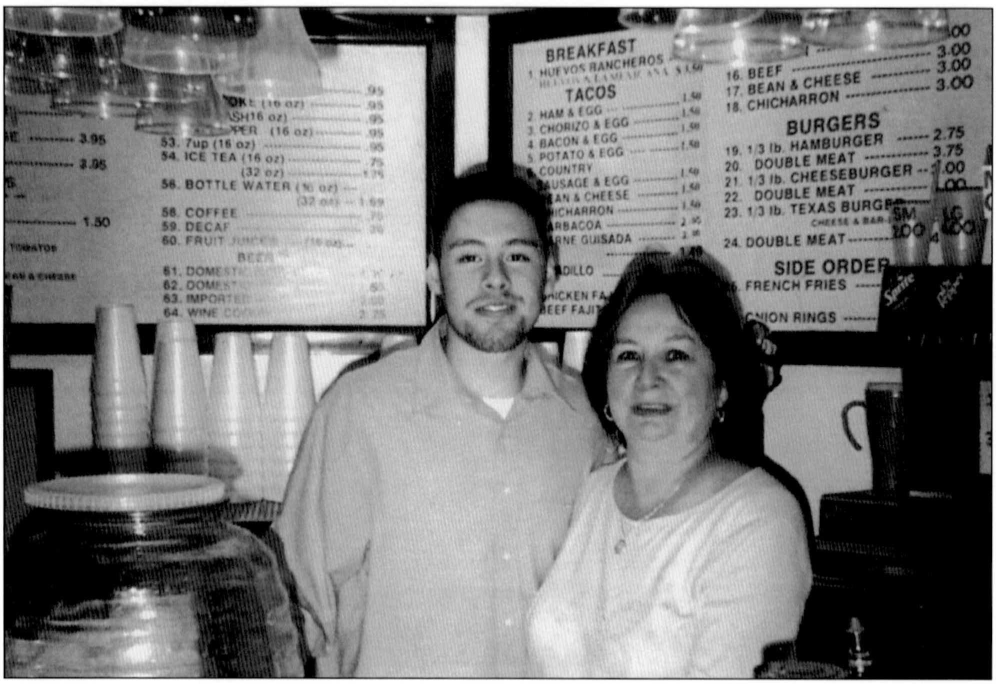

The Reyes family have been market vendors since the late 1950s. They are considered original vendors for being in business before the 1976 renovations. James Reyes is a third-generation market vendor; his grandparents sold produce, and his father founded The Pepper Tree. In the 1970s, his parents, Alex and Alicia Reyes, established Casa de Artes. Currently, James and his mother, Alicia (Alice), run Ranchero Grill & Tap. (Courtesy of Alicia Reyes.)

Six

Centro de Artes

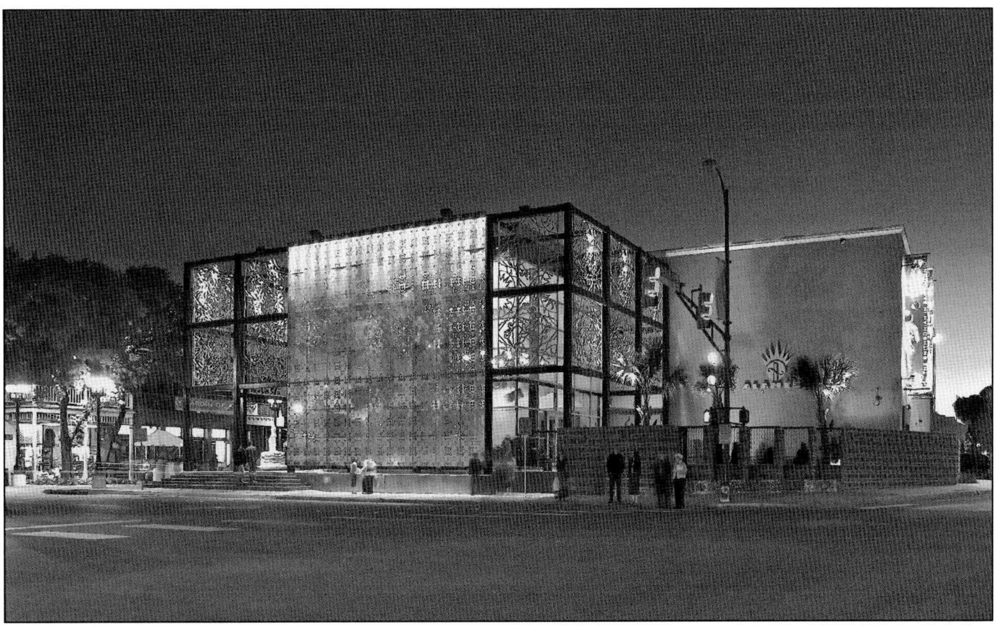

The Centro de Artes building provides a space to promote and preserve Latino culture. Before Museo Alameda opened in 2007, it could be rented for events. Most recently, it housed the Texas A&M University–San Antonio Educational & Cultural Arts Center. Currently, there is a television studio for KWEX 41 Univision and offices for the San Antonio Tricentennial Celebration Commission in the building. (Photograph by Al Rendon; courtesy of La Familia Cortez Restaurants.)

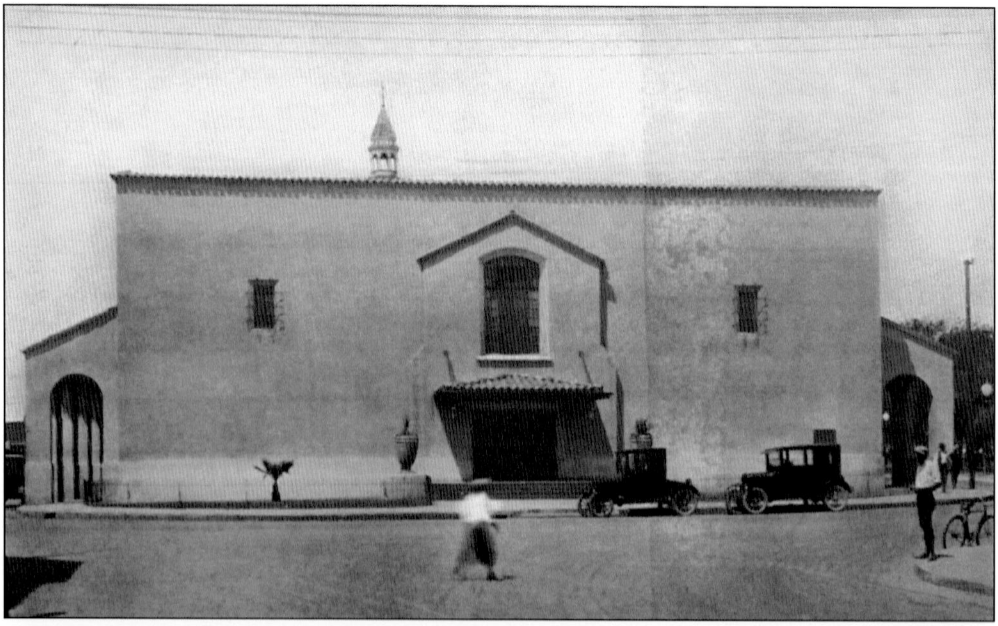

The Municipal Market House Annex was built in front of the old market in the 1920s. The cupola is visible in the background. Now that the market had a refrigerating plant, each stall had cold-storage space. The vendor stalls were on the first floor, and the restrooms were on the mezzanine. There was also an office for the market master, dry storage for each stall, and an area for music. (Courtesy of David Peché.)

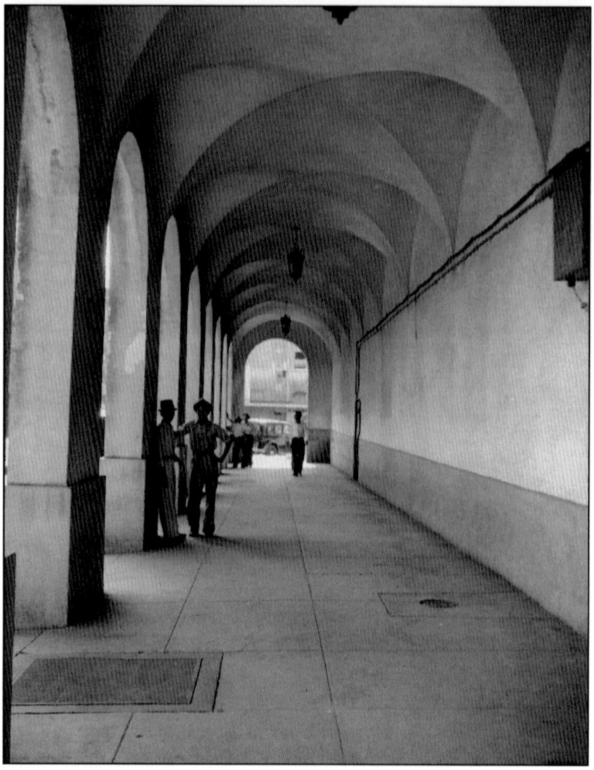

The building later known as Centro de Artes had arcaded passageways on both sides of the structure. This photograph, taken in the 1930s, shows what was lost during renovations to the building. In the original designs by architect Beverly W. Spillman, both annex buildings were to have arcades with vaulted ceilings over the sidewalks. (Courtesy of Texana Division, San Antonio Public Libraries, Postcard Collection.)

This late 1920s photograph shows the interior of the annex. There were stalls for meat, vegetables, milk, poultry, and fish. In the early 1940s, the stalls were occupied by Saenz Brothers Florist, Piggy Wiggly Store No. 34 (which had three stalls), City Market Café, Medellin's Market, Benjamin Pottery, and Theodore's Flower Shop. There were three fish markets—Auberlen's, Tarin's, and Alpert's. (Courtesy of David Peché.)

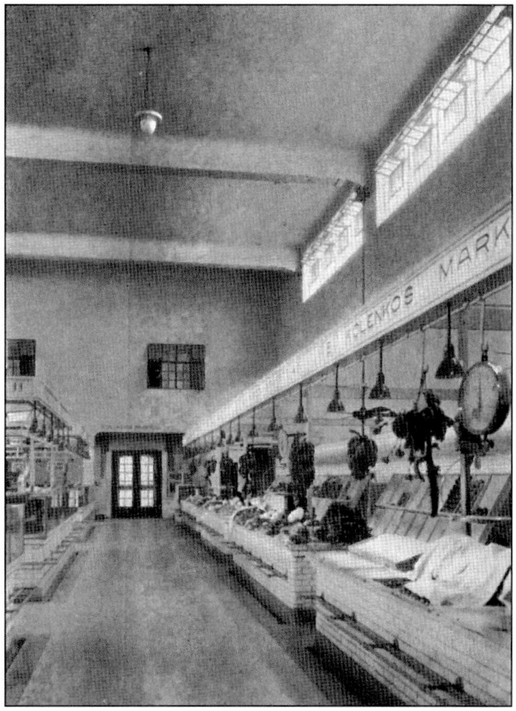

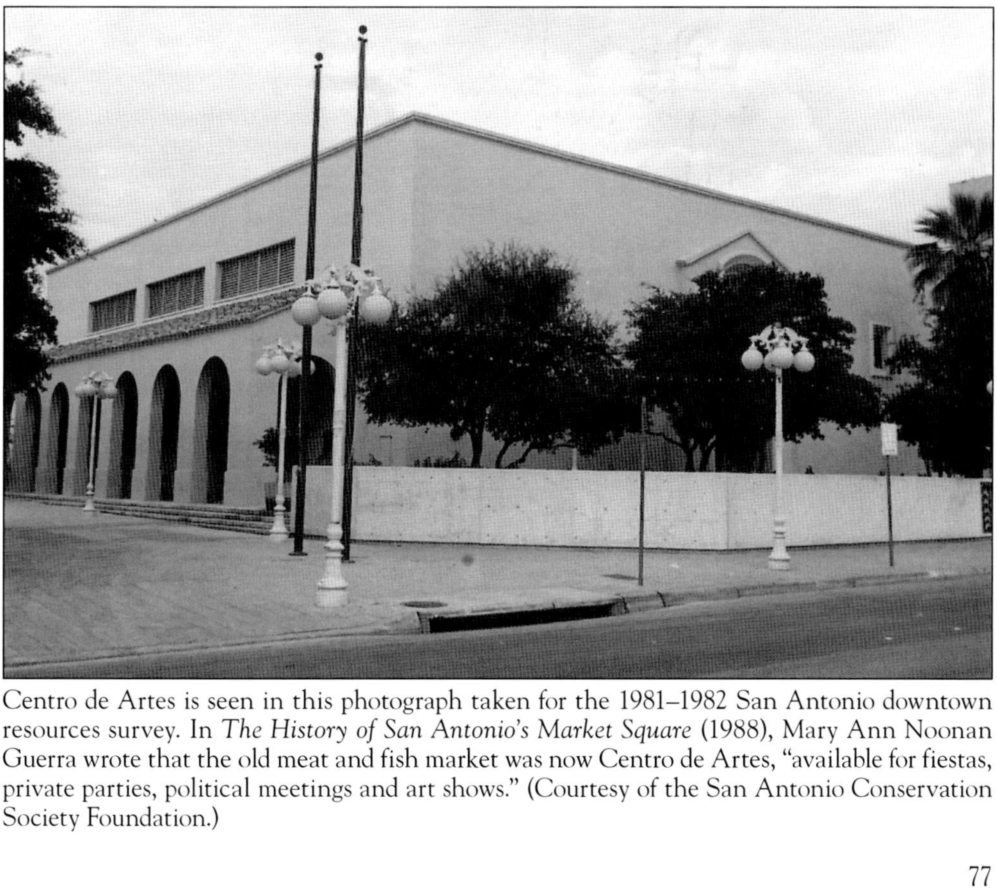

Centro de Artes is seen in this photograph taken for the 1981–1982 San Antonio downtown resources survey. In *The History of San Antonio's Market Square* (1988), Mary Ann Noonan Guerra wrote that the old meat and fish market was now Centro de Artes, "available for fiestas, private parties, political meetings and art shows." (Courtesy of the San Antonio Conservation Society Foundation.)

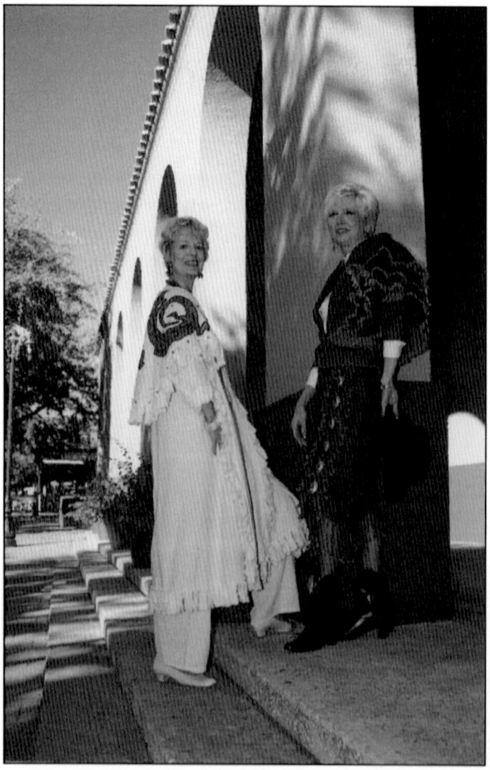

These models posing outside Centro de Artes on Produce Row in 1996 are wearing the latest in Southwestern apparel. The days of mule-drawn carts going down Produce Row disappeared in the early 1940s. In 1976, Produce Row and Concho Street were turned into a pedestrian mall. (Courtesy of the City of San Antonio, Office of the City Clerk Municipal Archives & Records.)

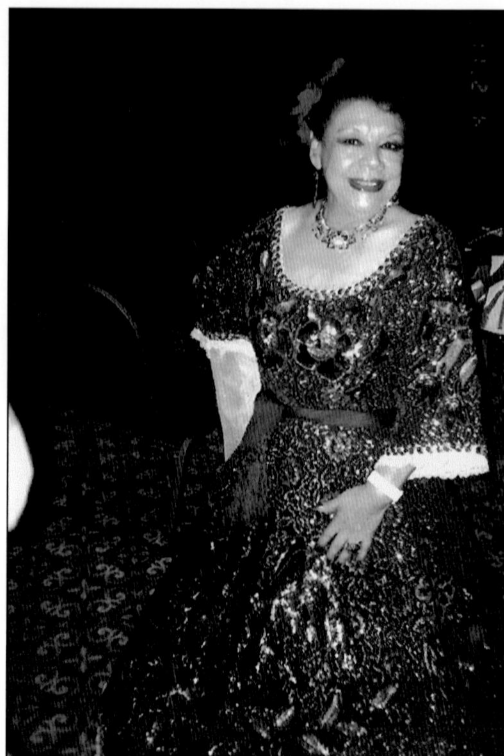

Beatriz Llamas, "La Paloma de Norte," has performed at Market Square throughout her career, which spans over five decades. Her dress was sewn by her mother, and she added all the embellishments by hand. When she was 15, Beatriz needed a *charro* outfit. It cost $68 that the family did not have, so her mother paid for the outfit by working for the lady who sold it to them. (Courtesy of Beatriz Llamas.)

Lydia Mendoza was a singer of Tejano, conjunto, and traditional Mexican music. Her family moved to San Antonio in 1928. Mendoza and her sisters performed around town, including at Plaza del Zacate (Hay Market Plaza). In 1999, she won the National Medal of Arts. Rita Vidaurri, of Las Tesoros de San Antonio, sang with Mendoza in Market Square. Mendoza died in 2007 in San Antonio. She was 91 years old. (Courtesy of Al Rendon.)

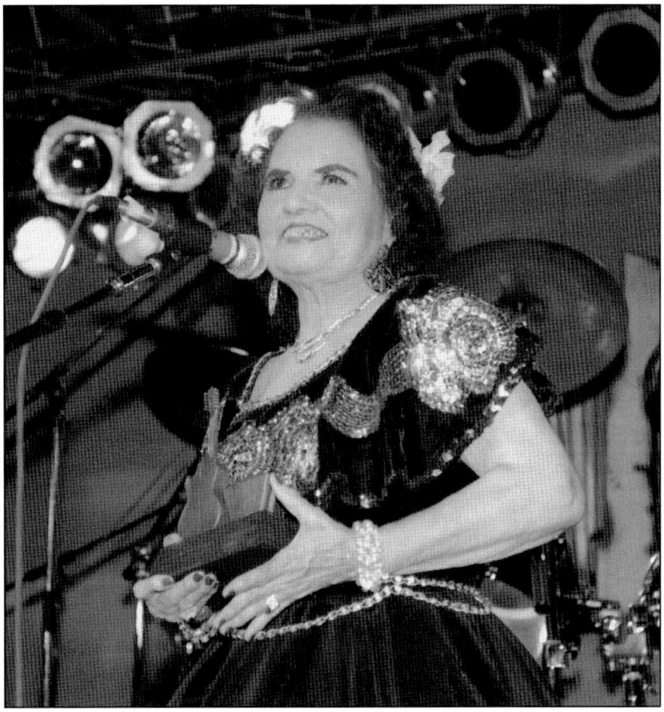

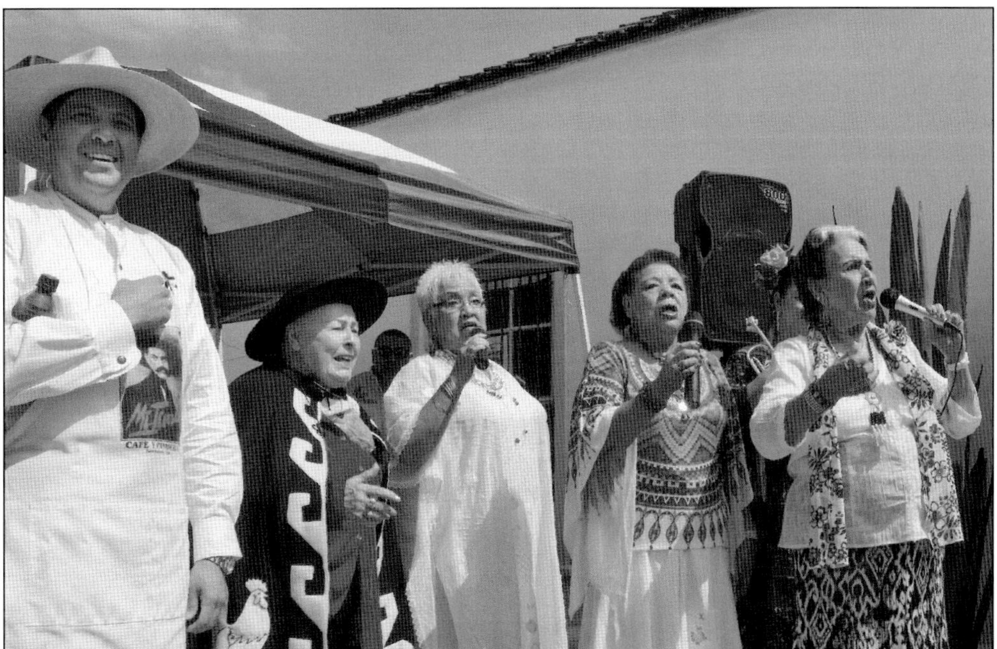

Each member of Las Teseros de San Antonio had international careers of their own. They teamed up through the Esperanza Peace and Justice Center, and some members are still preforming. From left to right are Michael Cortez, Janet Cortez ("Perla Tapatia"), Blanca Rodriguez ("Blanquita Rosa"), Beatriz Llamas ("La Paloma del Norte"), and Rita Vidaurri ("La Calandria"). Perla Tapatia passed away in 2014. (Photograph by Al Rendon; courtesy of La Familia Cortez Restaurants.)

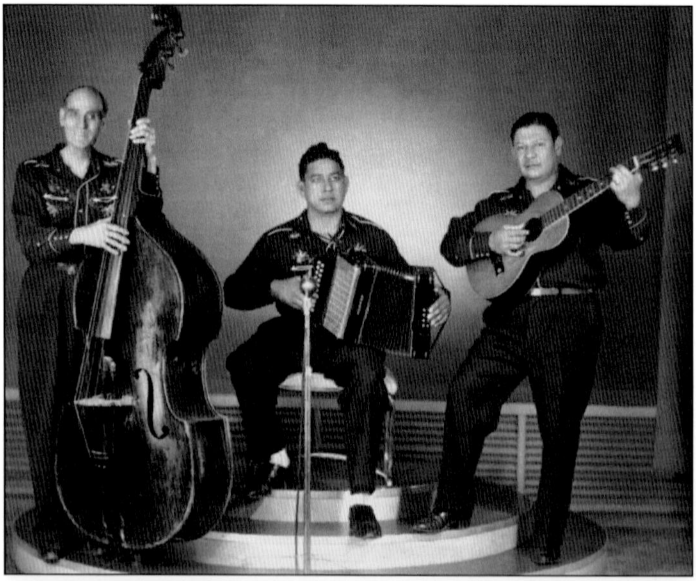

Santiago Jimenez Sr. y sus Valedores are pictured in the 1940s. From left to right are Ismael Gonzales, Santiago Jimenez, and Manuel Gonzalez. Santiago Jimenez Sr. was a pioneer of conjunto music. He was inducted into the Tejano Music Hall of Fame in 1993 and the Texas Conjunto Music Hall of Fame and Museum in 2003. His sons Santiago Jr. and Leonardo "Flaco" are both accordionists. (Courtesy of UTSA Special Collections–ITC, photograph 82-85.)

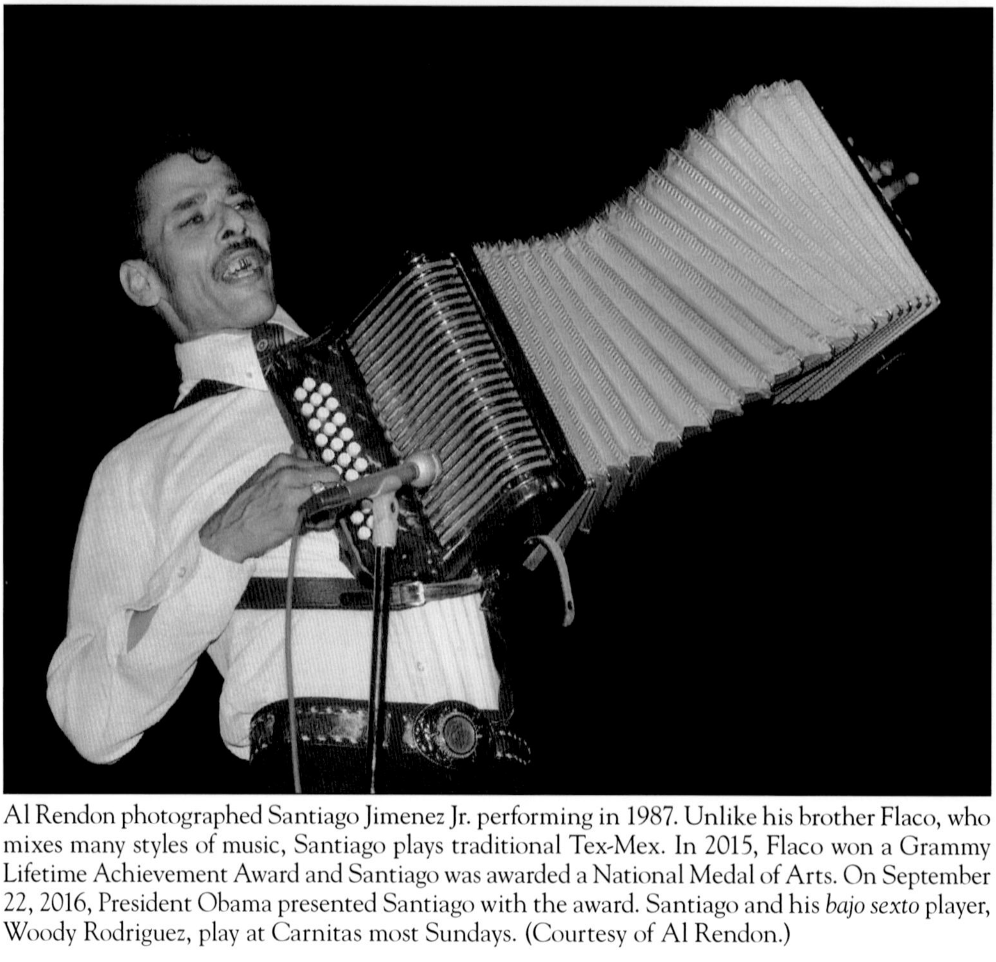

Al Rendon photographed Santiago Jimenez Jr. performing in 1987. Unlike his brother Flaco, who mixes many styles of music, Santiago plays traditional Tex-Mex. In 2015, Flaco won a Grammy Lifetime Achievement Award and Santiago was awarded a National Medal of Arts. On September 22, 2016, President Obama presented Santiago with the award. Santiago and his *bajo sexto* player, Woody Rodriguez, play at Carnitas most Sundays. (Courtesy of Al Rendon.)

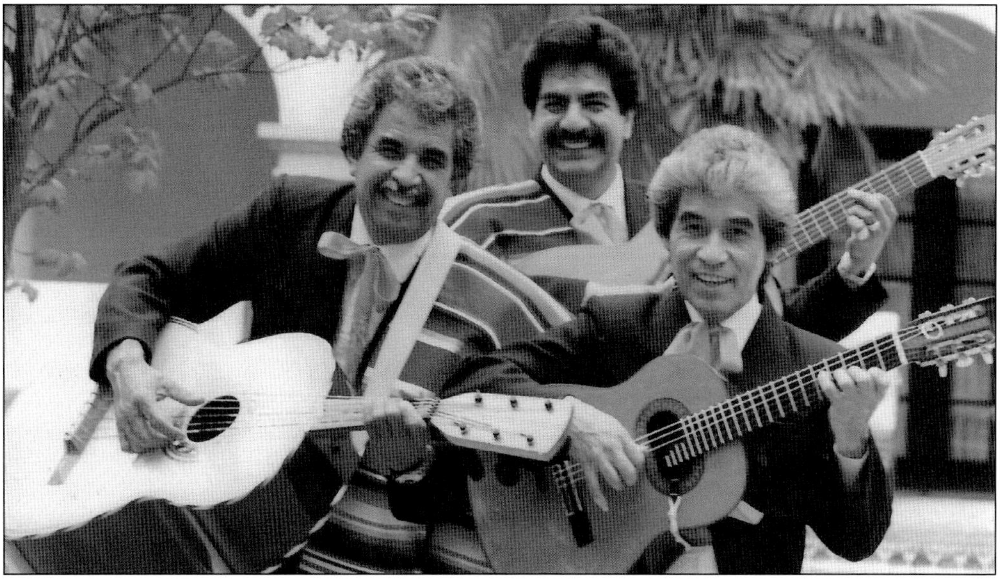

These troubadours have been playing in Market Square for decades. Pictured in 1983 are, from left to right, Francisco "Poncho" Perez with *guitaron*, Jose Lopez ("El Indio") with guitar, and Seferino "Chepe" Solis with *requinto*. Poncho came to San Antonio from Mexico in 1964 when he was 19. He remembers that the area was rough. There were prostitutes and *pachucos* who carried straight razors and were not afraid to use them. (Courtesy of Francisco Perez.)

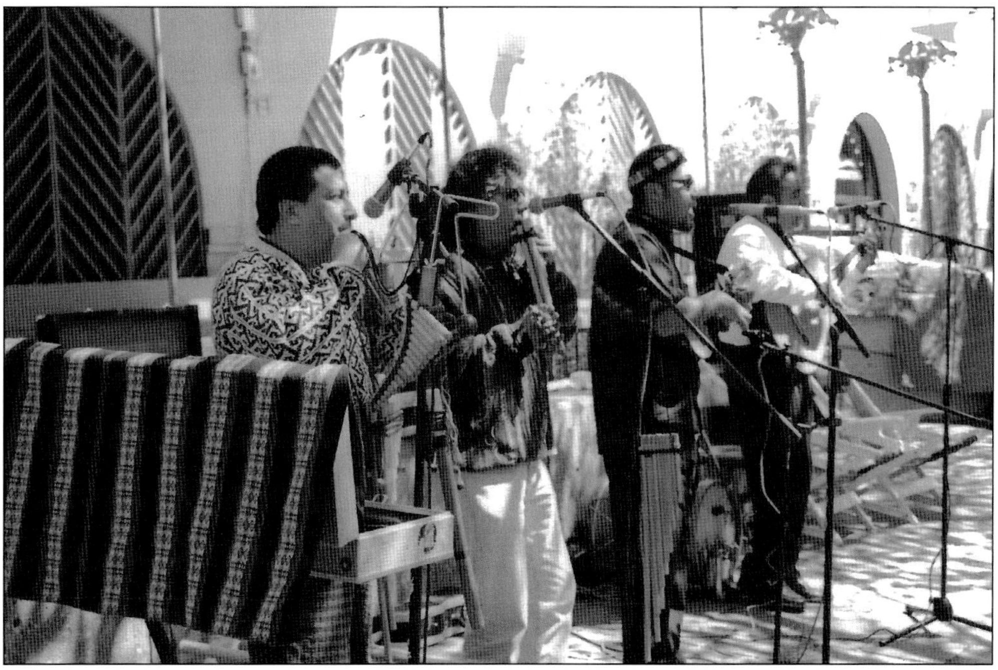

The 1990s brought a new sound to San Antonio and Market Square—music from the Andes. Most of these musicians came to the United States from Argentina, Bolivia, Chile, Colombia, Ecuador, and Peru. Since the music had Latin roots, it was well accepted and can still be heard at Rivercenter Mall on the San Antonio Riverwalk. This group is playing outside El Mercado on Produce Row. (Courtesy of Joanne Gonzales.)

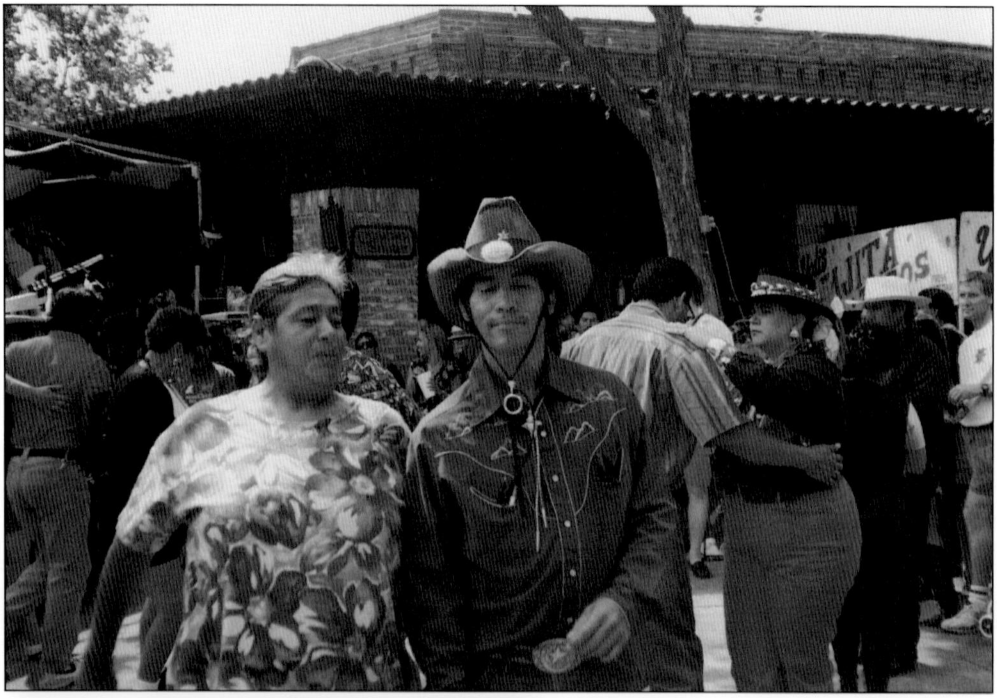

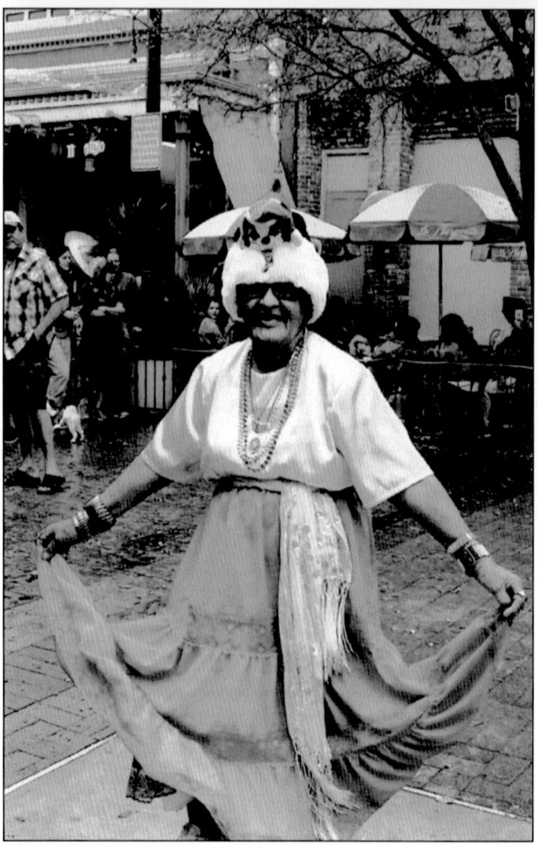

Dancing is a big part of the Tejano and Mexican cultures. In Market Square, one can enjoy dances from folklorico and conjunto to country and western. During Fiesta San Antonio and other festivals, the dancing takes place in the pedestrian mall. Two regular dancers pose here in 1994. There is also a gentleman who entertains the crowds dressed as Elvis Presley. The music and dancing bring people of all ages together. (Author's collection.)

Miss Margaret, as she is known by market regulars, enjoys dressing up in fiesta costumes and dancing. She has been dancing during events for the last five years. She is seen here in December 2015 during the Blessing of the Animals wearing a traditional Mexican skirt; her Santa Claus hat is adorned with a plush toy puppy. (Author's collection.)

It is not a party unless there is a piñata! Mary Perales and her mother, Elena, from Perales Imports, pose with their delivery. The Perales family bought their piñatas from a local maker, Mrs. Vasquez. In 1981, *Texas Monthly Magazine* mentioned Piñata Land at 709 South Alamo Street and Piñatas de Peña at 1832 Blanco Road. Most of the piñatas sold in the market today come from Mexico. (Courtesy of Mary Perales Valdez.)

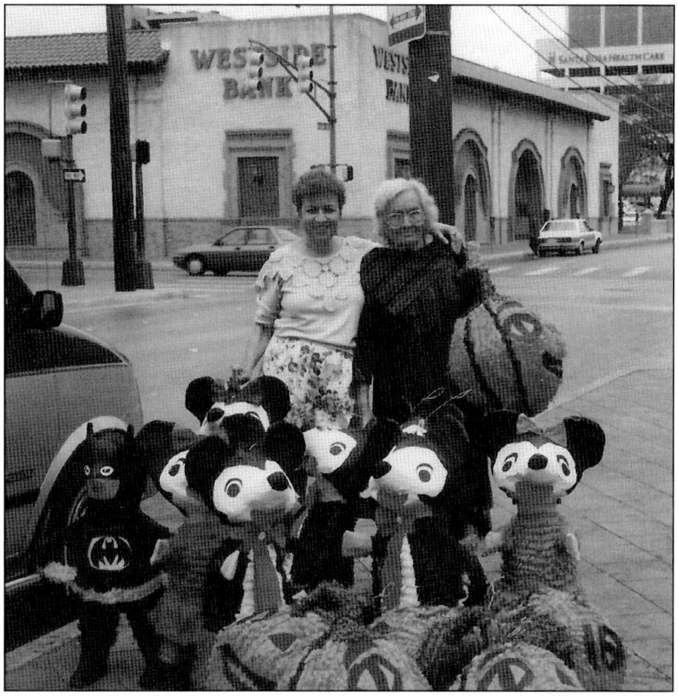

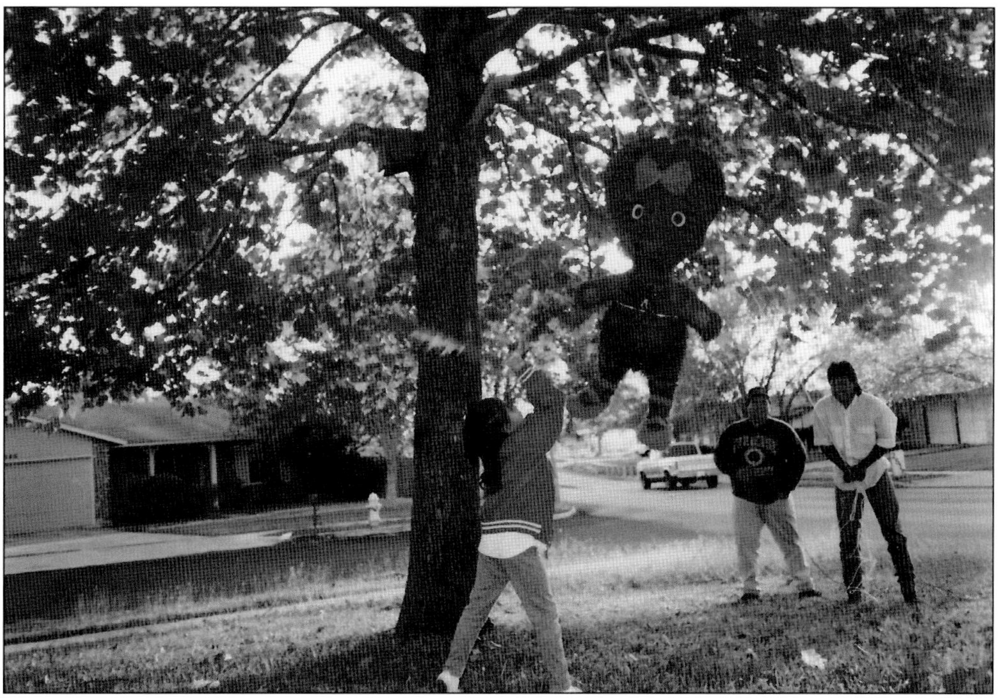

Piñatas are hung from trees or some type of beam. The object is to lower and raise the piñata and keep the person swinging the stick from breaking it. Sometimes the person with the stick is blindfolded. The piñatas are traditionally filled with candy and small toys. In this 1990s photograph, Phillip Leon Jr. mans the piñata while Paul Galvan looks on. (Courtesy of Phillip and Alice Leon.)

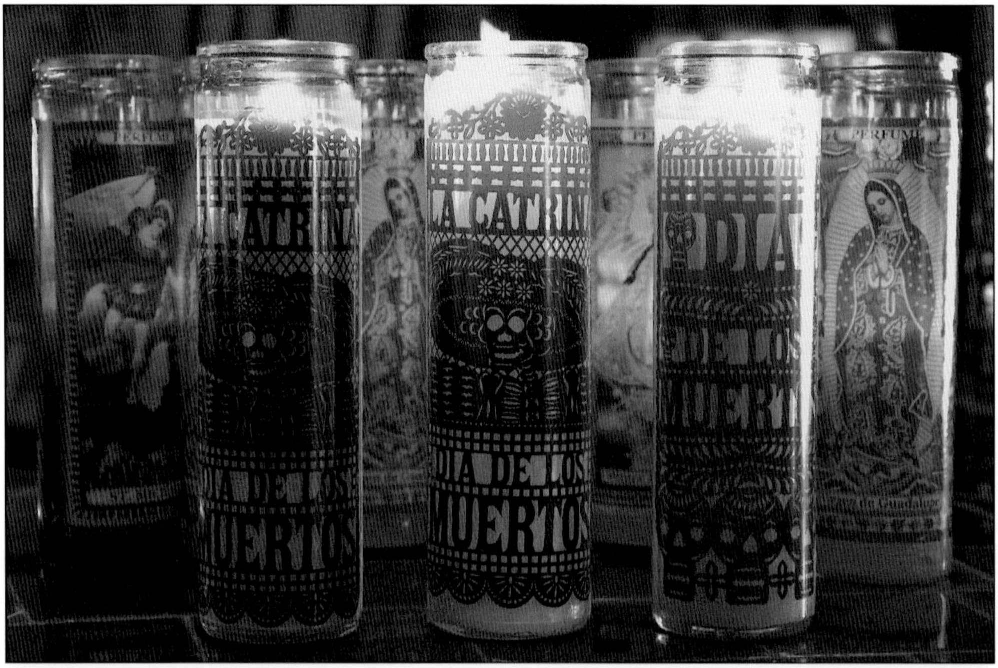

Day of the Dead, St. Michael, and Our Lady of Guadalupe candles light the way and guide the spirits back to earth for a visit with loved ones left behind. There are numerous Day of the Dead celebrations in San Antonio; one of the largest is at Market Square. The tradition has been preserved as a cultural heritage. (Photograph by Al Rendon; courtesy of La Familia Cortez Restaurants.)

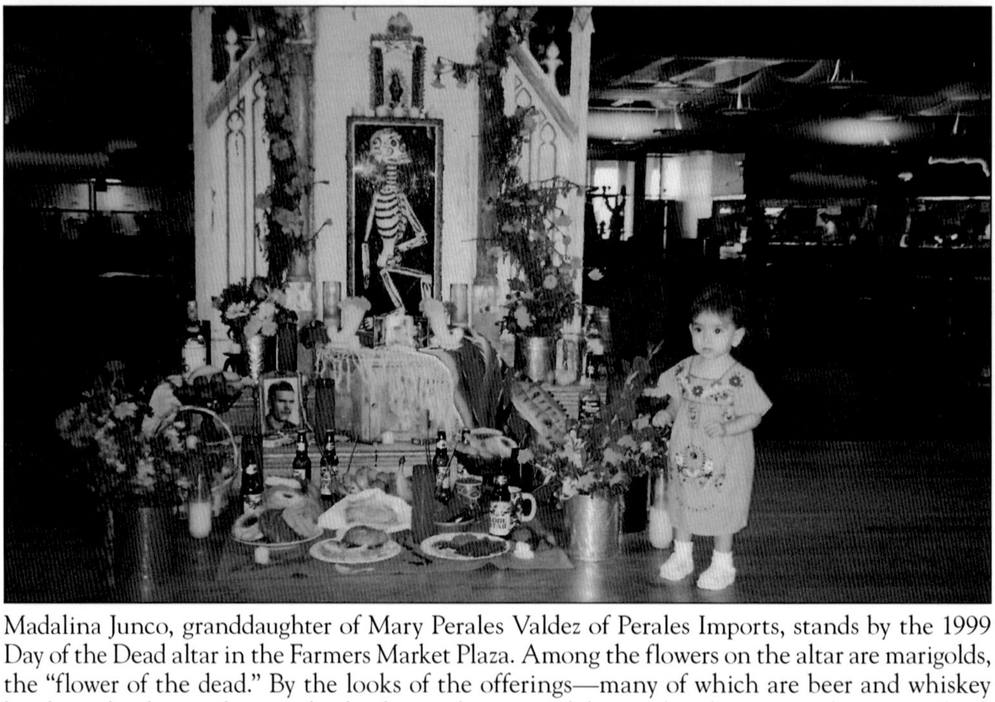

Madalina Junco, granddaughter of Mary Perales Valdez of Perales Imports, stands by the 1999 Day of the Dead altar in the Farmers Market Plaza. Among the flowers on the altar are marigolds, the "flower of the dead." By the looks of the offerings—many of which are beer and whiskey bottles—the departed enjoyed a drink. He also enjoyed donuts, hamburgers, and Mexican food. (Courtesy of Mary Perales Valdez.)

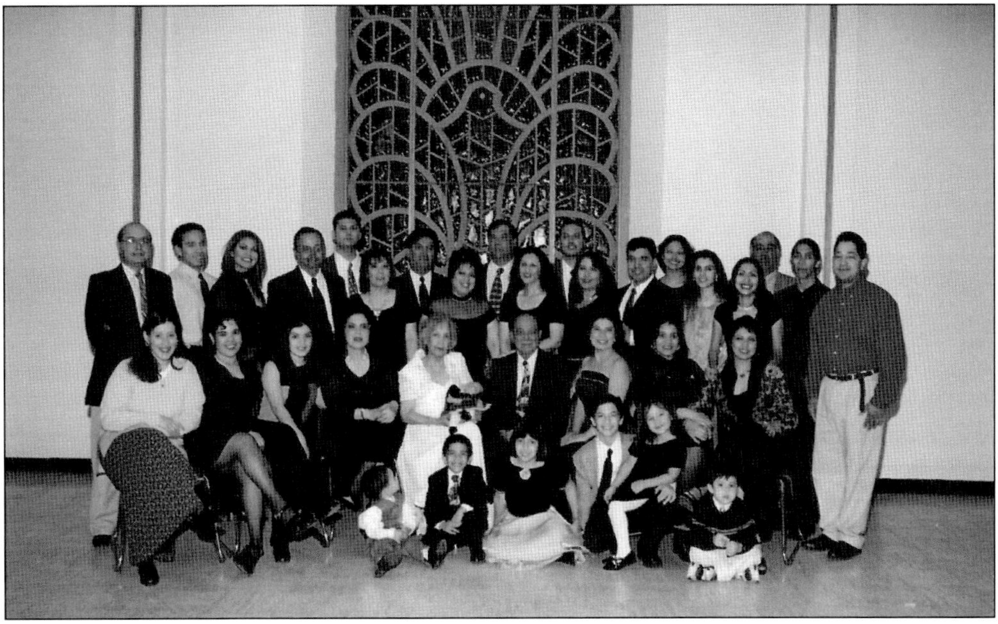

The Gonzalez family celebrates the 50th wedding anniversary of Susan and Rene Gonzalez (center) at Centro de Artes on December 28, 1997. Dela, Thelma, Rene, Blanca, Rita, and Ruth honored their parents with a reception and dance. The Market Square logo in the stained-glass window serves as the backdrop for the family portrait. (Courtesy of Thelma Gonzalez.)

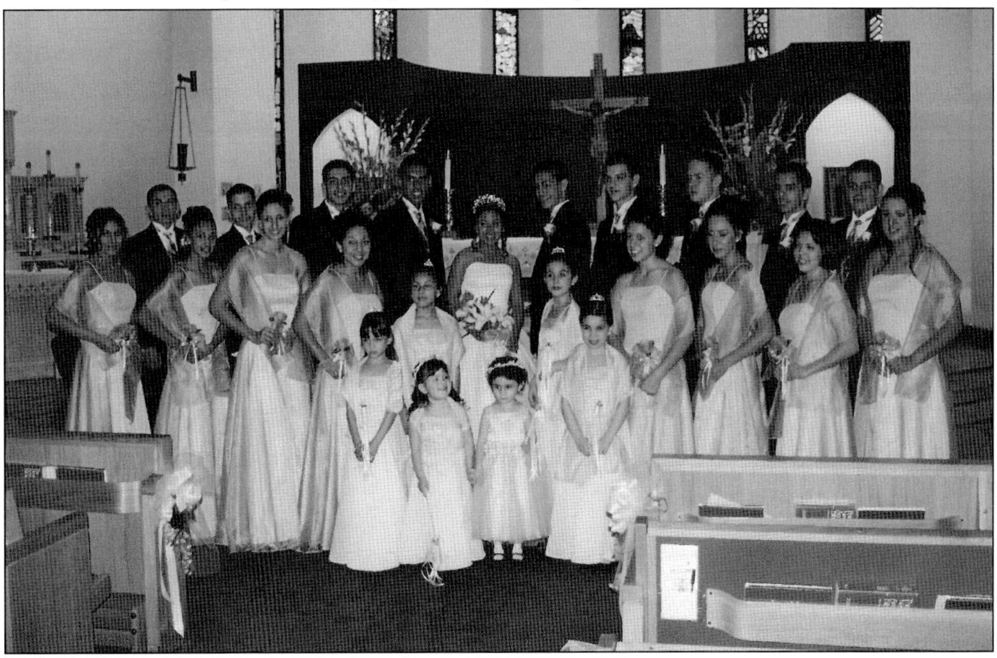

The Centro de Artes building was also rented out for *quinceañeras*. A quinceañera is a coming-of-age celebration in traditional Hispanic families. This religious celebration in 2003, honoring the 15th birthday of debutante Melessa Chriselda Rodriguez, took place at St. George Maronite Church. At center is Rodriguez and her escort, Nathaniel Jay Mireles. They are pictured with Rodriguez's court of honor. (Courtesy of Melessa C. Rodriguez.)

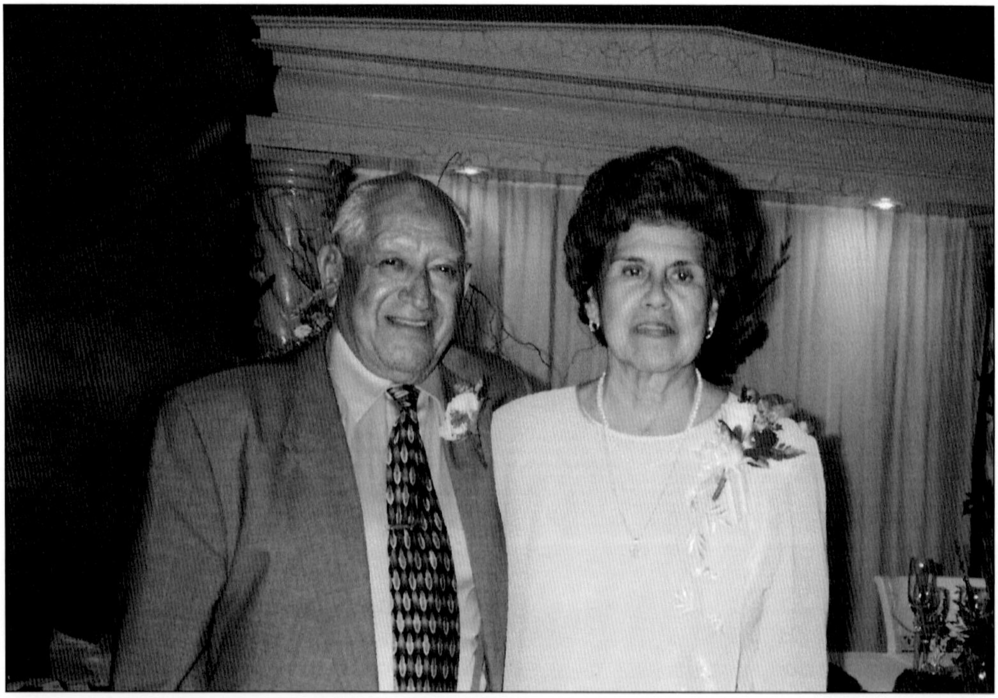

Centro de Artes has been a nucleus for Latino cultural education and has also been responsible for preserving traditions and telling stories. Family is very important, and grandparents play a very special role in a quinceañera, as they have had a hand in molding the girl into a young lady. Melessa Rodriguez's grandparents, Alexander O. and Alice Rodriguez, were sponsors of her princess dress. (Courtesy of Melessa C. Rodriguez.)

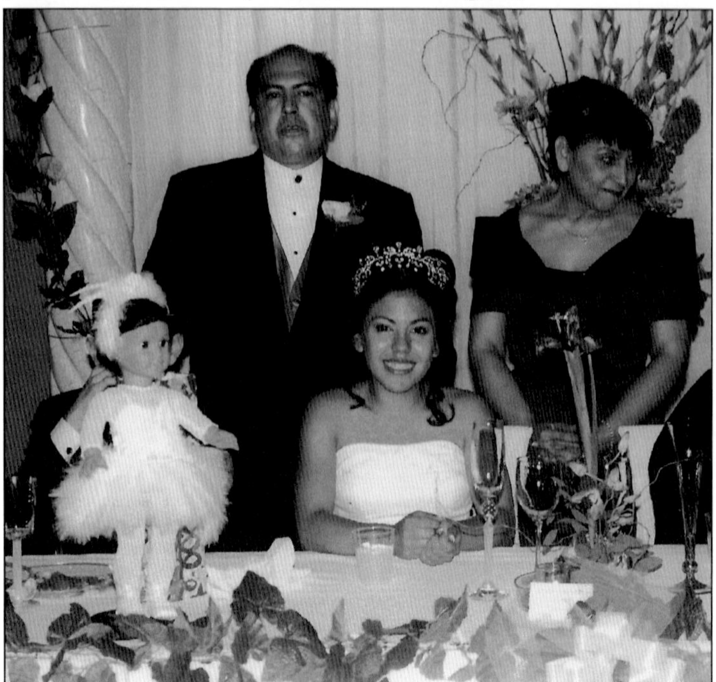

Part of the quinceañera ceremony is the last doll. It symbolizes stepping from childhood to adulthood. Melessa Rodriguez's doll was a gift from her maternal grandmother, Maria M. Flores. Pictured with Rodriguez and her last doll are her parents, Michael H. and Mary Lou Rodriguez. The tiara was a gift from Robert Kniejski and Irma Harnandez. Other ceremonial items were gifts from family and friends. (Courtesy of Melessa C. Rodriguez.)

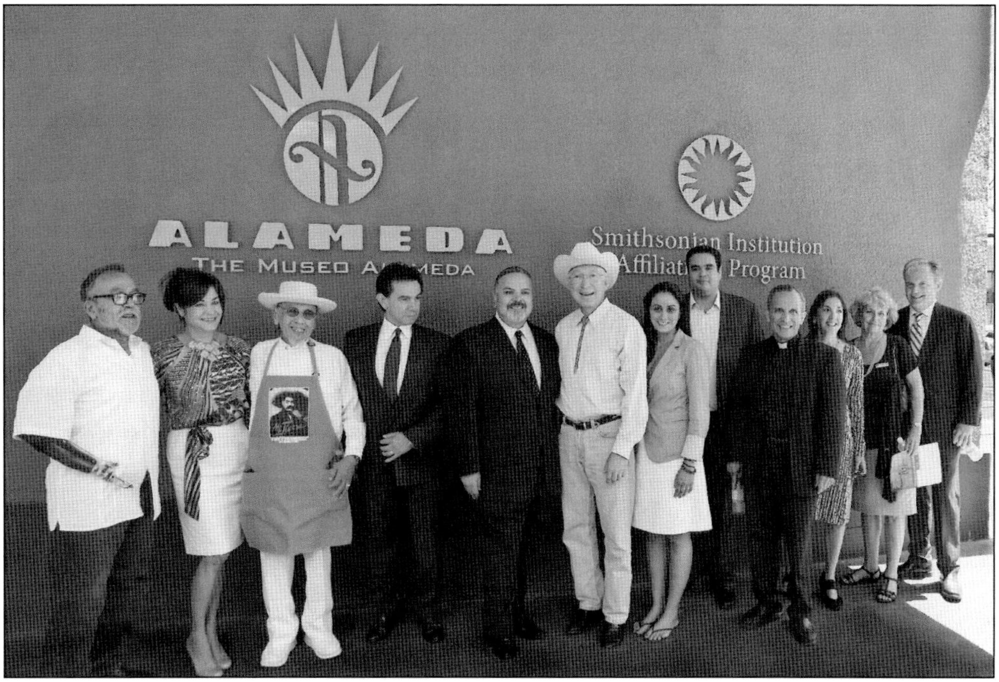

This group is pictured in April 2007 at the opening of Museo Alameda. This collaboration with the Smithsonian Institution had 11 galleries and 20,000 square feet of exhibit space telling the story of the Latino experience in America. It was a great concept, but the reality of financing the museum became apparent early on. On September 30, 2012, Museo Alameda closed its doors. (Photograph by Al Rendon; courtesy of La Familia Cortez Restaurants.)

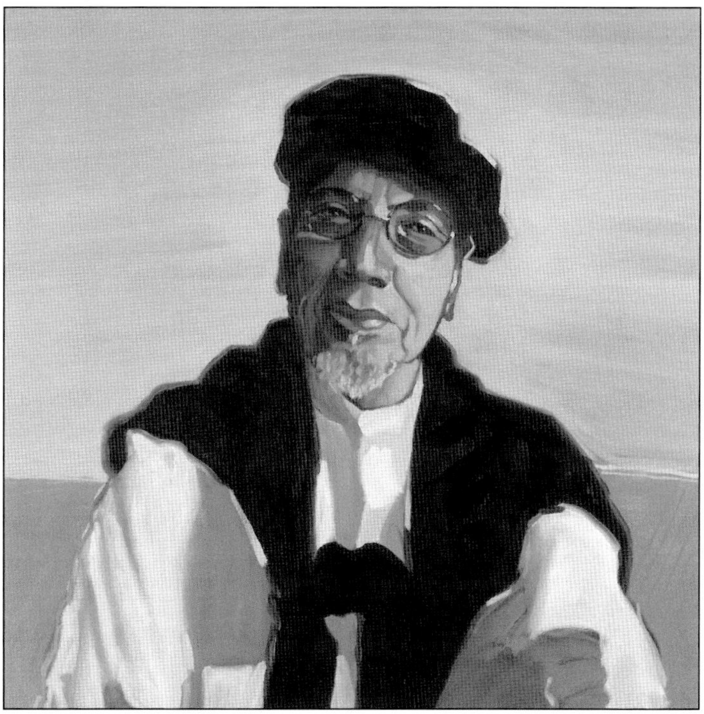

This portrait of Jorge Cortez, of La Familia Cortez Restaurants, was painted by Lionel Sosa in 2013. It was exhibited at Centro de Artes and Sosa Galleries. Sosa has had successful careers in marketing, writing, and painting. He is the founder of Sosa, Bromley, Aguilar & Associates, now Bromley Communications. This agency became the largest Hispanic advertising business in the United States. (Courtesy of Lionel Sosa.)

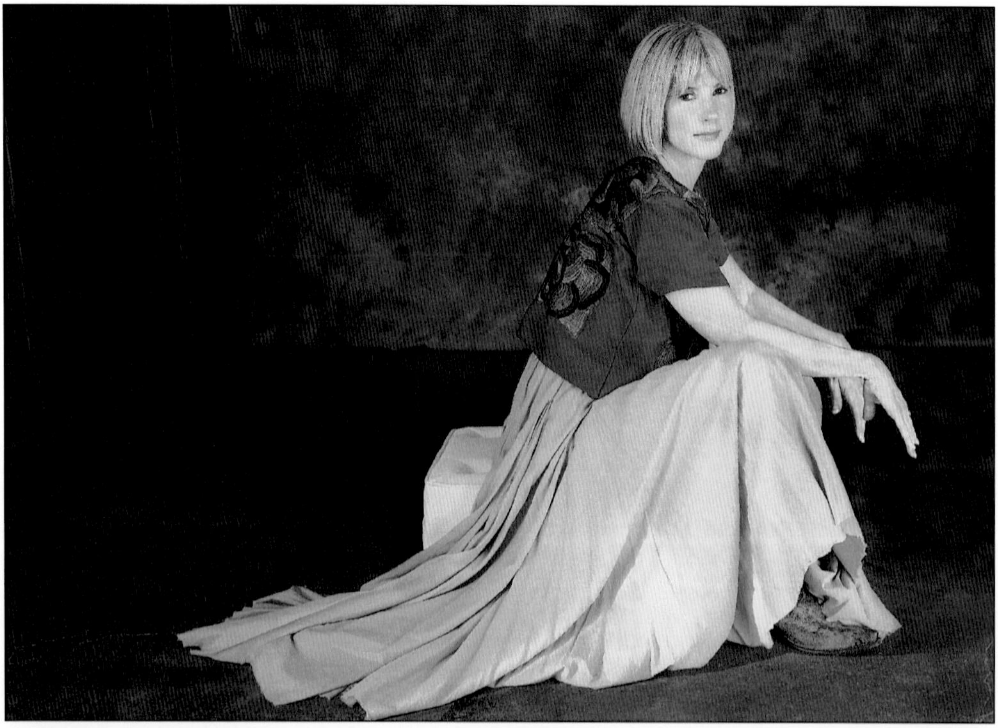

Kathy Sosa begun her career as a painter in 2006. She was commissioned to paint a portrait of Martha Stewart for the Texas Conference of Women. Sosa has exhibited throughout Texas and the United States. Between 2007 and 2008, she exhibited at Museo Alameda. In 2008, she exhibited in Market Square at Galeria Ortiz. In 2015, Sosa and Veronica Castillo showcased pieces in the Trees of Life exhibit at Centro de Artes. (Courtesy of Kathy Sosa.)

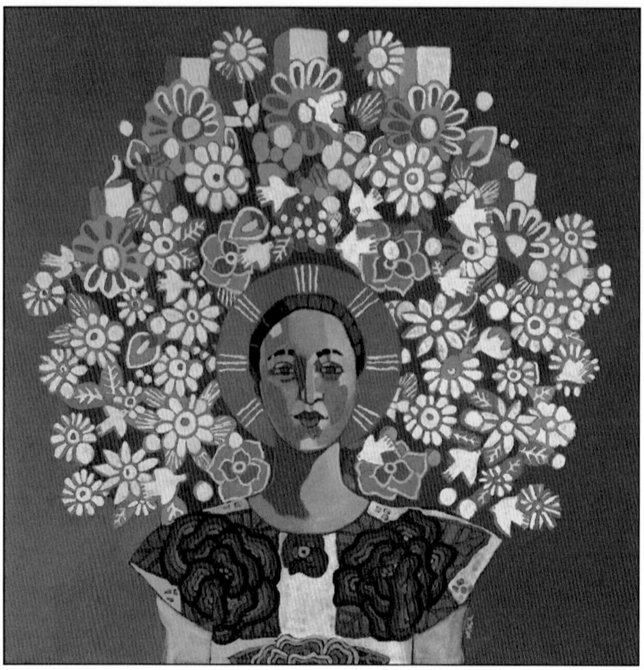

Reina De Las Flores No. 2 On My Mind by Kathy Sosa was on exhibit in the Trees of Life exhibit. This exhibit was a celebration of culture, tradition, and innovation. According to her biography, "in 2007 Sosa began to explore the artistic expression of *mestisaje*, the blending of peoples, races, ethnicities, languages, ideas, habits and cultures that characterizes the Texas-Mexico border region that has been her home since childhood." (Courtesy of Kathy Sosa.)

Seven

Cortez Family Dynasty

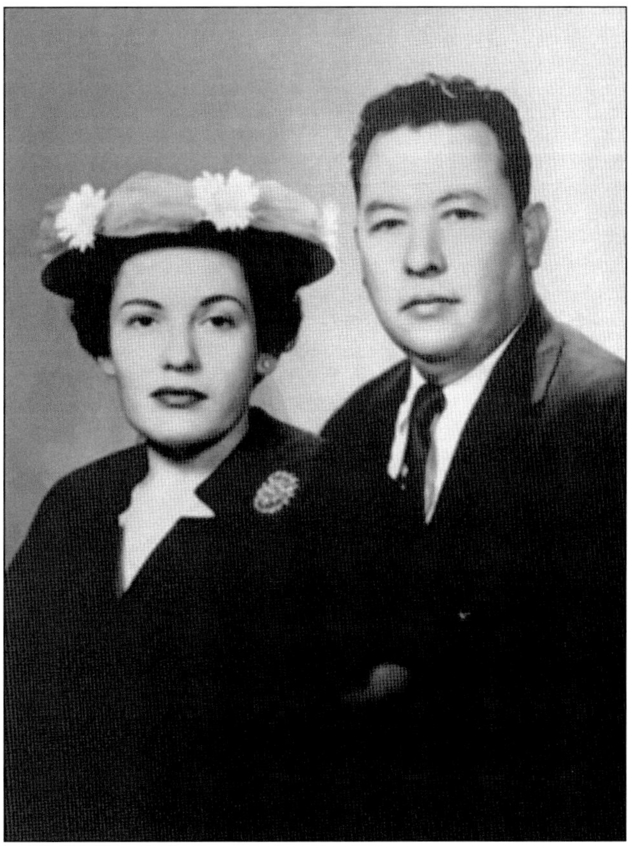

Landmark restaurant Mi Tierra celebrated its 75th anniversary in 2016. Pedro and Cruz Cortez founded the business in 1941. They opened a three-table Jamaica café to service farmers and workers at Municipal Market Annex. The Cortez family has been instrumental in keeping Market Square a vital part of San Antonio's history. Through the combined efforts of the city, the Cortez family, and vendors, Market Square is a tourist destination. (Courtesy of the La Familia Cortez Restaurants.)

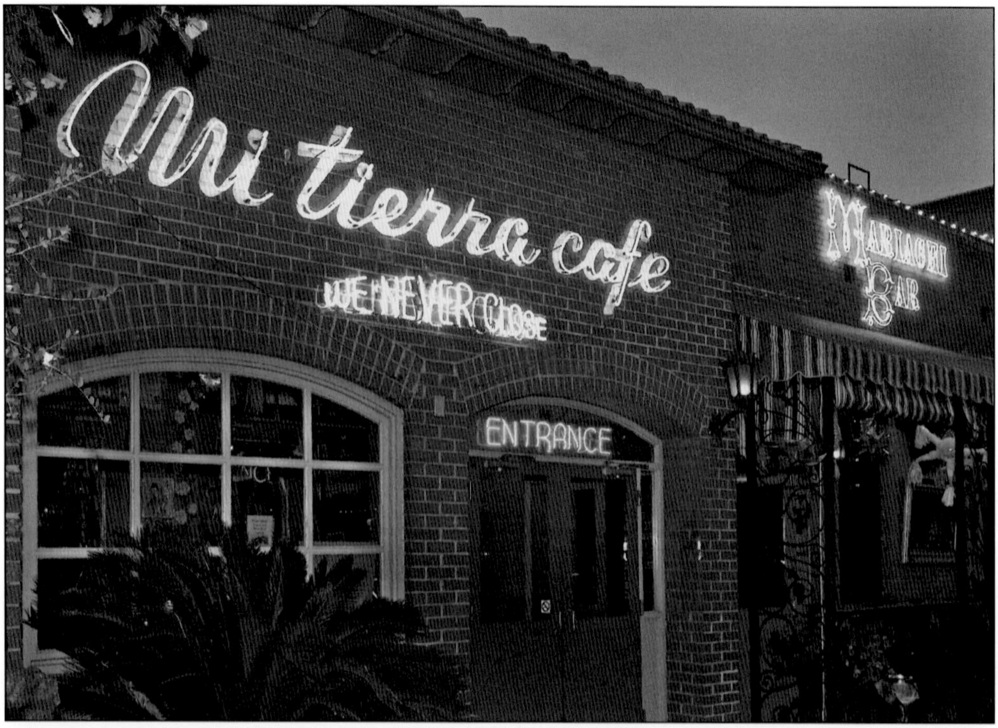

Mi Tierra Café began in 1951; the Jamaica café continued doing business. The entrance sign reads, "We never close." The restaurant is open 24 hours, 365 days a year. Mariachi Bar was added to Mi Tierra in 1989. Restaurant mariachi Henry Gomez plays the *vihuela* there at night; by day, Gomez is a respected composer. (Photograph by Al Rendon; courtesy of La Familia Cortez Restaurants.)

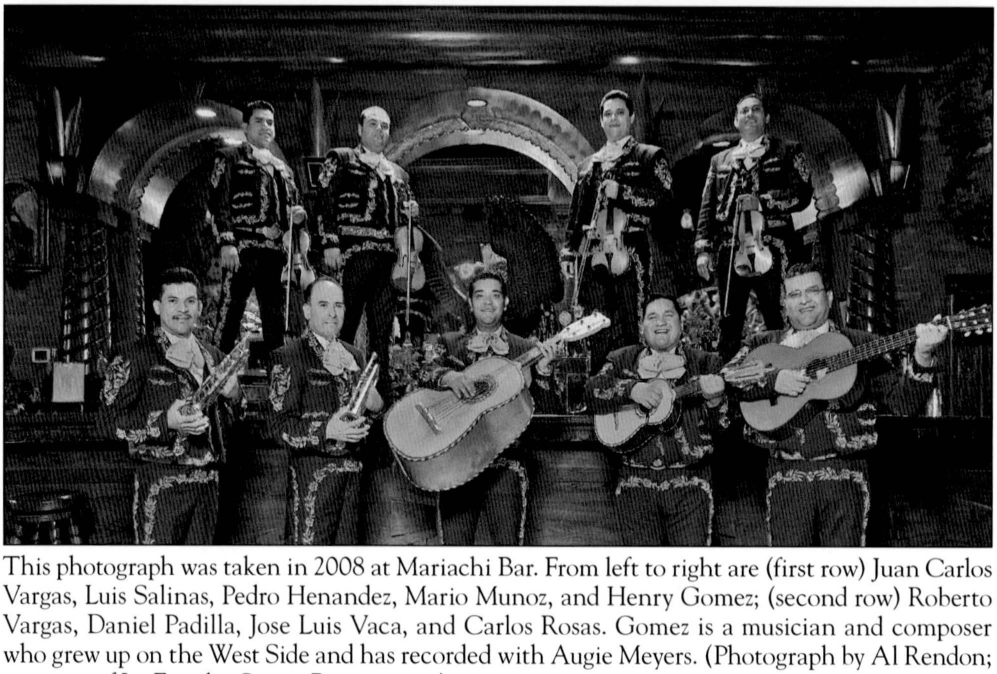

This photograph was taken in 2008 at Mariachi Bar. From left to right are (first row) Juan Carlos Vargas, Luis Salinas, Pedro Henandez, Mario Munoz, and Henry Gomez; (second row) Roberto Vargas, Daniel Padilla, Jose Luis Vaca, and Carlos Rosas. Gomez is a musician and composer who grew up on the West Side and has recorded with Augie Meyers. (Photograph by Al Rendon; courtesy of La Familia Cortez Restaurants.)

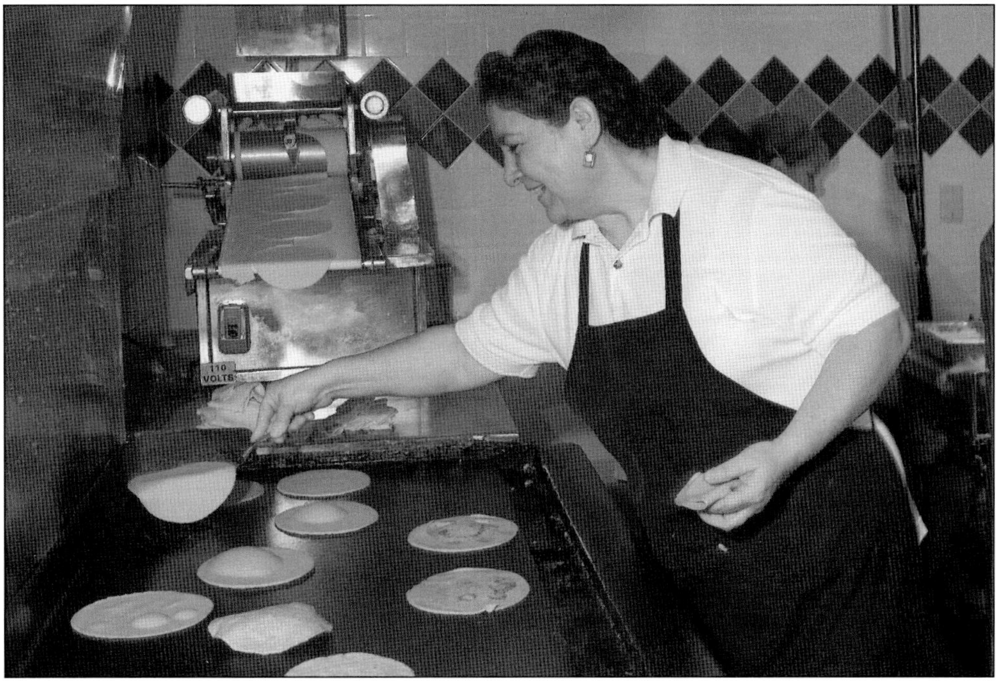

Making their own tortillas at Mi Tierra lines up with the principles of Don Pedro Cortez: "Take pride in your work. Do the very best you can. Plan your work properly. Do not cut corners at the expense of quality or safety." Anastasia Ortega is proud of her tortilla-making skills. She has been with Mi Tierra for 25 years. (Photograph by Al Rendon; courtesy of La Familia Cortez Restaurants.)

Tesero Torrentera makes pralines from scratch using Texas pecans. Torrentera has been making candy at Mi Tierra for over 25 years. The candy is made in the restaurant using natural ingredients and no preservatives. Other candies offered are coconut, caramel, peanut, candied orange peel, and pumpkin. These were the candies sold from glass cases by street vendors in the early days. (Photograph by Al Rendon; courtesy of La Familia Cortez Restaurants.)

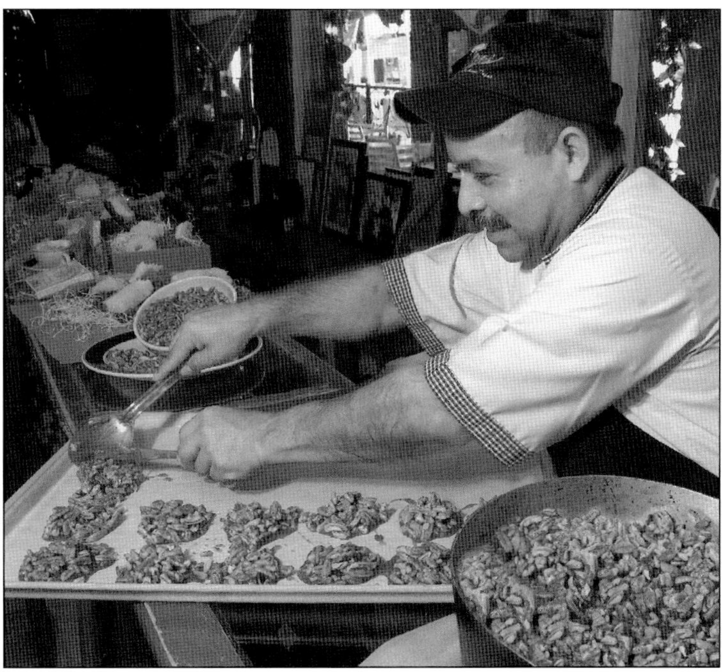

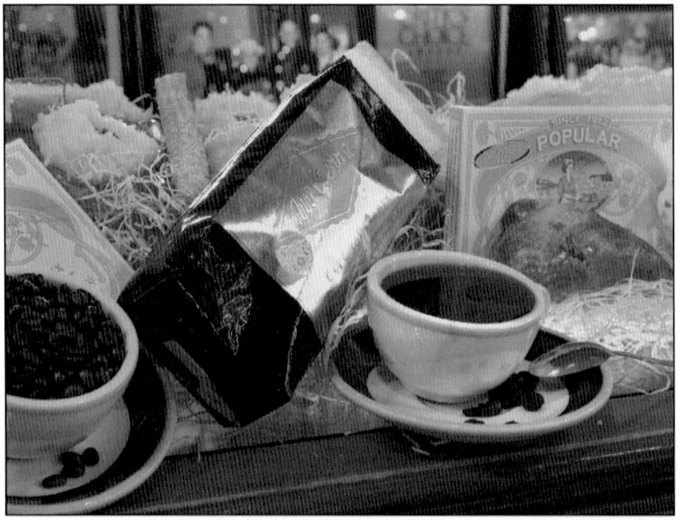

In 1941, the early-rising farmers and produce vendors wanted a strong cup of coffee. The special blend of coffee at Mi Tierra continued long after the produce vendors left the market. Customers wanted to brew this coffee at home. Ten years ago, Mi Tierra started offering their own line of whole coffee beans, a blend of Colombian and Chiapas Mexican beans. (Photograph by Al Rendon; courtesy of La Familia Cortez Restaurants.)

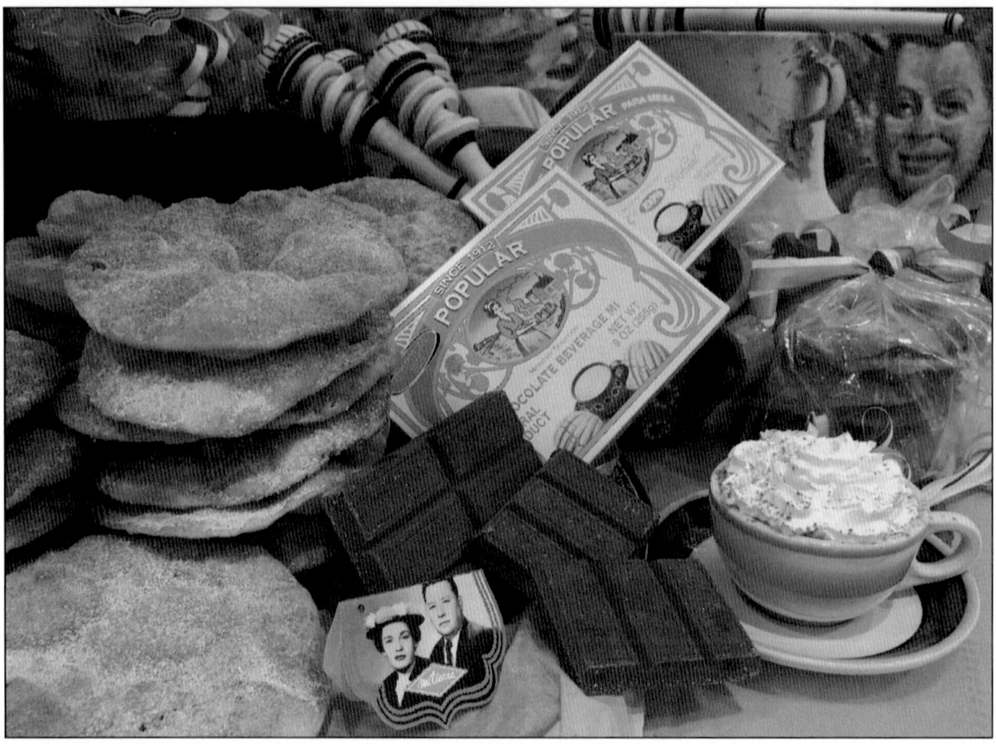

Mi Tierra uses La Popular authentic Mexican chocolate from Monterrey, Nuevo Leon. A few years ago, in appreciation of the product they have enjoyed since childhood, Michael and Pete Cortez toured the factory. Pete does not drink coffee or hot drinks. To cool the hot chocolate, he added whipped cream and sprinkled cinnamon on top. This became the signature chocolate drink served today. (Photograph by Al Rendon; courtesy of La Familia Cortez Restaurants.)

Day of the Dead bread is baked in late October and early November for Day of the Dead altars and festivities. The bread at Mi Tierra has been baked under the direction of two master bakers, Ricardo Montalvo and Jose Reynaga. This altar is in honor of Adela Gonzalez Gardena Mireles of Casa Mireles, Don Pedro, and Cruz Cortez. (Photograph by Al Rendon; courtesy of La Familia Cortez Restaurants.)

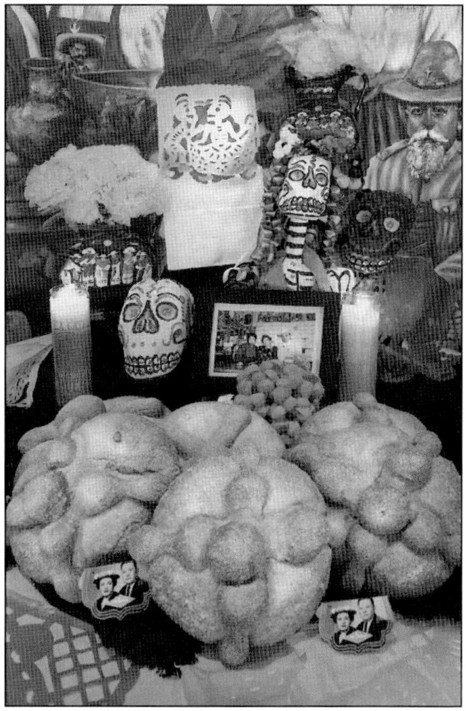

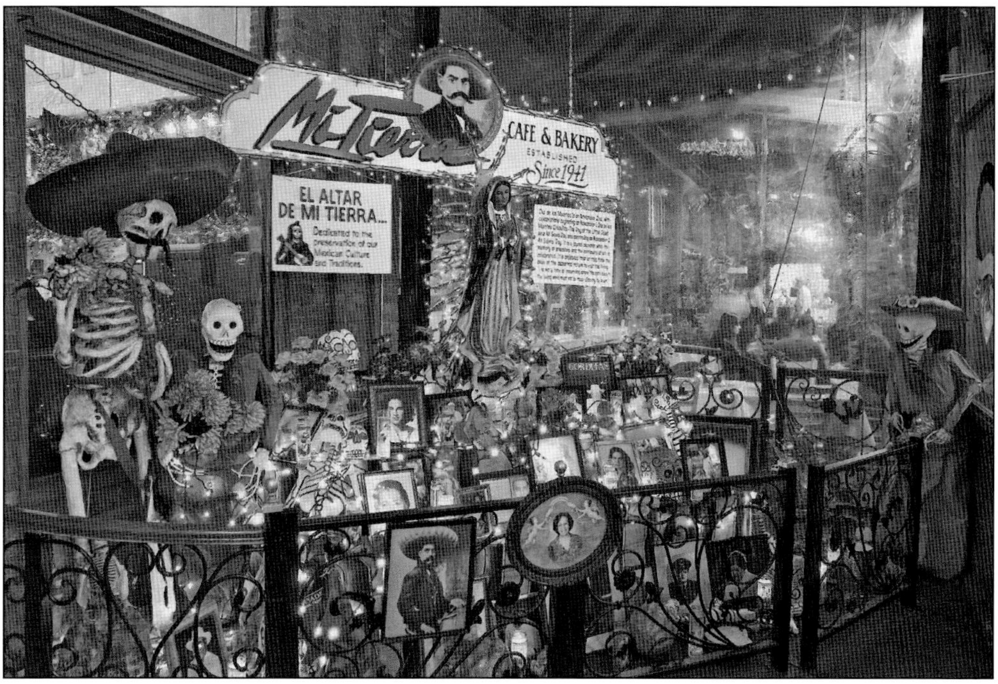

Michael Cortez's earliest memories of altars at Mi Tierra go back to the death of the queen of Tejano music, Selena Quintanilla. They put up Quintanilla's portrait at the restaurant, and people started bringing candles, flowers, and pictures of their loved ones, adding to the memorial. Currently, Deborah Cortez researches and designs the additions to the Cortez altars. (Photograph by Al Rendon; courtesy of La Familia Cortez Restaurants.)

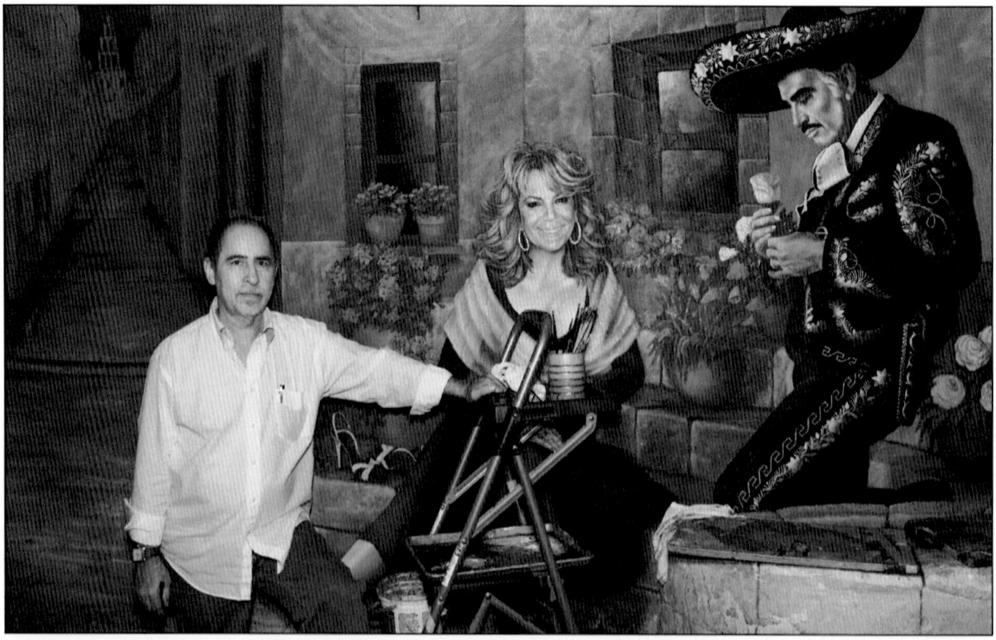

This mural of Vicki Carr and Vicente Fernández by artist Roberto Ytuarte was painted in 2010. It is part of the *American Dream* series for La Familia Cortez Restaurants, which began in 1990 with artist Jesus Garza. The murals are in line with the family's mission of serving good quality food while honoring and preserving Latino culture and traditions and the immigrant story. (Photograph by Al Rendon; courtesy of La Familia Cortez Restaurants.)

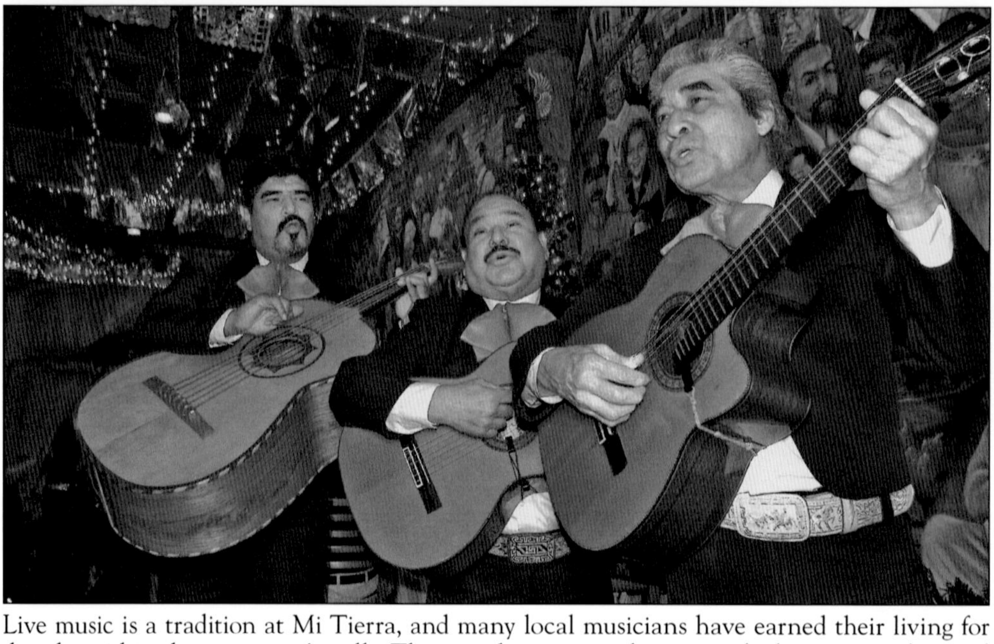

Live music is a tradition at Mi Tierra, and many local musicians have earned their living for decades within the restaurant's walls. There are lone guitar players, troubadours, mariachis, and trios. The musicians in this trio are, from left to right, Ismael Santander, Jose Uvalle, and Seferino "Chepe" Solis. Chepe has been playing at Market Square and Mi Tierra for 60 years. (Photograph by Al Rendon; courtesy of La Familia Cortez Restaurants.)

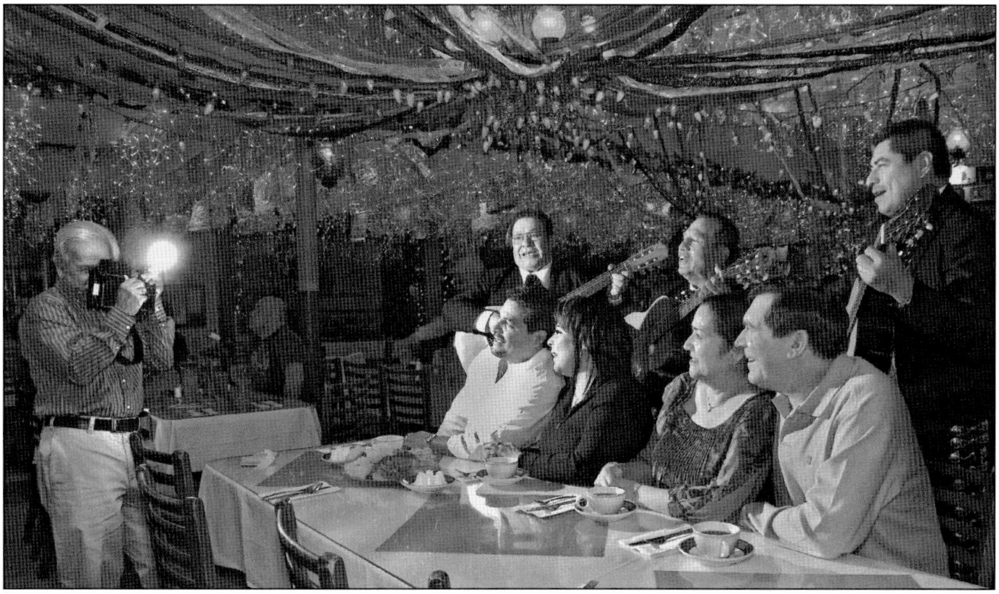

Photographer Antonio Garcia is known as "Hollywood" at Mi Tierra. He documents celebrations and gatherings for visitors. The musicians are, from left to right, Jose Luis Frausto Sr., Francisco Martinez, and Adrian Lopez. In the 1970s, Frausto played with Mariachi Chapultepec and founded Trio Los Pepes. He performed at Mi Tierra for over 40 years. (Photograph by Al Rendon; courtesy of La Familia Cortez Restaurants.)

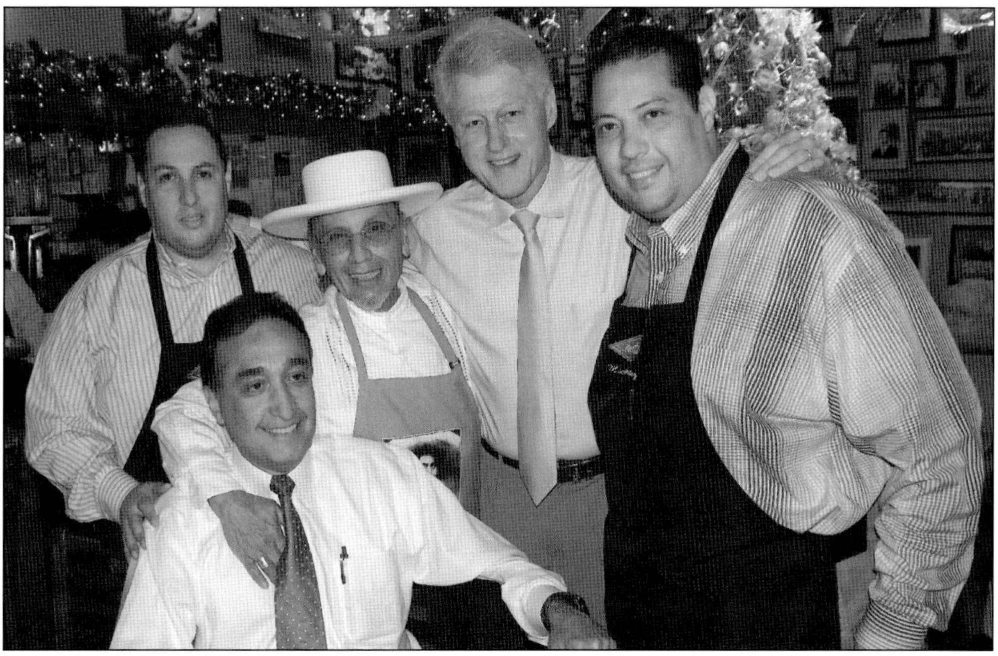

Former president Bill Clinton meets with Henry Cisneros at Mi Tierra in 2010. In 1993, Clinton appointed Cisneros as secretary of Housing and Urban Development, a position he held until 1997. Cisneros was mayor of San Antonio from 1981 to 1989. From left to right are Pete Cortez, Cisneros, Jorge Cortez, Clinton, and Michael Cortez. (Photograph by Al Rendon; courtesy of La Familia Cortez Restaurants.)

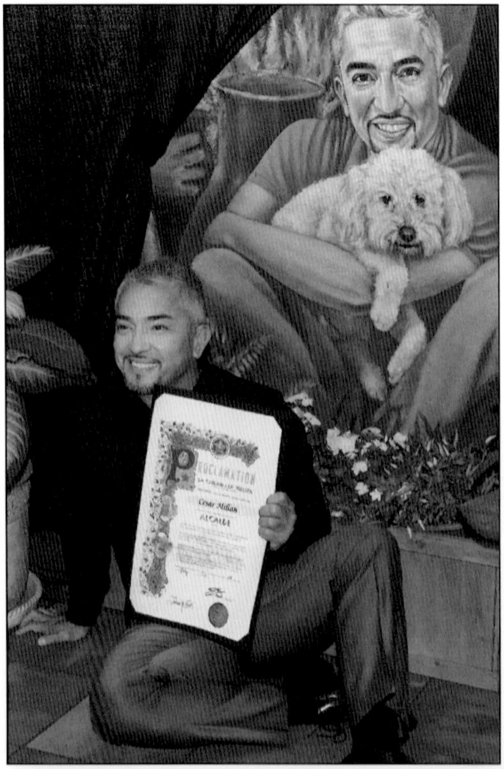

Cesar Millan, known as the "Dog Whisperer," sits in front of his mural at Mi Tierra holding the proclamation he was issued by the mayor of San Antonio on July 18, 2013. Millan was declared mayor of San Antonio for the day. His success story is right in line with the immigrant stories La Familia Cortez Restaurants works to preserve. (Photograph by Al Rendon; courtesy of La Familia Cortez Restaurants.)

Mi Tierra employee Abel Elizalde and his helper were in charge of placing the Virgin de Guadalupe on the restaurant's altar. *La Virgin* is at the Produce Row entrance. The altar at the Dolorosa Street entrance features a case originally in Berta Mireles's store, later owned by artist Franco Mondini-Ruiz, then used in a botanic exhibit at the former Museo Alameda. (Photograph by Al Rendon; courtesy of La Familia Cortez Restaurants.)

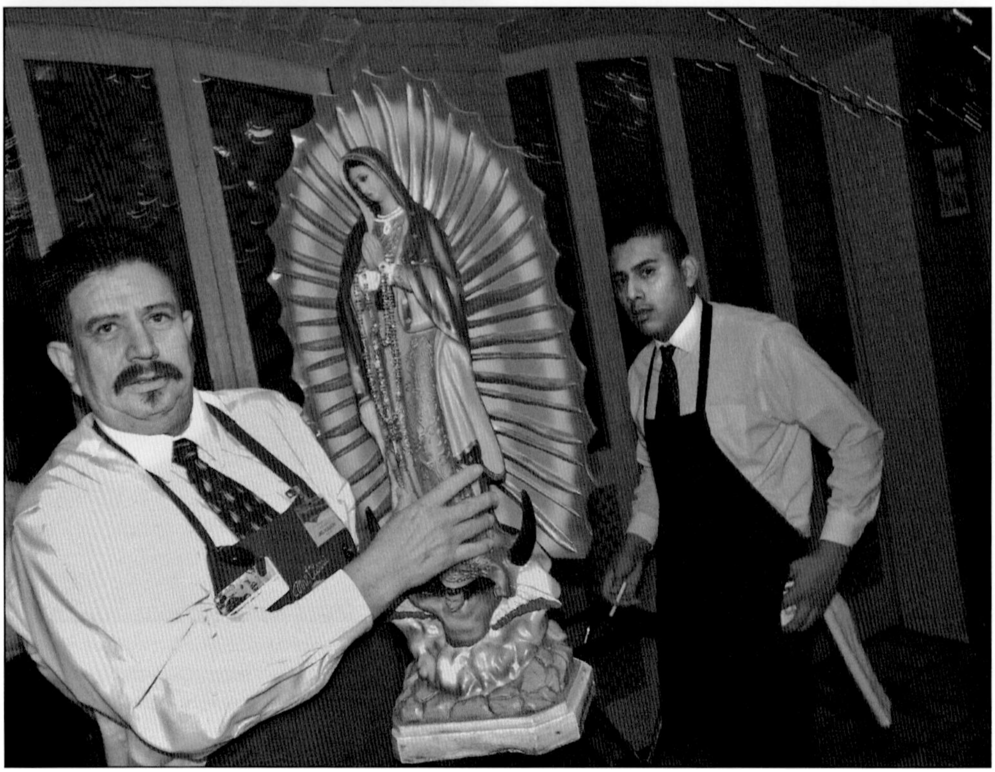

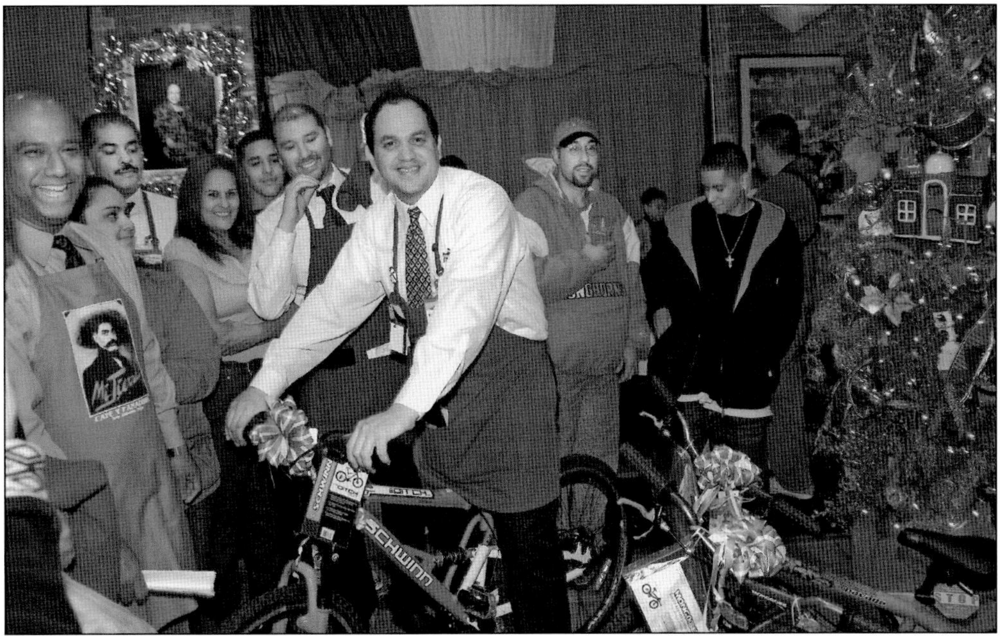

The annual Christmas party takes a lot of planning and must be done in shifts. Mi Tierra is open year-round, seven days a week, for 24 hours a day. Employees look forward to drawing for gifts, which could be anything from bicycles to big screen televisions. At far left wearing a Mi Tierra apron is Brian Vanderputt. (Photograph by Al Rendon; courtesy of La Familia Cortez Restaurants.)

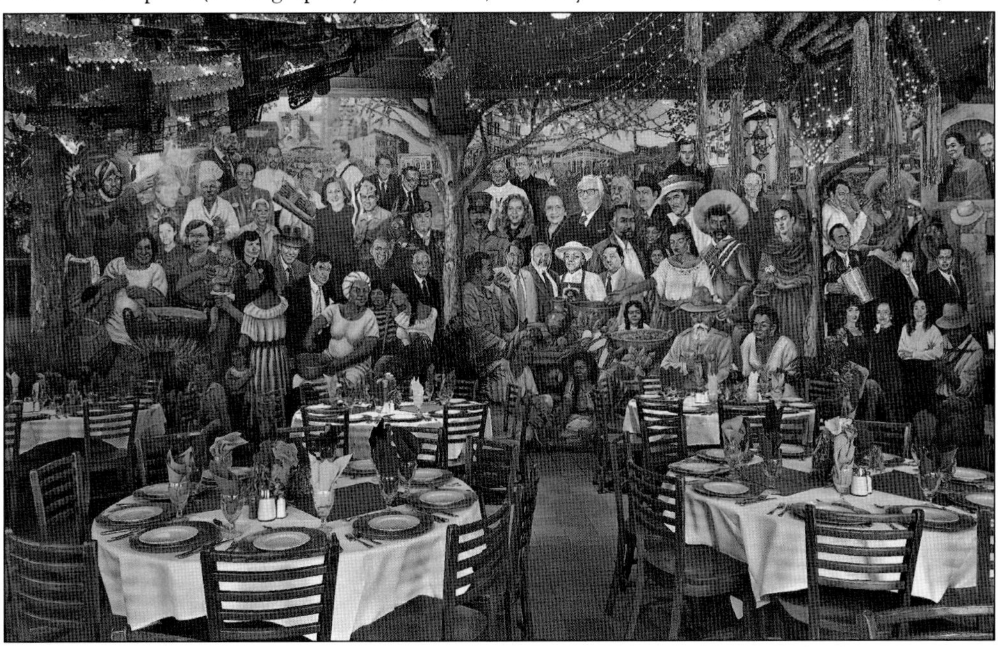

The murals at Mi Tierra celebrate the lives of local, national, and international celebrities; Cortez family members; and friends and politicians, all adding to the festive atmosphere. Families come from all over to celebrate birthdays, holidays, weddings, and after funeral receptions. The fiesta never stops; the decorations of lights, decorative paper on string banners, and piñatas stay up year-round. (Photograph by Al Rendon; courtesy of La Familia Cortez Restaurants.)

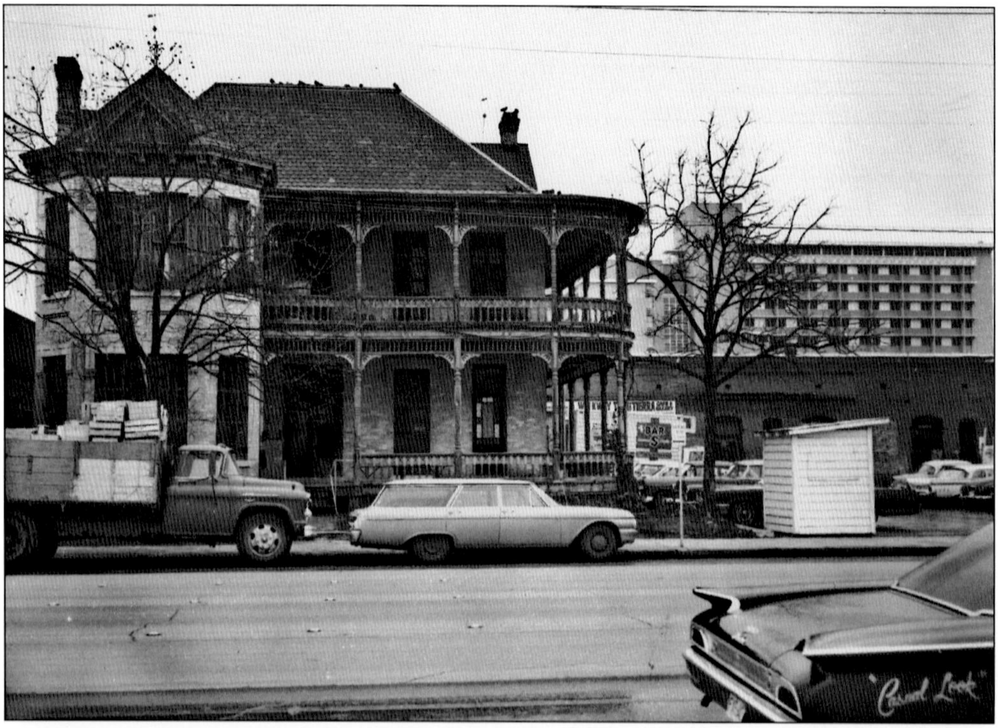

The Eli Arnaud house at 217 Buena Vista Street is pictured here in November 1970. Mi Tierra is visible in the background. Arnaud built the house for his wife, Willomena, and their eight children. Later, the house would be known as the residence of Charles Arnaud. In 1961, Don Pedro Cortez purchased the entire block. The house was later demolished to expand the parking lot of Mi Tierra. (Courtesy of UTSA Special Collections–ITC; photograph 82-533.)

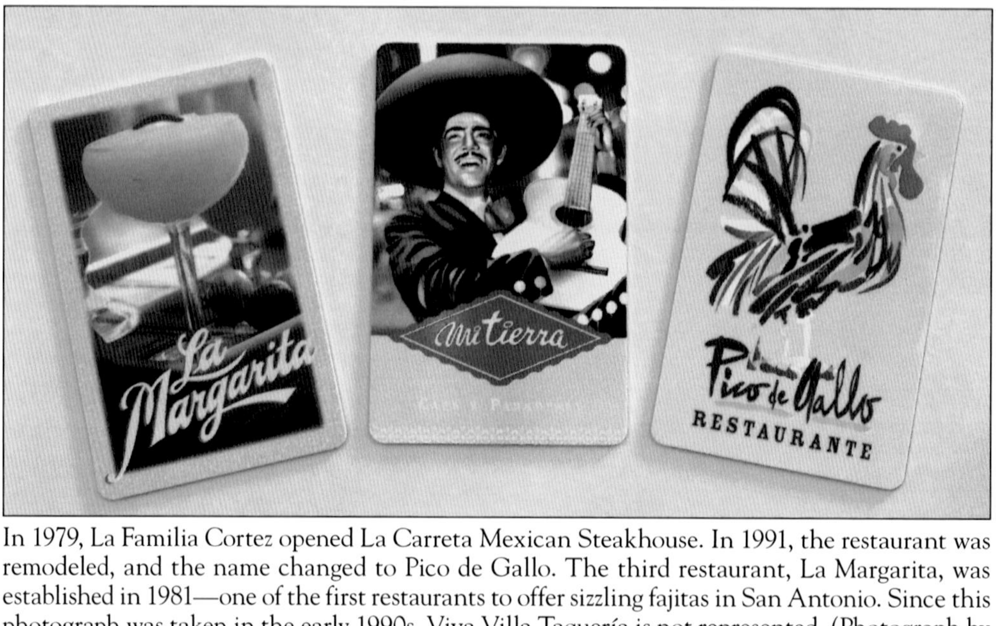

In 1979, La Familia Cortez opened La Carreta Mexican Steakhouse. In 1991, the restaurant was remodeled, and the name changed to Pico de Gallo. The third restaurant, La Margarita, was established in 1981—one of the first restaurants to offer sizzling fajitas in San Antonio. Since this photograph was taken in the early 1990s, Viva Villa Taquería is not represented. (Photograph by Al Rendon; courtesy of La Familia Cortez Restaurants.)

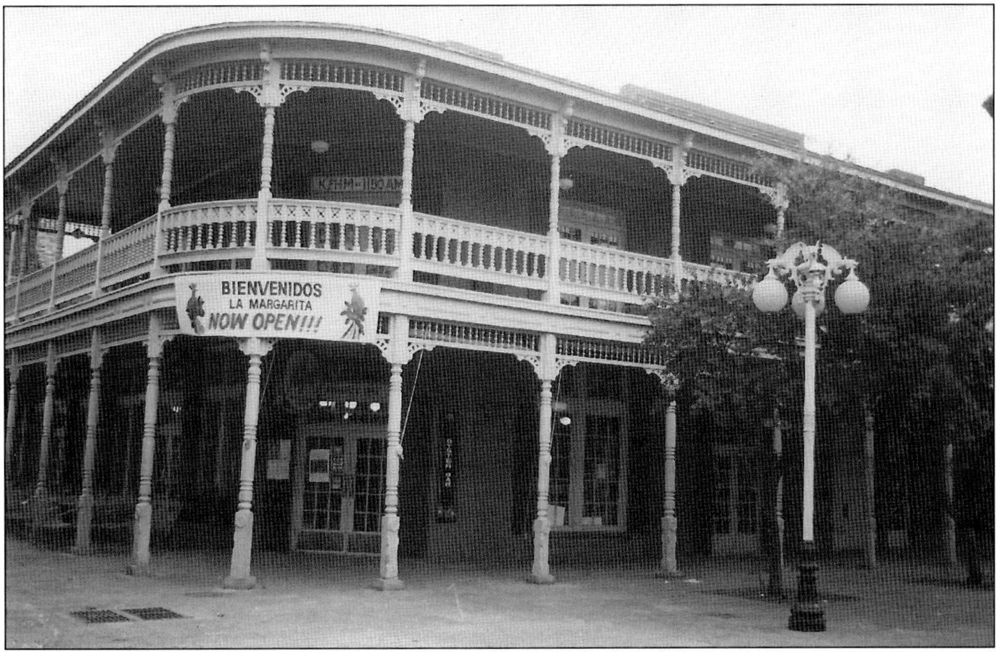

This photograph was taken in 1981. The porch supports, balustrades, and other decorative details were salvaged by the Cortez family when the Arnaud house was demolished, and then added to La Margarita's exterior at 120 Produce Row. The 1927 city directory listed Wah Yuen Quong at 120 Produce Row. In 1948, the Quong family was still there, but by 1977, the building was vacant. (Courtesy of the San Antonio Conservation Society Foundation.)

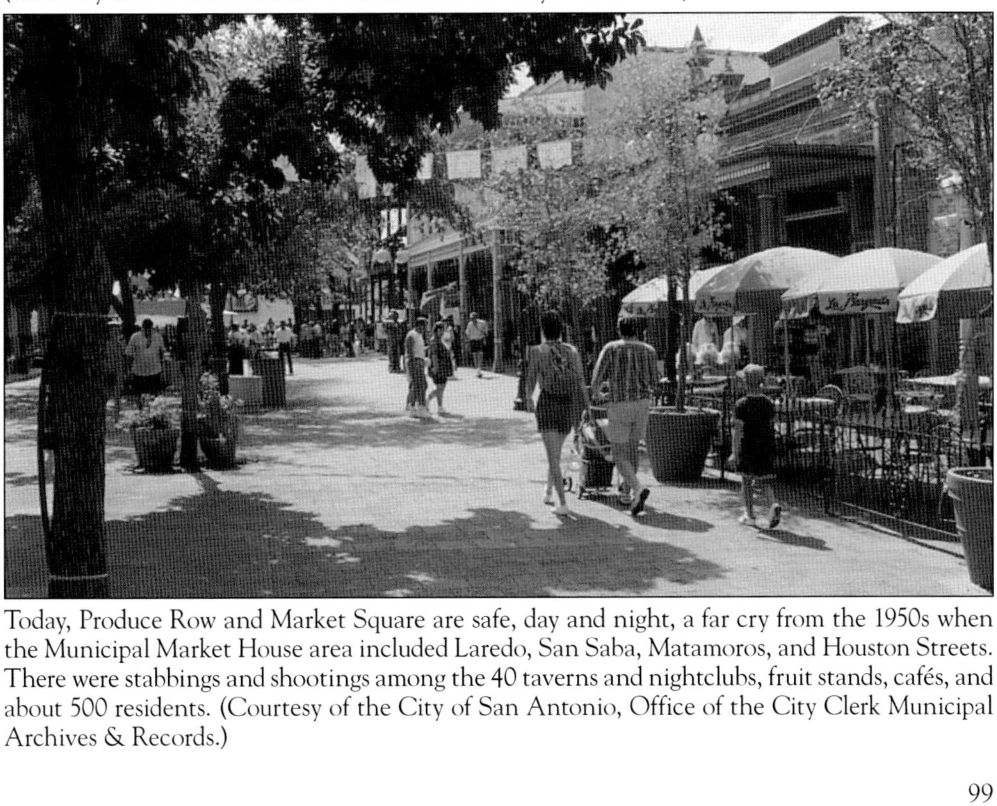
Today, Produce Row and Market Square are safe, day and night, a far cry from the 1950s when the Municipal Market House area included Laredo, San Saba, Matamoros, and Houston Streets. There were stabbings and shootings among the 40 taverns and nightclubs, fruit stands, cafés, and about 500 residents. (Courtesy of the City of San Antonio, Office of the City Clerk Municipal Archives & Records.)

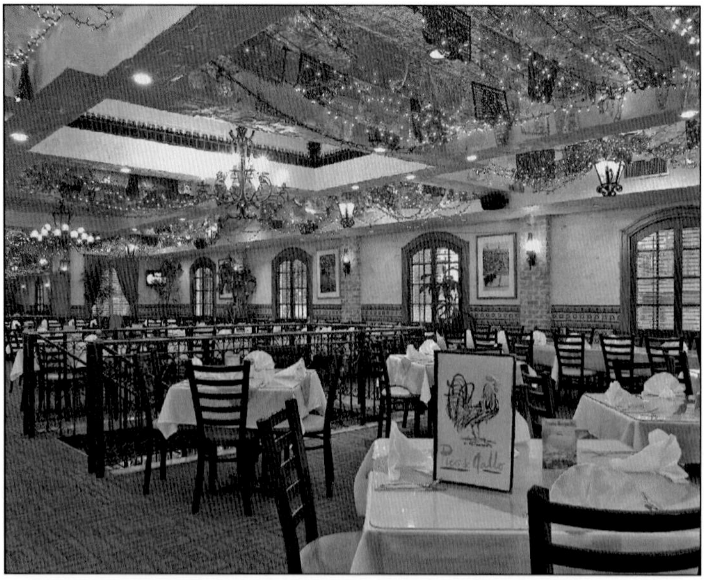

Pico de Gallo is the former Cortez family restaurant La Carreta Mexican Steakhouse, which opened in 1979. In 1991, it was remodeled and renamed. The upstairs party room has hosted decades of families celebrating life. The restaurant is located a few blocks from Market Square at 111 South Leona Street. There is nightly mariachi music. (Photograph by Al Rendon; courtesy of La Familia Cortez Restaurants.)

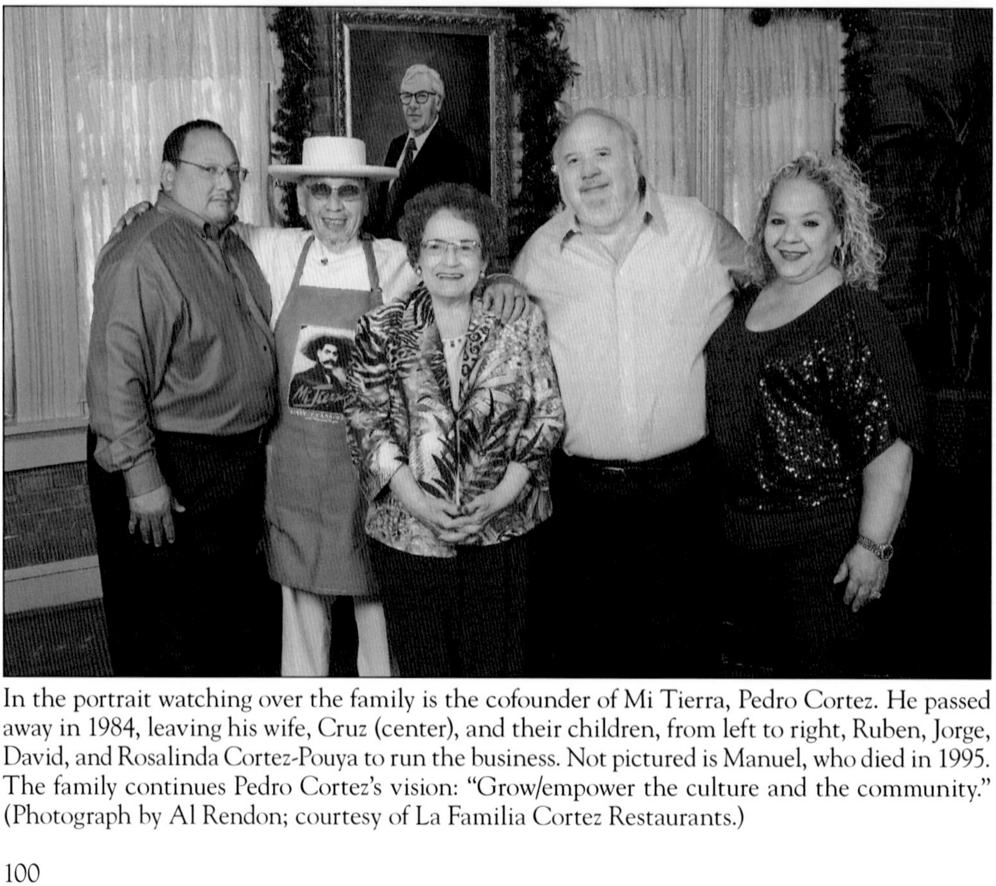

In the portrait watching over the family is the cofounder of Mi Tierra, Pedro Cortez. He passed away in 1984, leaving his wife, Cruz (center), and their children, from left to right, Ruben, Jorge, David, and Rosalinda Cortez-Pouya to run the business. Not pictured is Manuel, who died in 1995. The family continues Pedro Cortez's vision: "Grow/empower the culture and the community." (Photograph by Al Rendon; courtesy of La Familia Cortez Restaurants.)

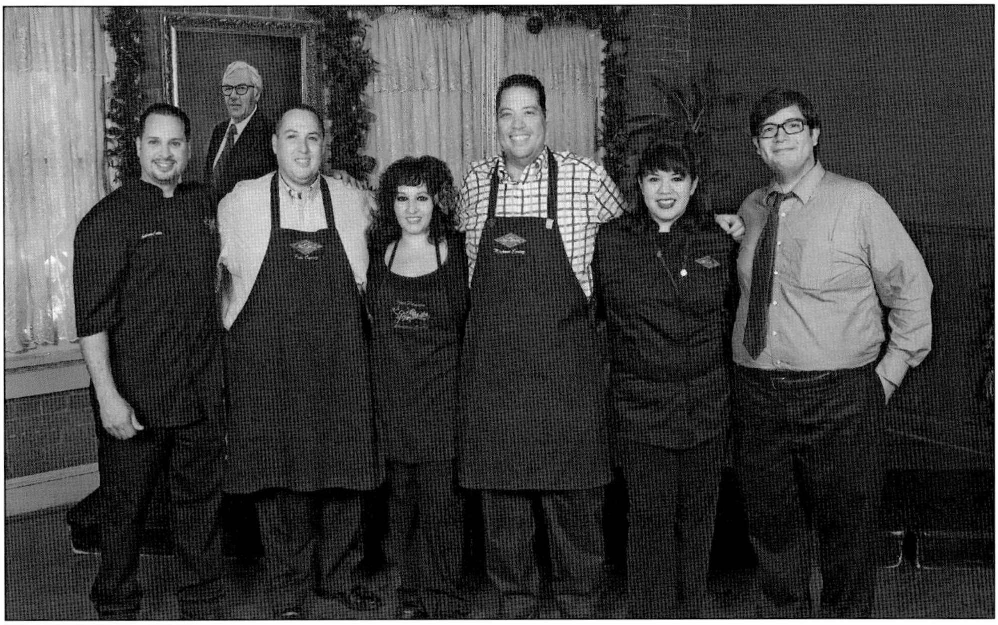

The third generation of the Cortez family is pictured here. From left to right are Anthony, Pete, Christina de la Fuente, Michael, Angelica, and Jonathan. Chef Raul Salazar, of Mi Tierra, watched the grandchildren grow up. Most worked summers in the family business. Salazar has been with the Cortez family for 45 years. Fifteen years ago, the family rewarded his loyalty with a key to the restaurant's spice room. (Photograph by Al Rendon; courtesy of La Familia Cortez Restaurants.)

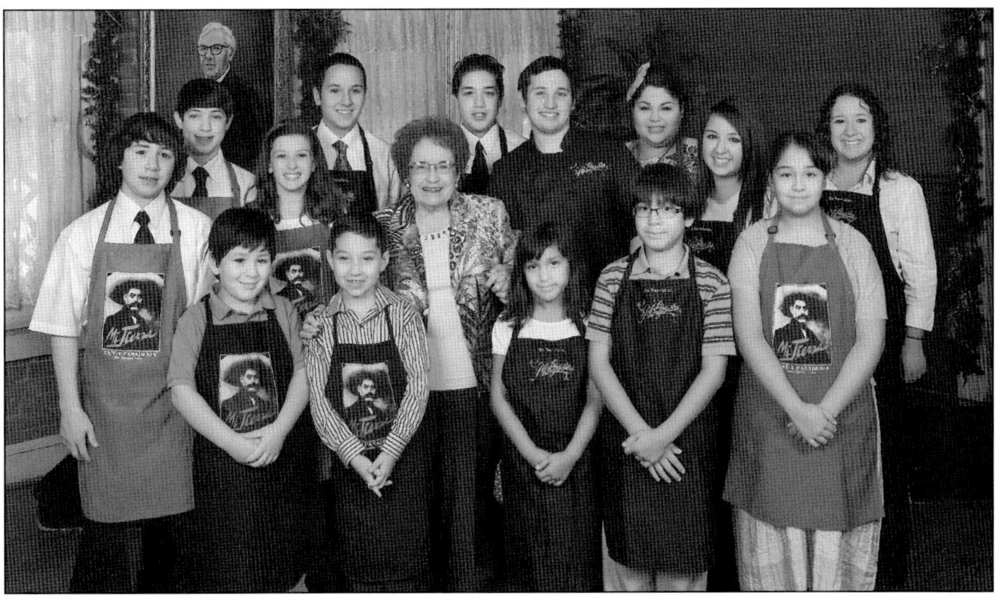

The matriarch of the Cortez family, Cruz (center), is pictured here with the fourth generation: Noah de la Fuente, George Peter Cortez, Sophia Pacheco, Ashley Cortez, Christopher de la Fuente, Sarah Cortez, William de la Fuente, Yasmin Pouya, Victoria Cortez, Anthony Cortez, Manuel Cortez, Elijah Cortez, Audrey Cortez, and Joshua Pacheco. This generation will celebrate La Familia Cortez Restaurants' 100th anniversary in 2041. (Photograph by Al Rendon; courtesy of La Familia Cortez Restaurants.)

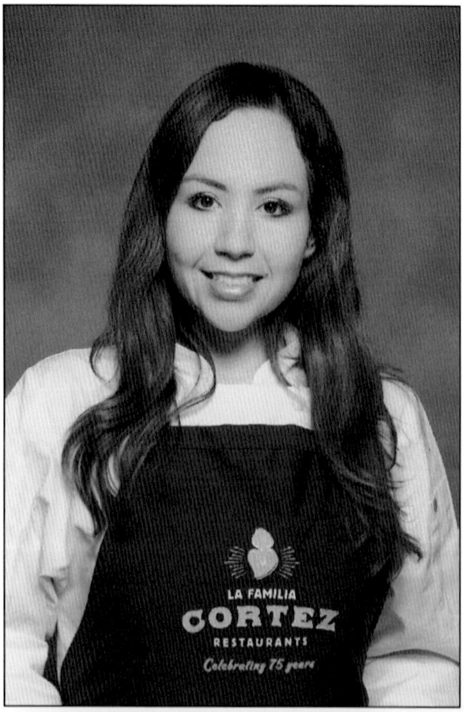

Cariño Cortez-Haass, daughter of Jorge Cortez, is the project manager of the family's latest food venture. Viva Villa Taqueria, the home of "Revolutionary Tacos," opened in 2015. As a graduate of the Culinary Institute of America at Hyde Park, Chef Cariño uses her culinary initiatives and marketing skills to attract a new generation of foodies. (Photograph by Al Rendon; courtesy of La Familia Cortez Restaurants.)

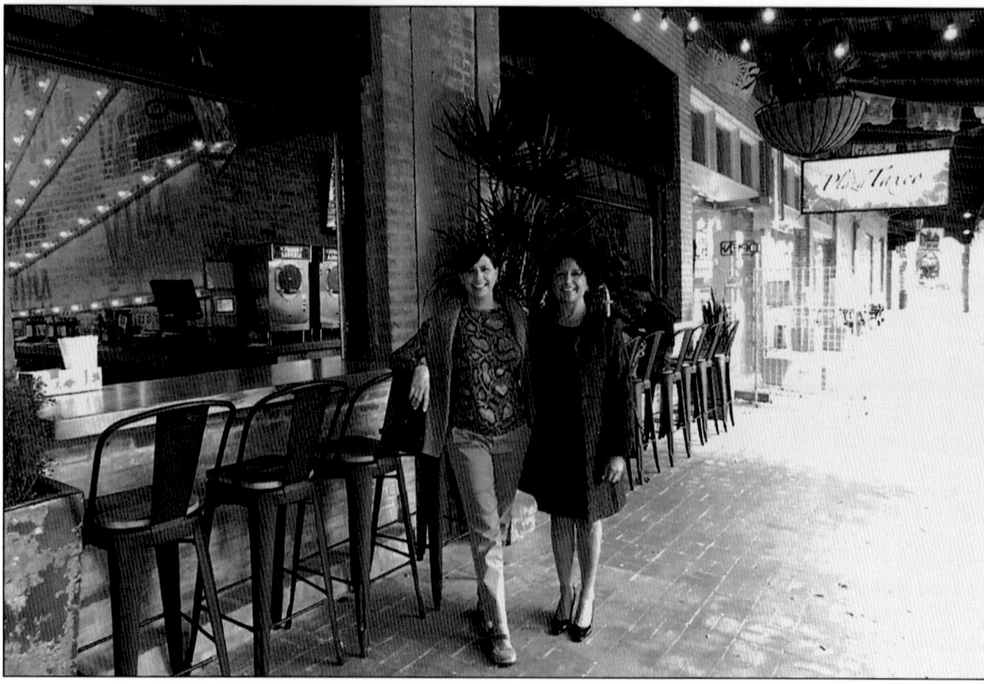

Nancy Lara (left) and Edna Campos Gravenhorst, founders of Sazón in the City, pose at the outdoor bar of Viva Villa Taqueria. Nancy and Edna are both certified tourism ambassadors for the city of San Antonio. The event planners focus on local history, heritage, and hospitality. Next to Viva Villa Taqueria is Plaza Taxco, followed by the television studio of *SA Live* on KSAT 12. (Author's collection.)

Eight

Urban Renewal

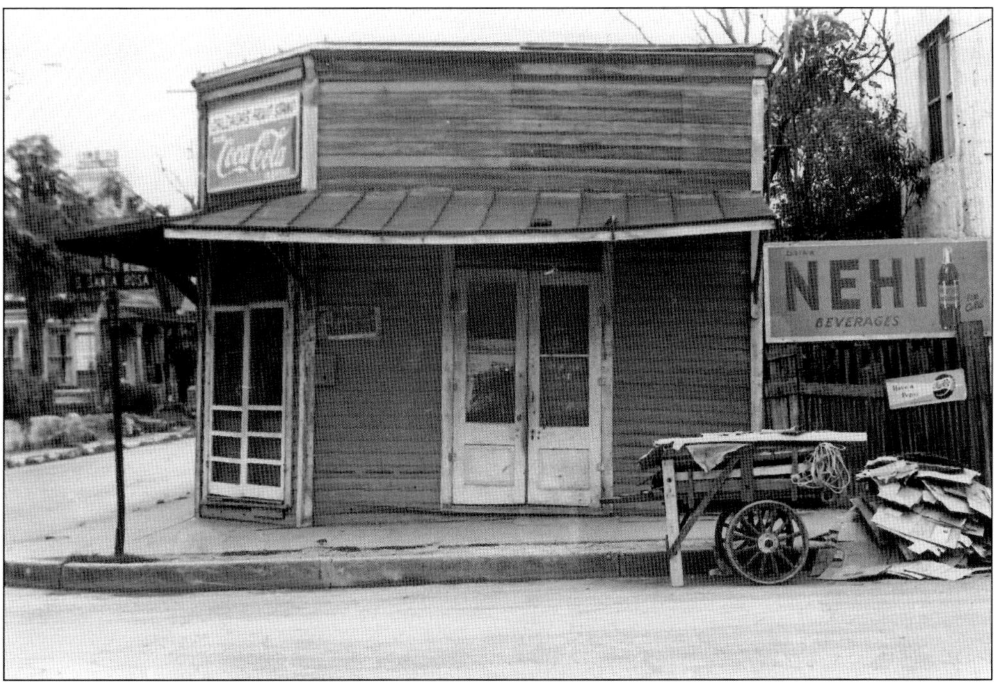

Urban renewal changed Market Square and the surrounding areas. Many businesses relocated, others disappeared. A 1966 document in the Francisco Chapa Collection on the Rosa Verde Project states, "Urban Renewal is a means of revitalizing and modernizing our city and eliminating blight and deterioration through the redevelopment or rehabilitation of declining areas." Calzadas Fruit Stand, at 300 South Santa Rosa Avenue, relocated to 529 Fredricksburg Road. (Courtesy of Texana Division, San Antonio Public Libraries.)

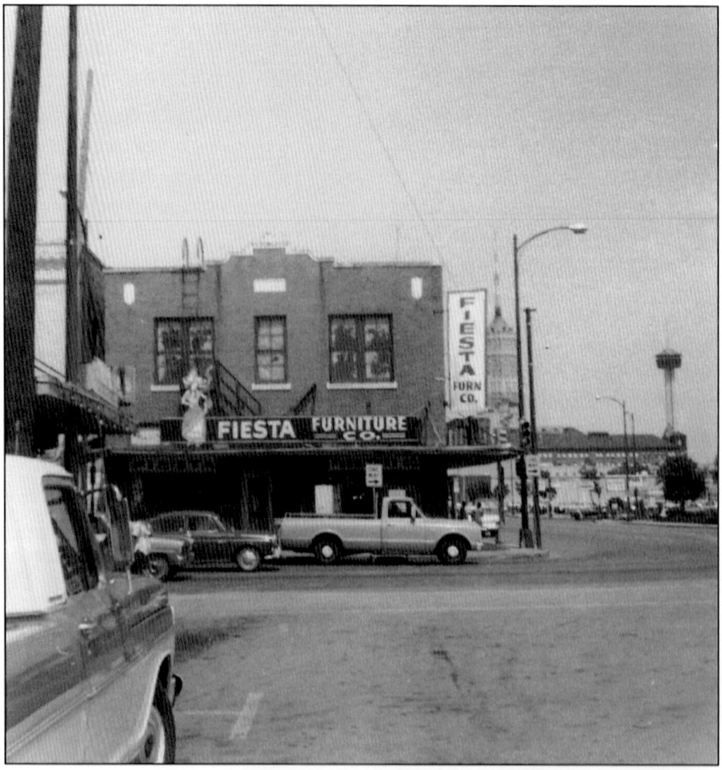

Fiesta Furniture Company, pictured in 1970, was located at 126 South Santa Rosa Avenue. To the right is the Tower Life Building and the Tower of the Americas. The store moved four employees from a 4,000-square-foot building to a 3,000-square-foot space at 114 North Medina Street. The owner remarked, "My business will remain in the central business area." (Courtesy of Texana Division, San Antonio Public Libraries.)

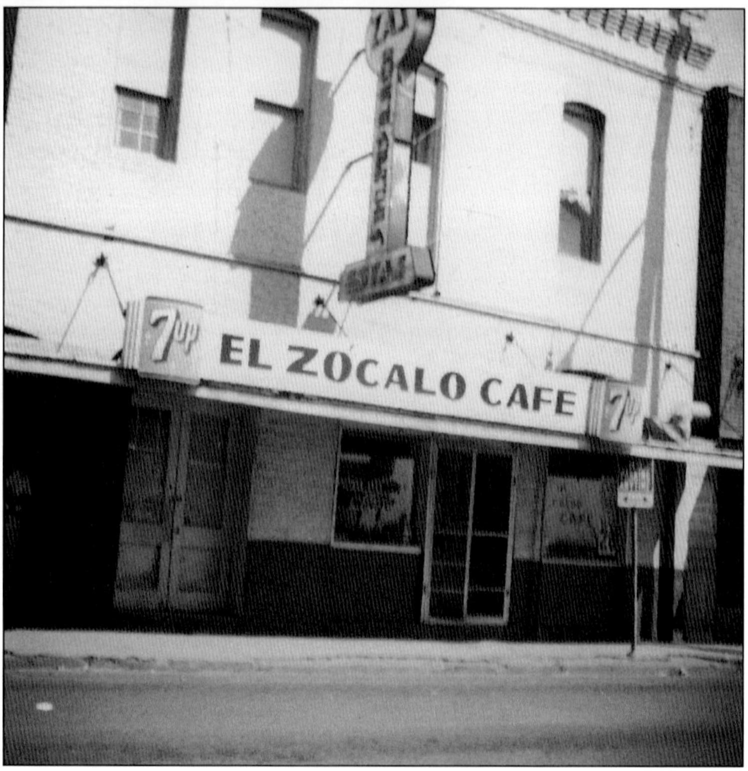

In 1970, El Zocalo Cafe, at 120 South Santa Rosa Avenue, was owned by Elena Renteria. Renteria lived in the five-room apartment upstairs. On the urban renewal project worksheet, she stated her business income as $300 and her rent at $200. She was relocated to an apartment at 214 Palo Blanco Street. There is no mention of a business relocation. (Courtesy of Texana Division, San Antonio Public Libraries.)

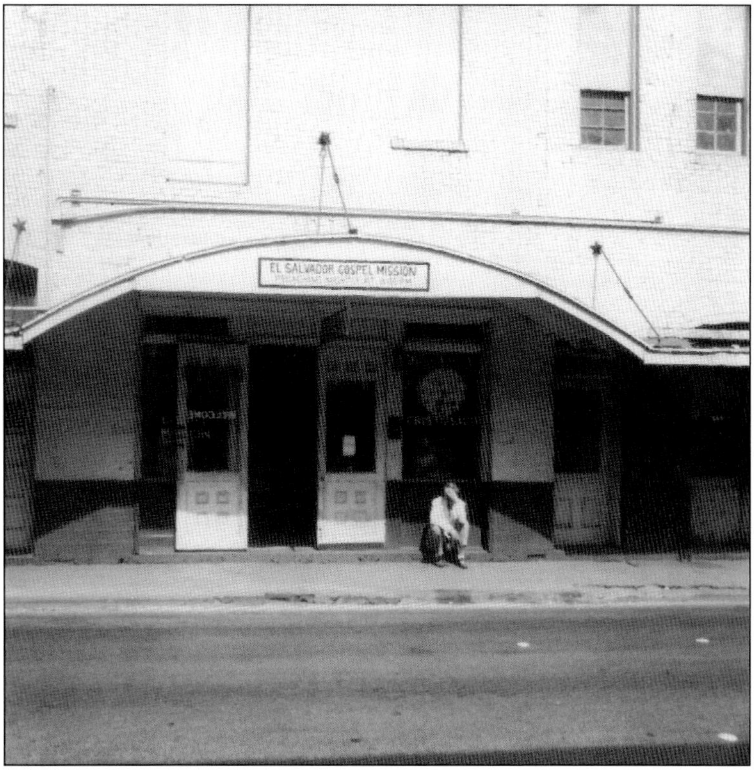

El Salvador Gospel Mission at 112 South Santa Rosa Avenue closed after this photograph was taken in 1970. Due to his age, the preacher decided to retire instead of relocating. The sign on the 3,500-square-foot building announces preaching every night at 8:00 p.m. (Courtesy of Texana Division, San Antonio Public Libraries.)

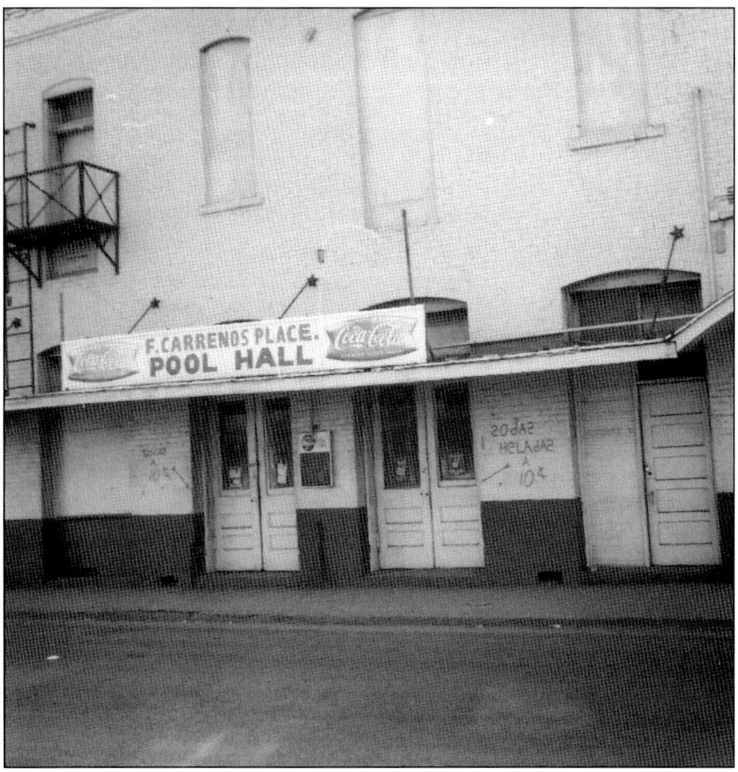

F. Carreno's business at 110 South Santa Rosa Avenue started to decline before 1970. As sole proprietor, it was hard for Carreno to maintain a 4,000-square-foot building. On his urban renewal worksheet, he stated his gross annual income as $3,600. Instead of relocating his business, he elected to close down the pool hall where he sold cold sodas for 10¢. (Courtesy of Texana Division, San Antonio Public Libraries.)

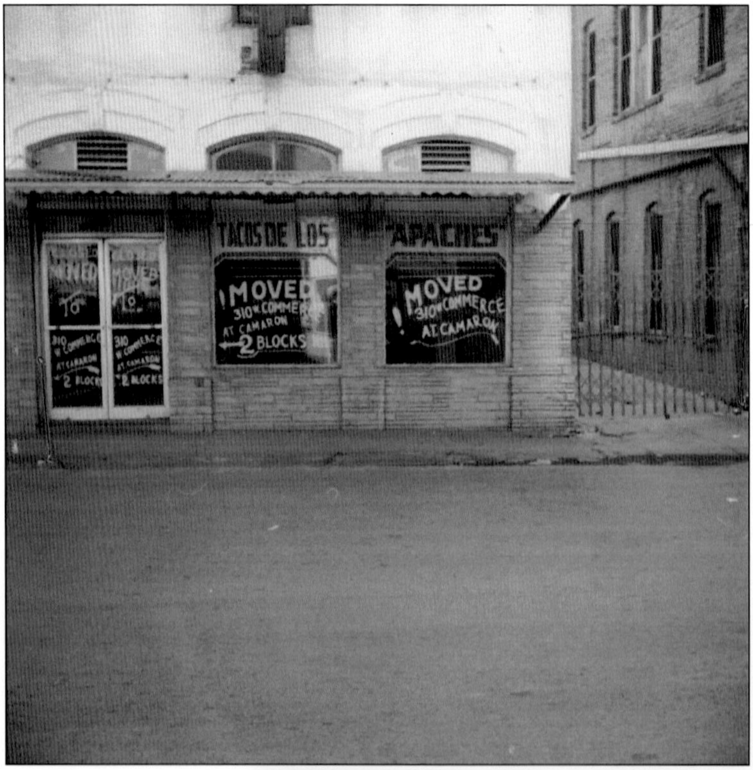

In 1969, when Tacos De Los Apaches at 104 South Santa Rosa Avenue was photographed, the windows announced its relocation to 310 West Commerce Street. Rogelio Gonzales, owner of the café, rented the 24-by-70-foot space for $175 per week. When it came time for relocation, Gonzales's health was declining. He decided to liquidate instead of moving. (Courtesy of Texana Division, San Antonio Public Libraries.)

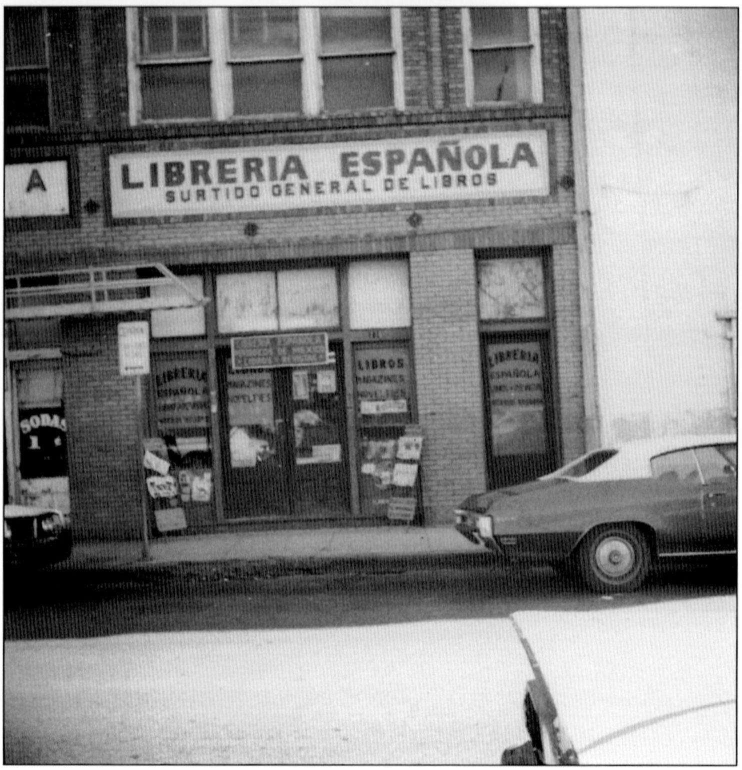

Libreria Española, the Spanish bookstore at 116 North Santa Rosa Street, employed two people and did well in an area of 525 square feet. In 1970, its gross annual income was reported at $46,266. The relocation to 219 West Houston Street gave the business extra room, 650 square feet, in a more modern building and increased street traffic. (Courtesy of Texana Division, San Antonio Public Libraries.)

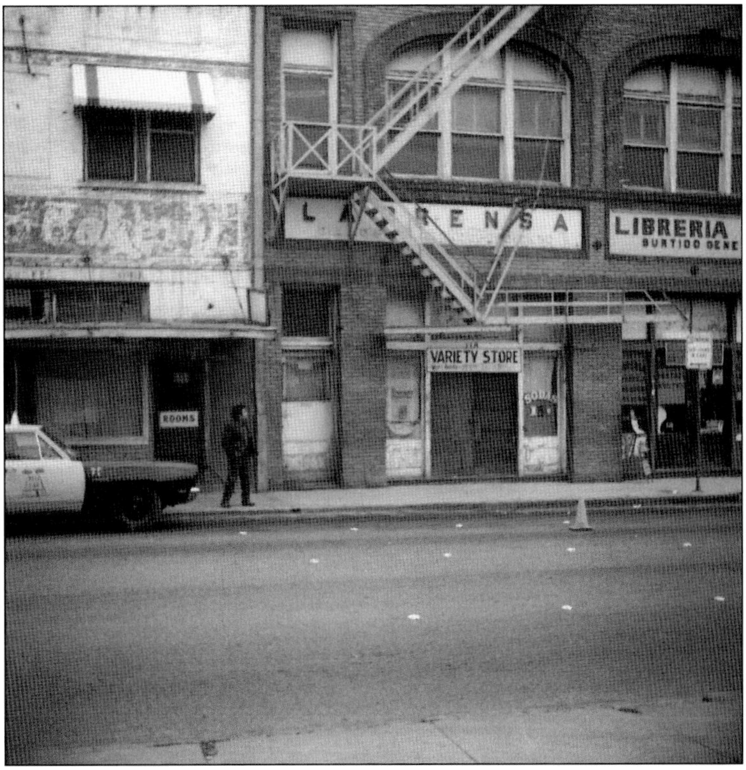

La Prensa, a Spanish-language newspaper, was founded by Ignacio Lozano in 1913. In 1927, it was located at 118–120 North Santa Rosa Street. In 1942, it was at 120 North Santa Rosa Street, with Lozano Book Store next door at 118 North Santa Rosa Street. The officers were Ignacio Lozano, president; Leonides Gonzalez, vice president; and Alicia Lozano, secretary. In 1971, *La Prensa* was located at 120 North Santa Rosa Street. (Courtesy of Texana Division, San Antonio Public Libraries.)

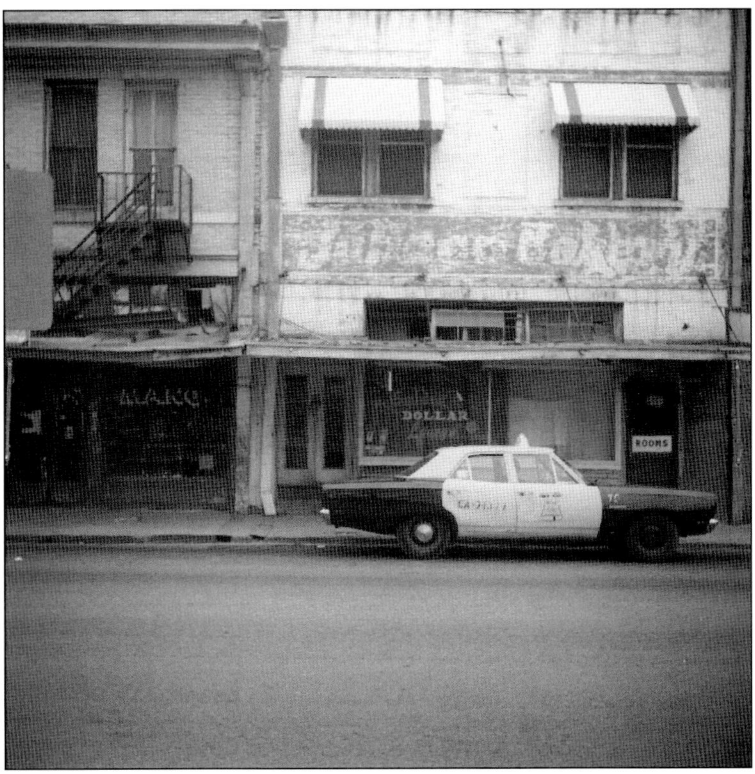

A Mrs. Vargas was the owner of the Golden Dollar Lounge in 1971. The building, with rooms for rent upstairs, was located at 122 North Santa Rosa Street. It was a small business with annual sales of $12,464; the owner was the only employee. Instead of relocating, Vargas decided to close the lounge in order to pursue other business interests. (Courtesy of Texana Division, San Antonio Public Libraries.)

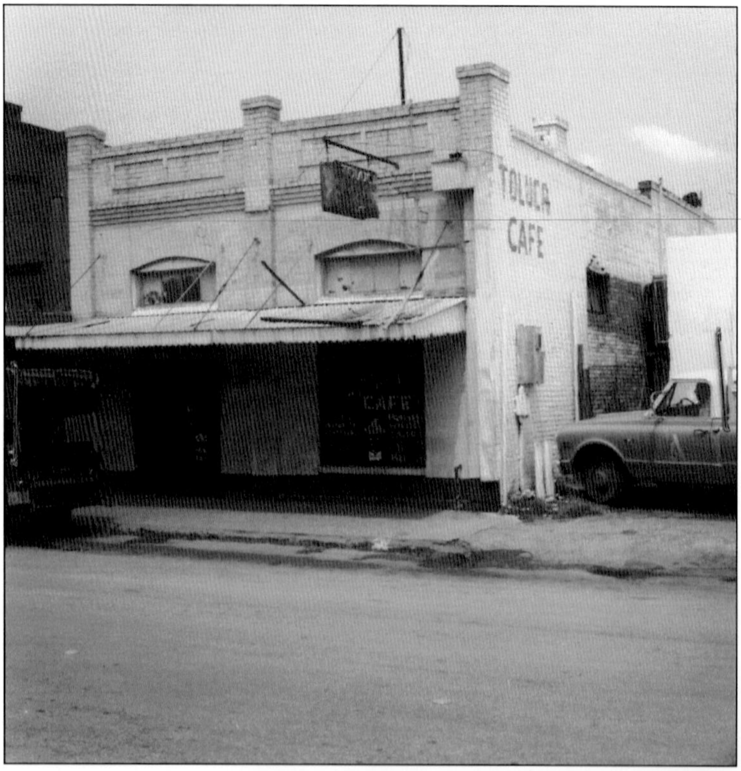

In 1970, Arthur Siller's business, Toluca Café, was in decline. The building at 110 South Concho Street housed the Western Poultry Company in 1908. In 1927, it was the location of Lee Yee Café. By 1942, the Toluca Café & Bar sold beer there, and Lorenzo Garza's restaurant provided the food. Pascual De Leon sold fruits at 110 ½ South Concho Street in 1942. (Courtesy of Texana Division, San Antonio Public Libraries.)

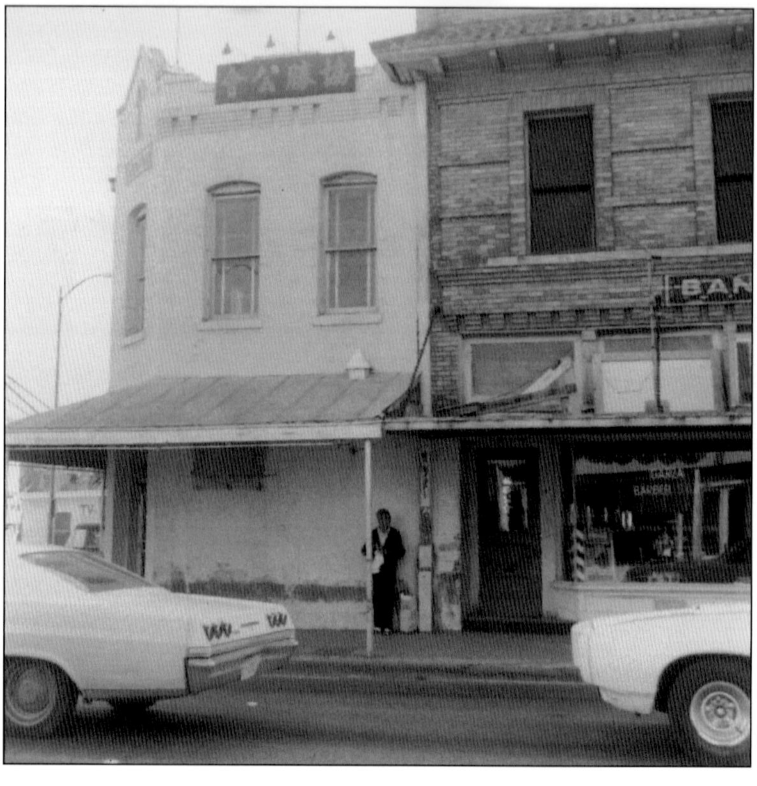

In 1942, the Hip Sing Association was located at 607 ½ West Houston Street; Henry Woo was the secretary. When this photograph was taken in 1969, the association was located at 127 North Laredo Street, next to Garza Barber Shop. The association had a new building constructed at 414 Buena Vista Street. It was the same size as the old one, 8,000 square feet. (Courtesy of Texana Division, San Antonio Public Libraries.)

In 28 years, Cohen's Army Store expanded into two more storefronts. In 1942, the store was listed at 105–107 South Pecos Street and managed by Harry Cohen. In 1970, the address extended from 103 to 109 South Pecos Street. When it relocated to 506 North Elmendorf Street, the store downsized from 14,000 to 8,000 square feet and went from employing three people to two. (Courtesy of Texana Division, San Antonio Public Libraries.)

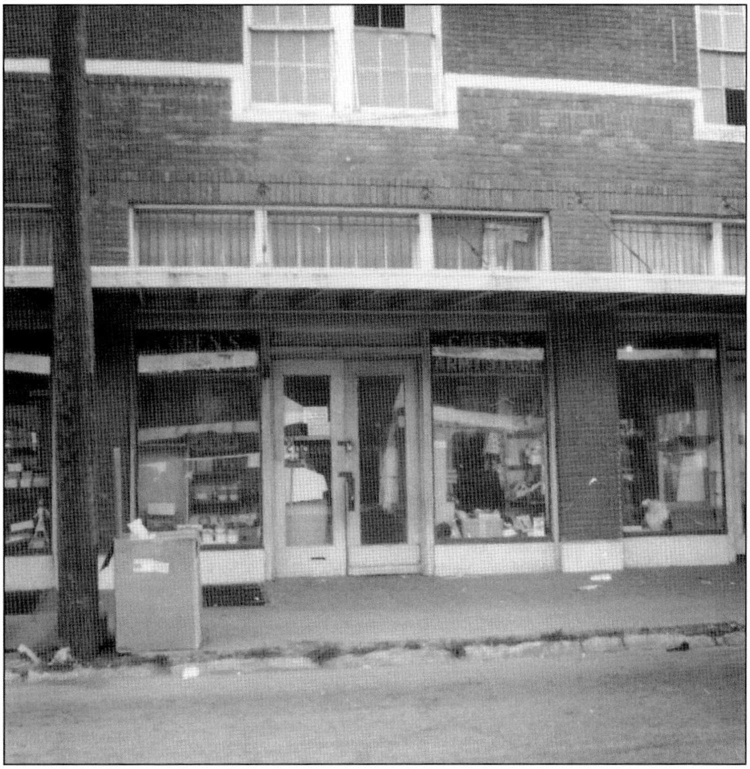

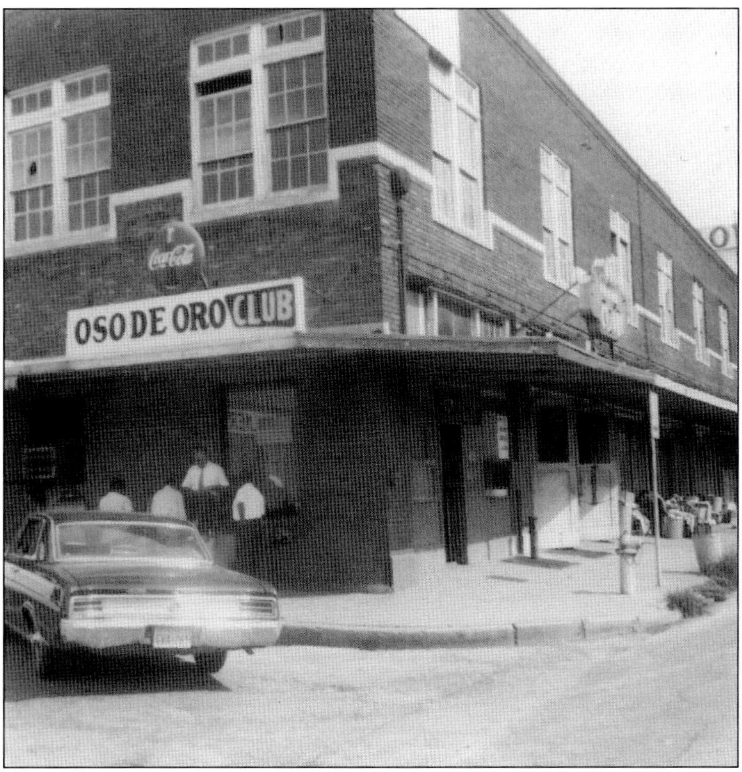

Until 1970, gentlemen who came for beer at the Oso De Oro Club could get their shoes shined in front of the bar. In 1927, this building was the residence of Leon Lee. Next door at 111 South Pecos Street was the Juvenile Manufacturing Company. In the 1940s, this was the location of the Pecos Restaurant. Next door to it was the New Twentieth Century Club. (Courtesy of Texana Division, San Antonio Public Libraries.)

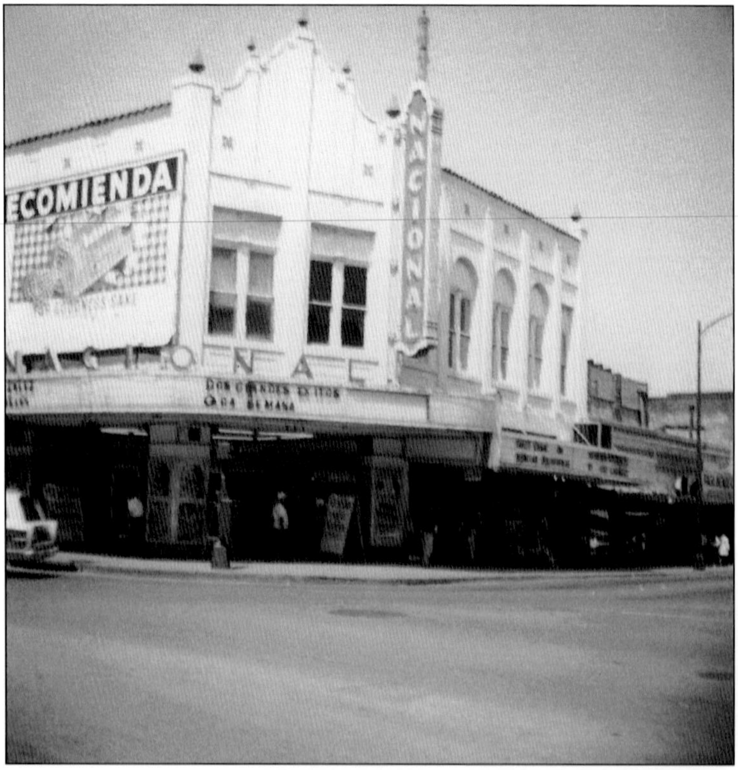

El Teatro Nacional, at 819 West Commerce Street, featured first-run Mexican movies. It also hosted road shows starring Mexican entertainers who made only one American appearance. El Teatro Nacional was photographed in 1970 as part of urban renewal because of the two apartment tenants upstairs who were being relocated. Rosalio Moreno moved to 1115 North Zarzamora Street and Jose Prado to an apartment at 602 Devine Street. (Courtesy of Texana Division, San Antonio Public Libraries.)

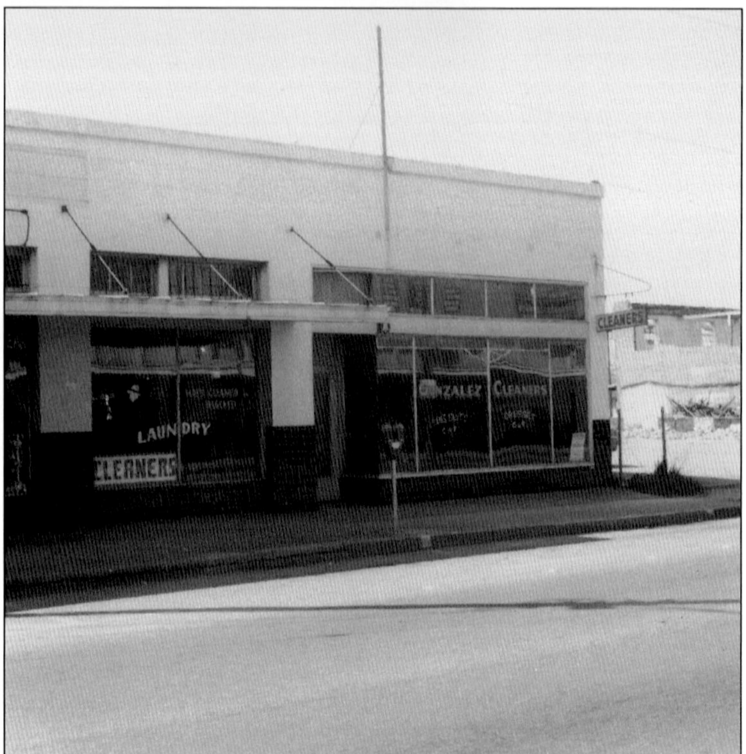

This building at 1212 West Commerce Street, which housed Gonzalez Cleaners in 1970, was the location of Henry C.S. Tire Dealer and Sieberling Rubber Company in 1942. Henry C.S. Smith sold wholesale tires. When Elena Gonzales was asked to remark on relocating, she stated she would retire from the cleaning business. (Courtesy of Texana Division, San Antonio Public Libraries.)

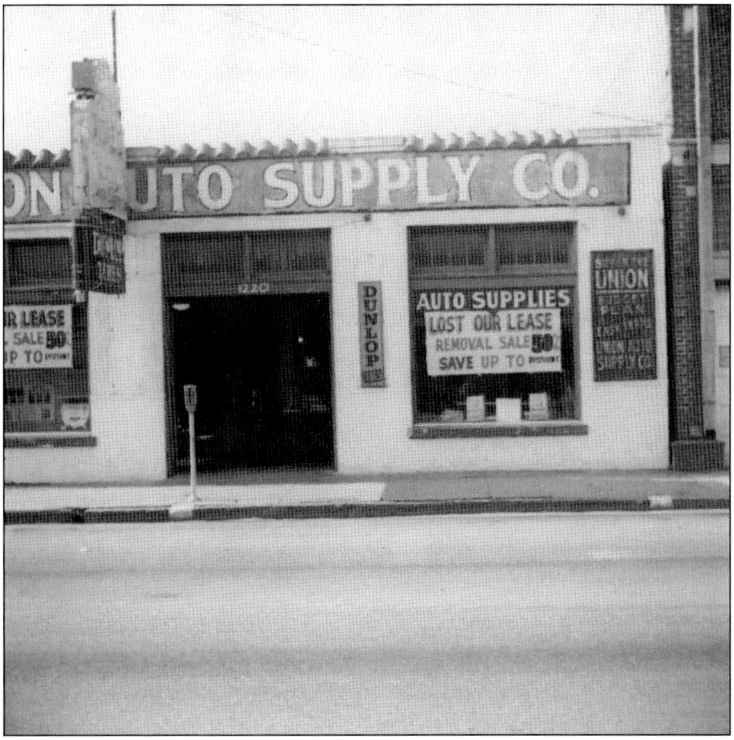

In the 1940s, this location at 1220–1226 West Commerce Street was the Union Auto Supply & Furniture Company. Officers were Shrolly Goodman, president, and Benjamin Lessor, secretary-treasurer. The second location was at 1316–1318 South Flores Street. In 1969, Israel Goodman and Ben Lessor had a second business, G. & L. Investment Company. Due to old age, instead of relocation, they closed the business. (Courtesy of Texana Division, San Antonio Public Libraries.)

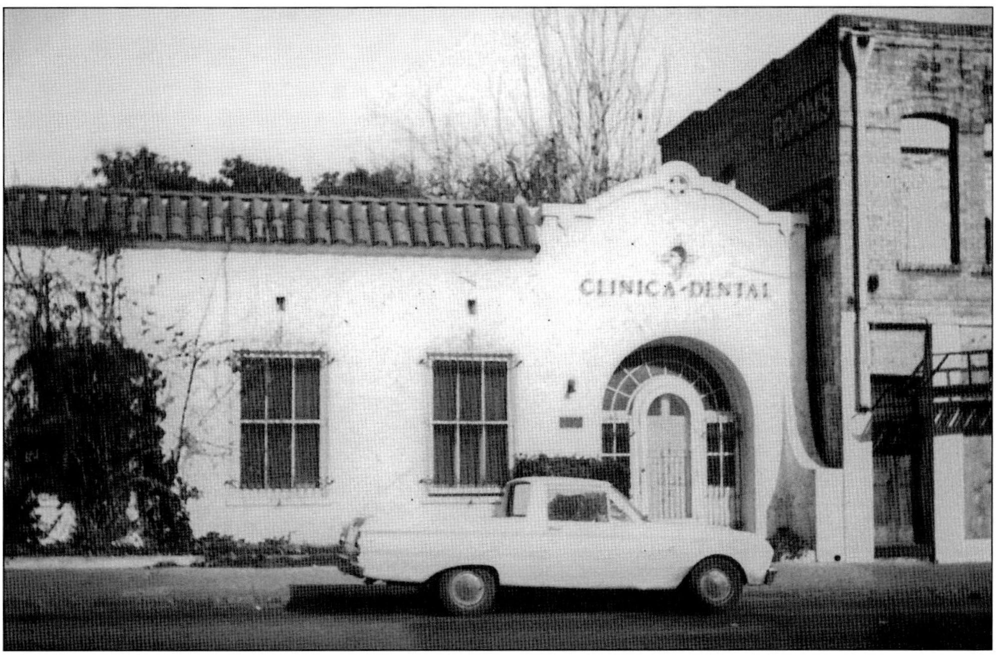

Dr. Hector Urrutia's dental office was at 415 West Houston Street in 1970. In 1942, he was down the road at 609 West Houston Street. Dr. Urrutia later moved his practice to suite 823 in the Medical Arts Building located at 705 East Houston Street. The Medical Arts Building, constructed in the 1920s, is now the Emily Morgan Hotel. (Courtesy of Texana Division, San Antonio Public Libraries.)

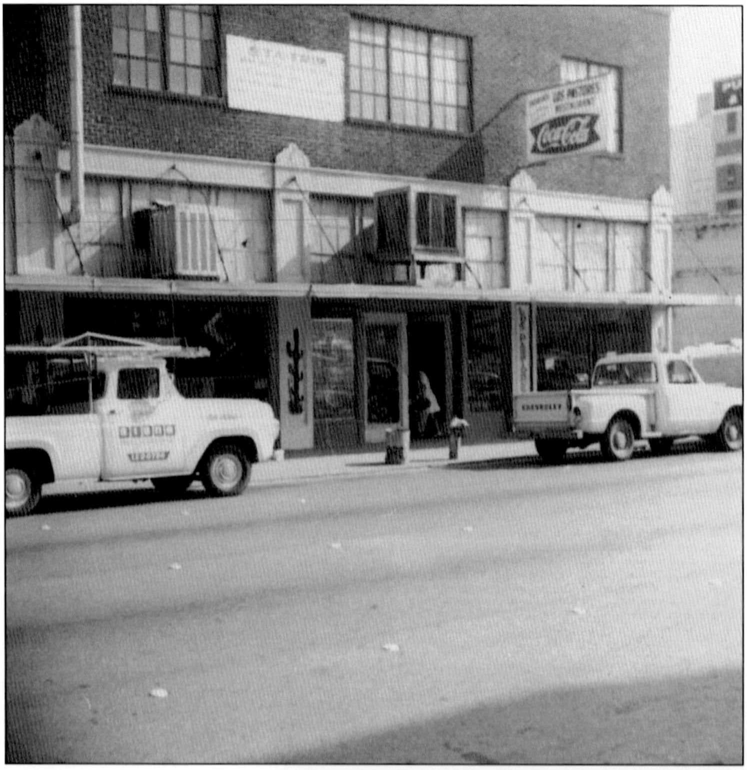

In 1969, with the help of the Relocation Department, Charles Doria obtained a Small Business Administration loan to move Los Pastores Restaurant from 309 West Houston Street to 119 Camaron Street. The restaurant space expanded from 28,000 square feet to 37,000 square feet. Doria's wife, Corrine, was also a business owner. In 1942, Corrine's Beauty Shop was located at 510 ½ North Leona Street. (Courtesy of Texana Division, San Antonio Public Libraries.)

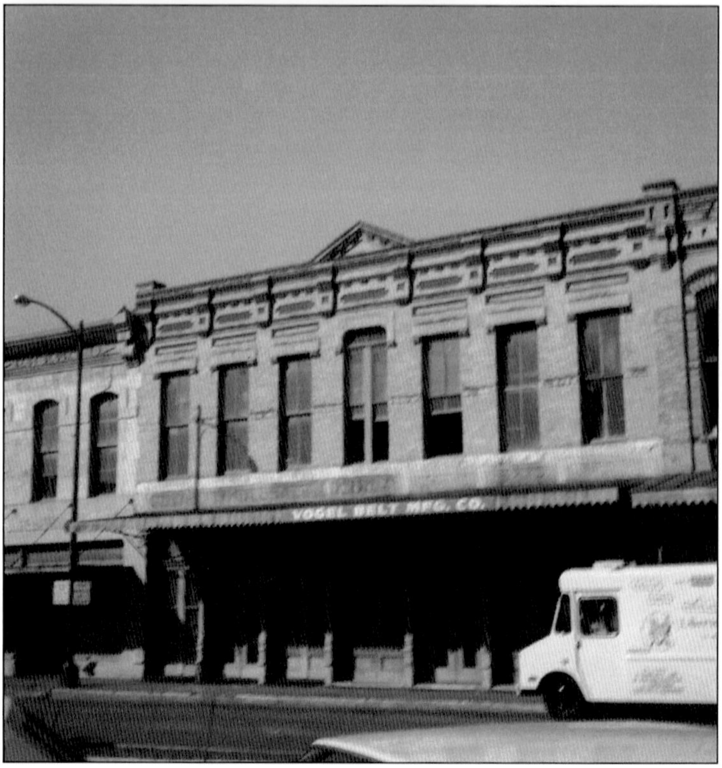

Adolf Vogel Leather Goods was founded in 1909 as manufacturers of leather goods and leather clothing. It was located at 119 Military Plaza in the 1940s. When this photograph was taken in 1970, it was listed at 115–117 Military Plaza and the name had changed to Vogel Belt Manufacturing Company. At the time, it had 52 employees. Vogel Belt Manufacturing Company later moved to its present location at 1819 South Flores Street. (Courtesy of Texana Division, San Antonio Public Libraries.)

Nine

Festivals and Celebrations

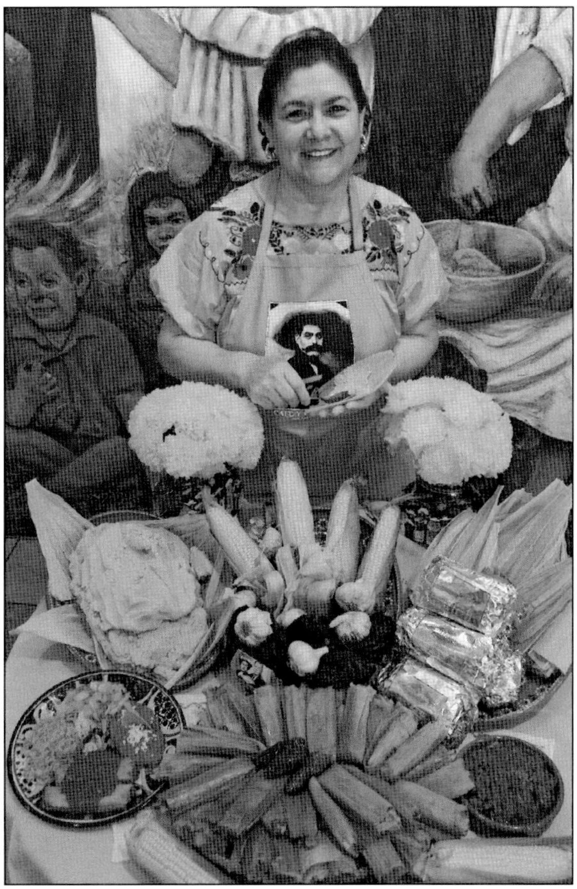

In honor of ancestors and to help preserve Mexican and Tex-Mex traditions, Market Square has provided a stage for fiestas and celebrations for over a century. Fiestas include all or some of these elements: ethnic food and drinks, music, dancing, parades, and decorations. Anastacia Ortega, from Mi Tierra, displays dough for tamales, corn, garlic, tamales, rice, and guacamole. (Photograph by Al Rendon; courtesy of La Familia Cortez Restaurants.)

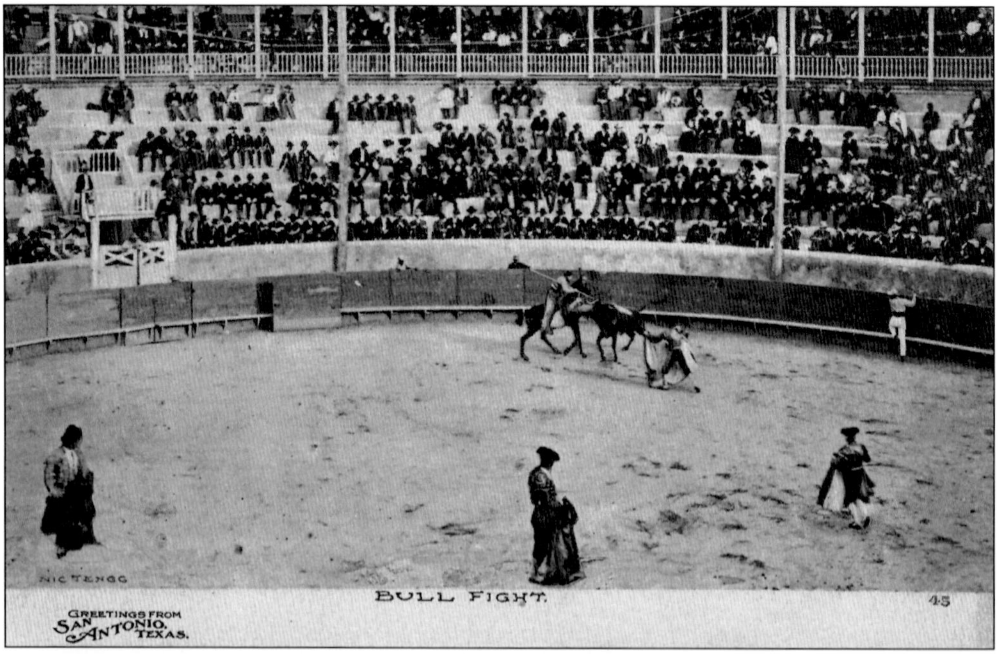

The Market Square of today was once the Municipal Market House grounds and Hay Market Plaza. In the early 1900s, bullfighting brought a festive mood to the market. On April 19, 1904, an advertisement in the *San Antonio Light* announced, "Grand Bull Fight, west side of hay market." The *San Antonio Daily* advertised the event at Plaza de Toros, on southwest corner of Hay Market Plaza, at 5:00 p.m. (Author's collection.)

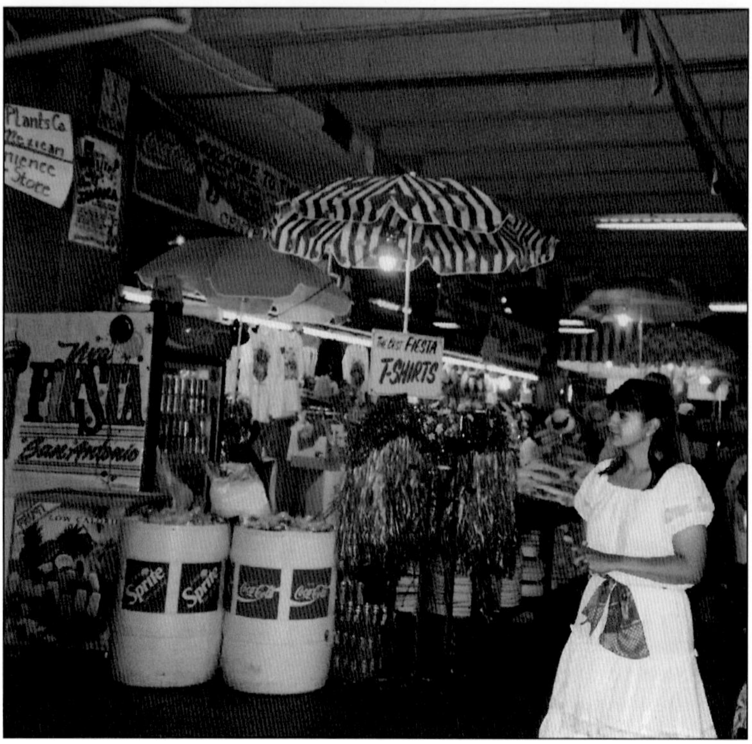

In honor of the heroes of the Alamo and Battle of San Jacinto, Fiesta San Antonio was started in 1891. Numerous events are featured throughout the city for the annual festival held every April. Market Square is host to Fiesta de los Reyes, as well as other events during this time as part of Fiesta El Mercado. (Courtesy of Phillip and Alice Leon.)

Fiesta is a time for family and friends to gather. George and Connie Rivera start planning their group of attendees for the Battle of Flowers Parade months in advance. Since friends have moved all over the United States, invitations have to be sent out in time to commit for reserved seating at the parade. The oldest and largest Fiesta parade attracts crowds of over 350,000. (Courtesy of Nancy Lara.)

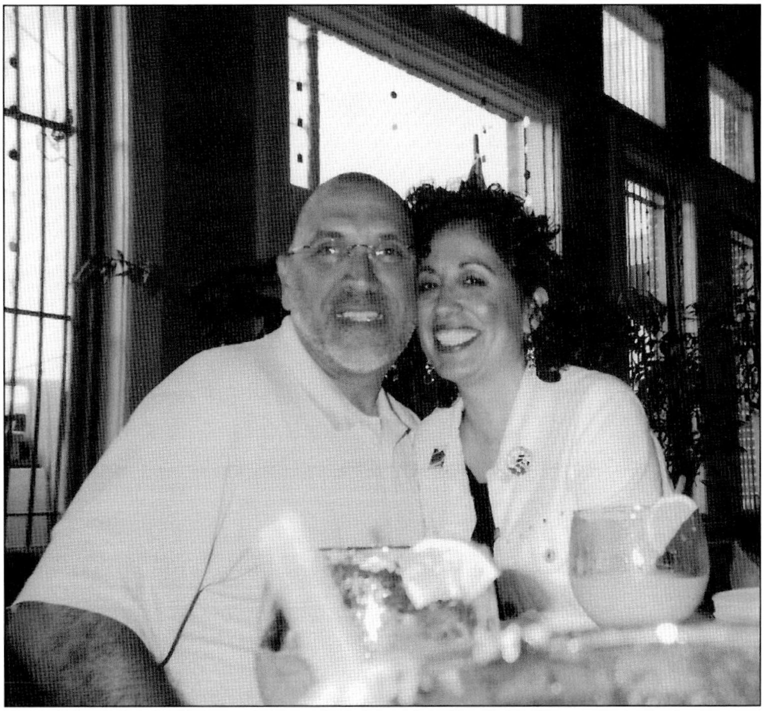

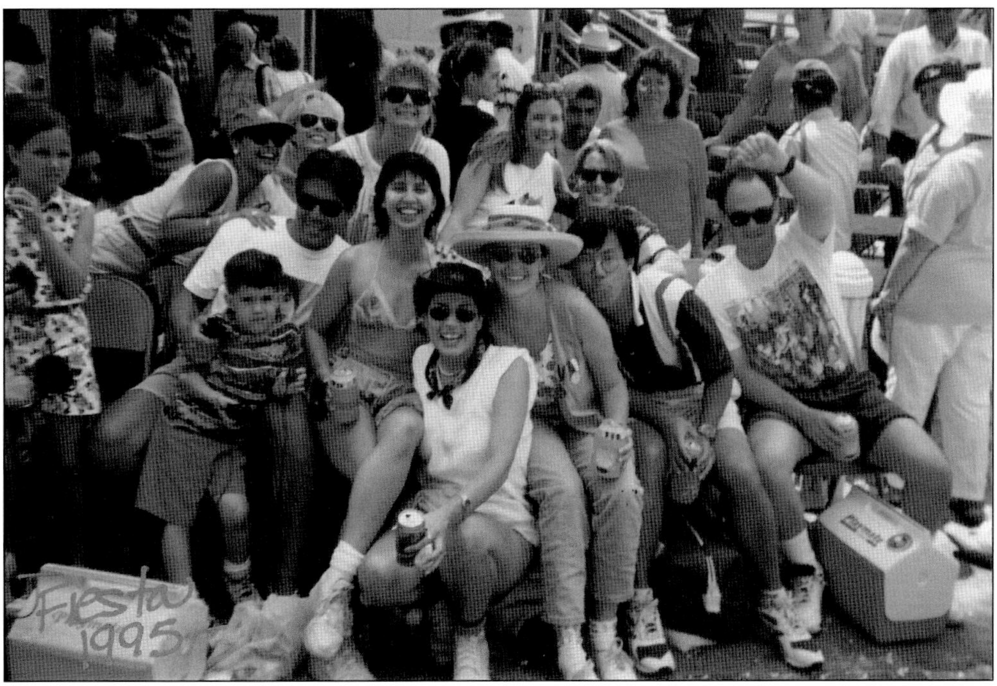

In 1995, the Riveras hosted a group at the Battle of Flowers Parade. Pictured are, from left to right, (first row) Eddie Arriola, Nancy Lara, Alicia Tsandoula, Cherie DeVries, and Roger Teng; (second row) Edna Campos Gravenhorst, Sue Lagomarsino, Carol Hawkins, and Julie and Kevin Kleck. After the parade, it is a tradition to party at Fiesta El Mercado. (Courtesy of Nancy Lara.)

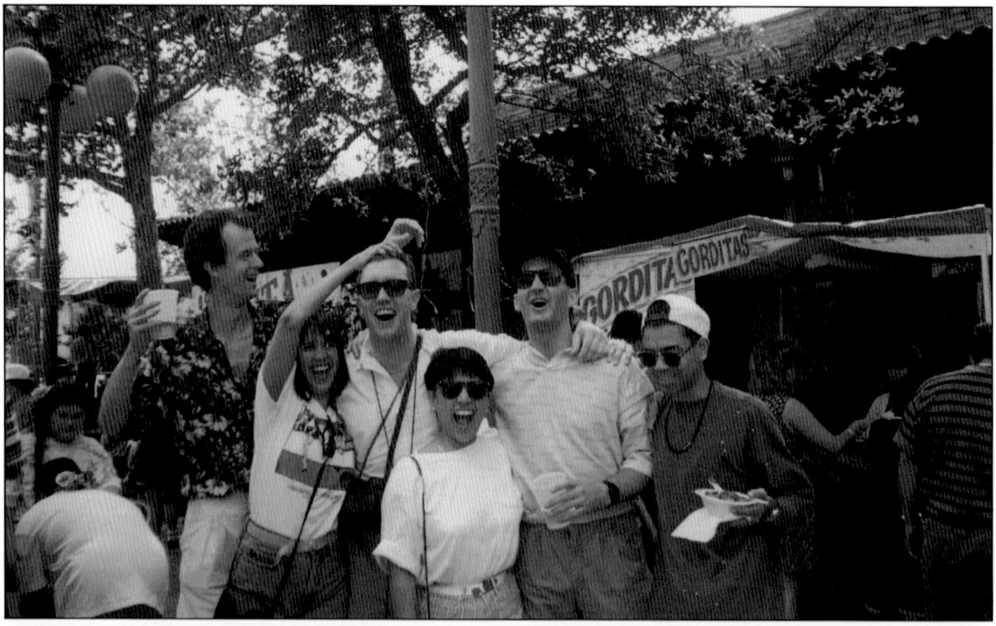

The Fiesta celebration begins with the breaking of *cascarones* on friends' heads! Cascarones are colored and decorated eggshells filled with confetti. They are used for celebrations, traditionally at Easter. At Fiesta El Mercado in 1994, friends gathered to eat, drink, and celebrate. From left to right are Randy Capps, Nancy Lara, Michael Dyer, Sue Carrisalez, Kevin Rickerson, and Ken Smith. (Author's collection.)

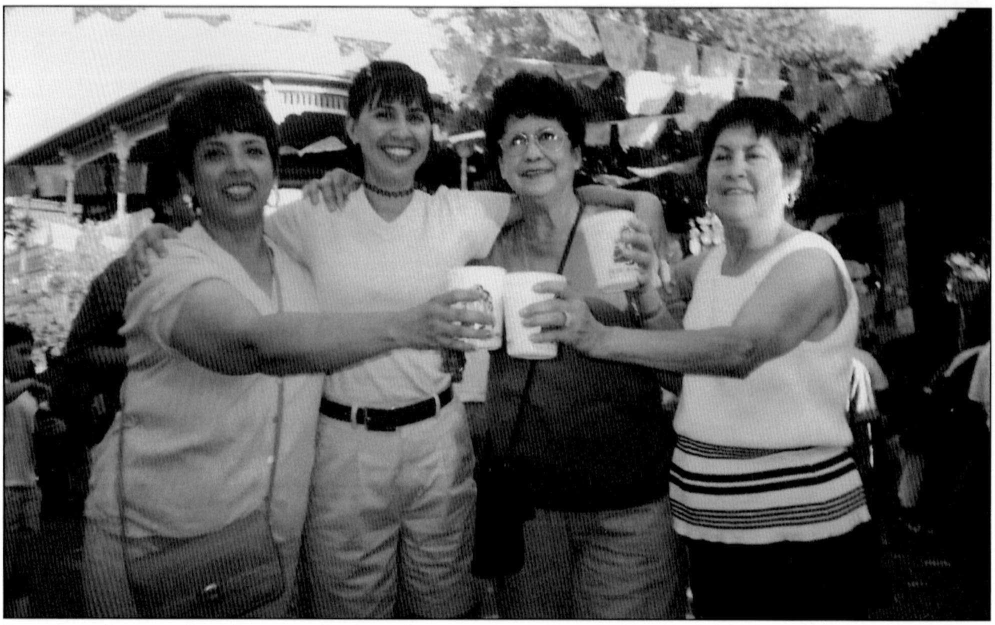
Papel picado is used to decorate both indoors and outdoors. Sheets of paper or thin plastic are cut into elaborate designs and hung on a string to create banners. Rosie Amaro, Nancy Lara, Mary Lara, and Lupe Amaro are standing under the banners in Market Square during Fiesta 1999. Papel picado is commonly displayed for holidays, weddings, quinceañeras, and on altars for Day of the Dead. (Courtesy of Nancy Lara.)

In the Latino community, one of the most important celebrations is the Fiesta de Quince Años. A girl's 15th birthday marks her passage to womanhood. In this photograph, Melessa Chriselda Rodriguez smiles for her official portrait. This is her special day. Customs for this celebration in San Antonio emphasize God, family, friends, and godparents, with a religious mass, ethnic food, and mariachi music. (Courtesy of Melessa C. Rodriguez.)

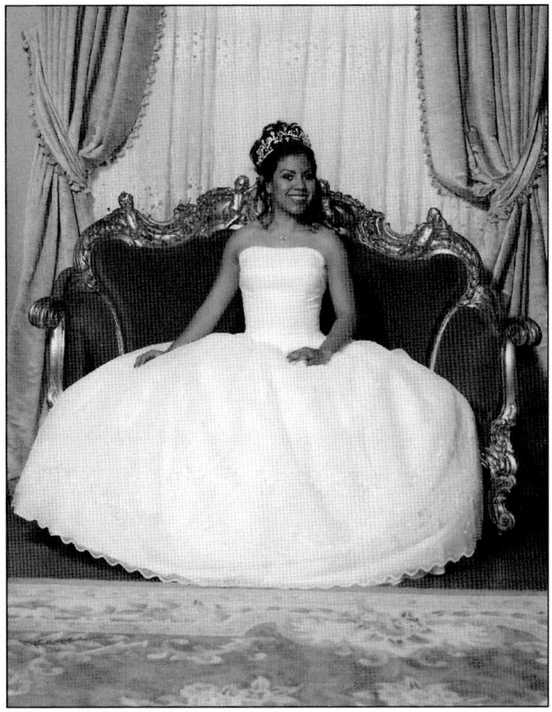

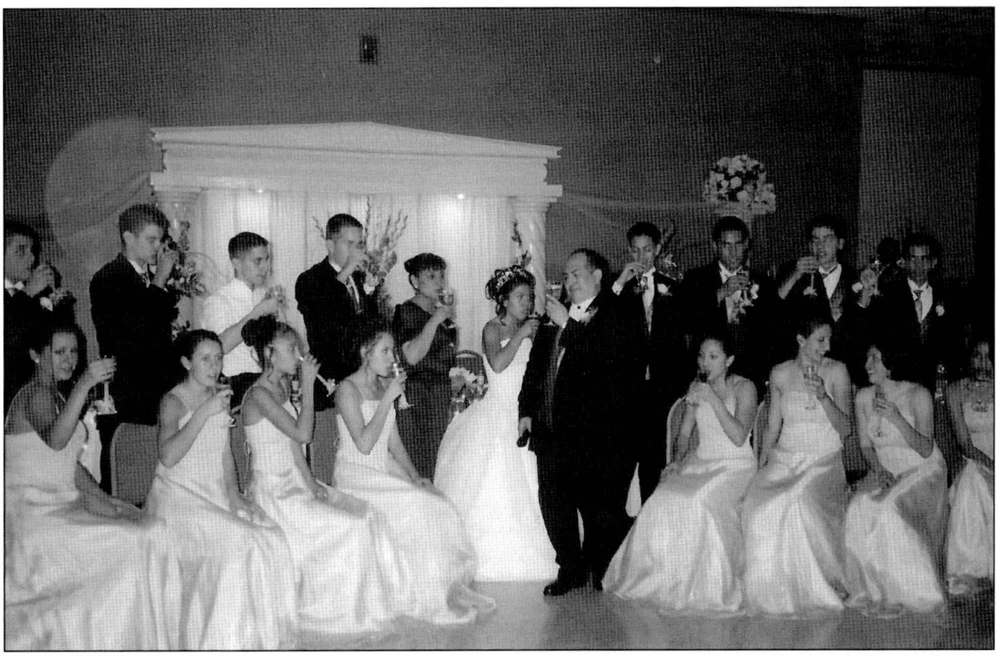

The quinceañera's parents, Michael H. and Mary Lou Rodriguez, toast to their daughter's coming of age. Melessa Rodriguez's court of honor included her escort Nathaniel Mireles, Amanda Rodriguez, Lauren Kniejski, Tess Rodriguez, Ashley Vera, Lauren Gonzales, Ashley Phipps, Dayna Fogle, Karen Rodriguez, Logan Barnes, Salvador Cuellar II, Michael Sandford, Javier Villegas, Jacob Ayala, Juan Padilla, Randall Zamora, and Rudy Valenzuela. (Courtesy of Melessa C. Rodriguez.)

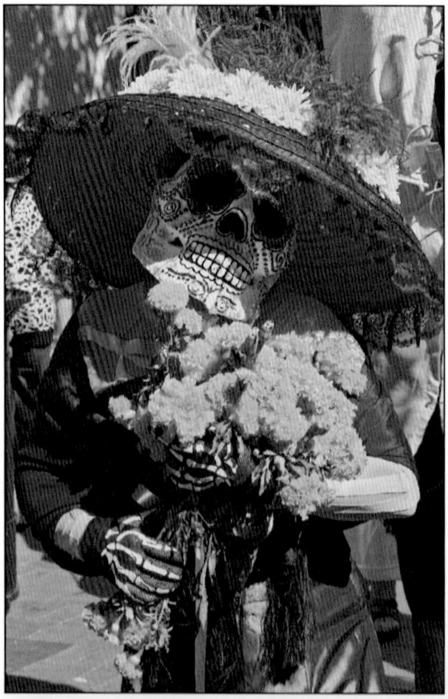

Day of the Dead is a multi-day Mexican holiday mixing Christian beliefs with ancient indigenous rituals. It is a time to honor and pray for family members and friends who have died. Mexico's Grand Dame of Death is La Calavera Catrina, a female skeleton wearing a plumed hat. This Catrina was photographed at Market Square. (Photograph by Al Rendon; courtesy of La Familia Cortez Restaurants.)

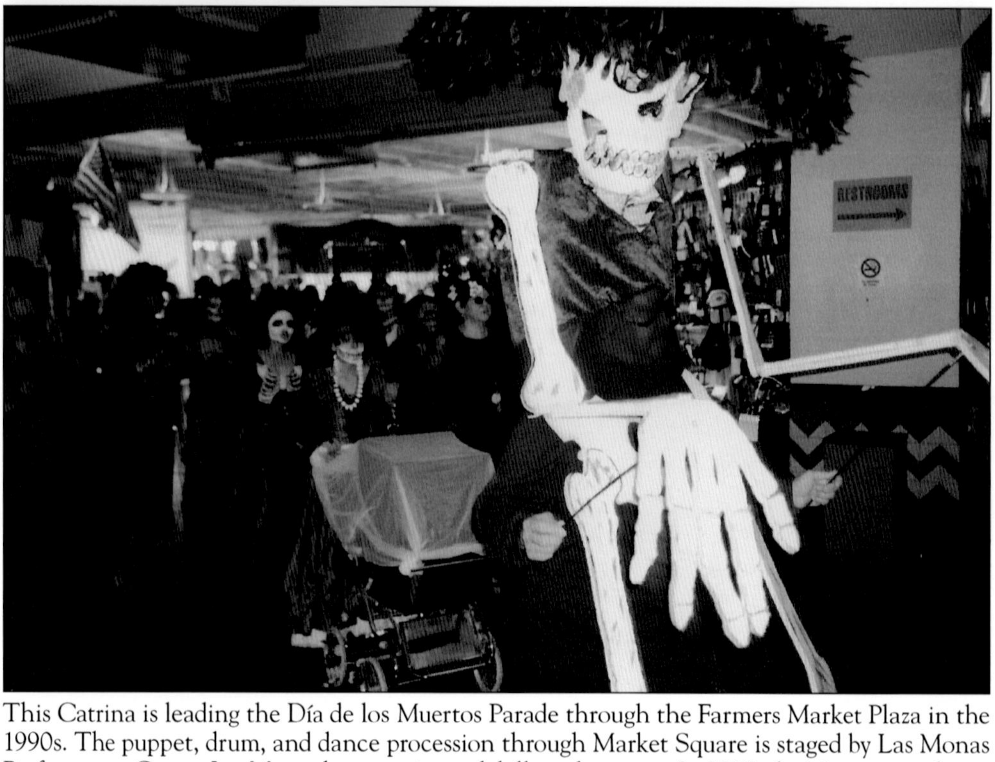

This Catrina is leading the Día de los Muertos Parade through the Farmers Market Plaza in the 1990s. The puppet, drum, and dance procession through Market Square is staged by Las Monas Performance Group. Las Monas honor animated dolls and puppets. In 2008, the Mexican tradition of Day of the Dead was inscribed in the List of the Intangible Cultural Heritage of Humanity by UNESCO. (Courtesy of Thelma Gonzalez.)

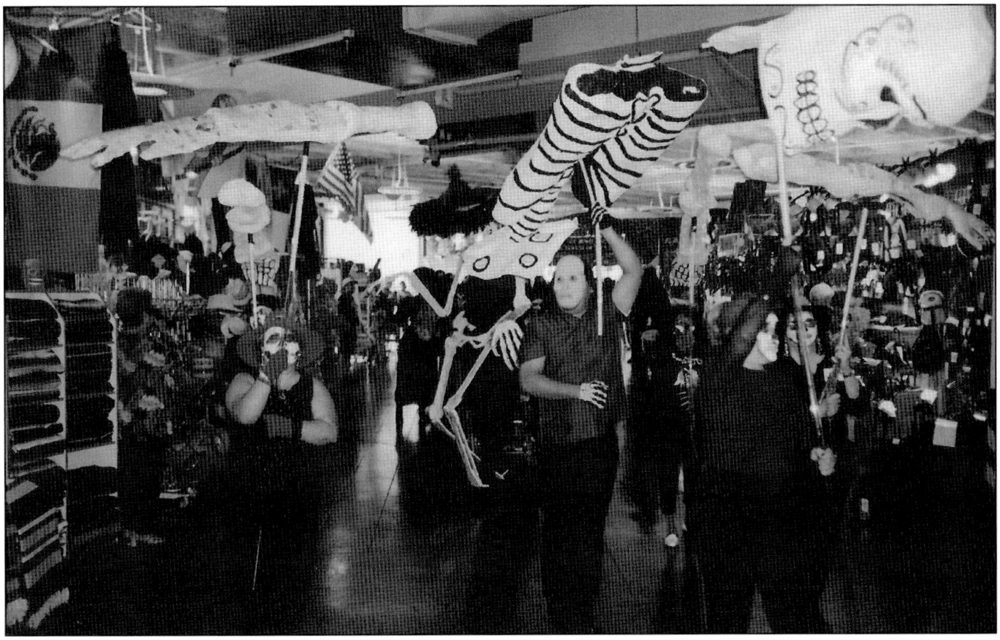

Members of Las Monas Performance Group march through the aisles of Farmers Market Plaza and impress spectators with their mobile pieces of art. Las Monas has also led parades at La Villita and the Houston Museum of Fine Arts. In 2008, it was awarded the Parade Director's Award in the Fiesta Flambeau Parade. In 2009, Las Monas won first place with their Las Vegas recreation. (Courtesy of Thelma Gonzalez.)

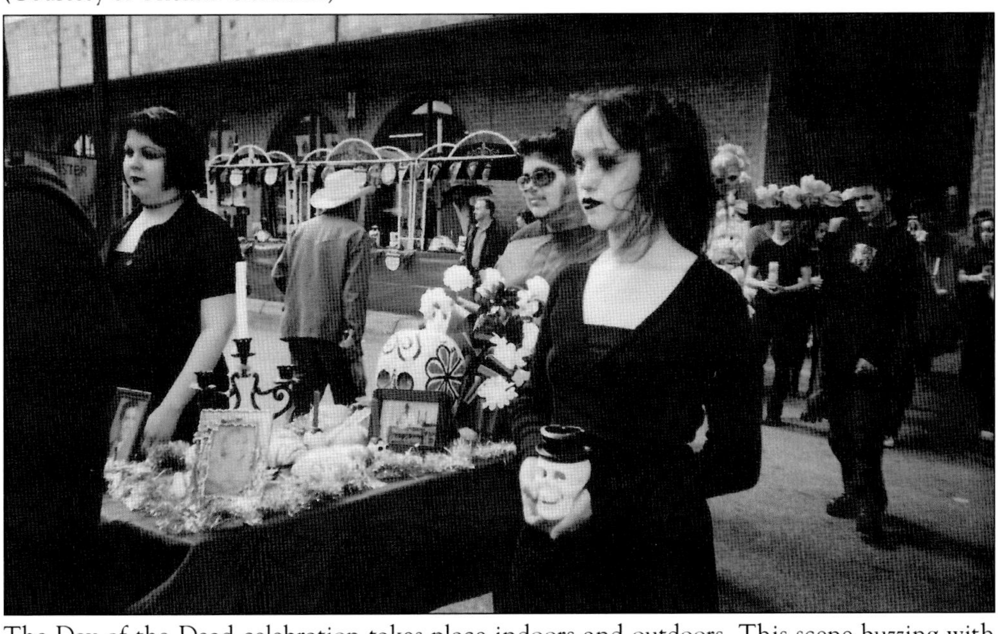

The Day of the Dead celebration takes place indoors and outdoors. This scene buzzing with activity on San Saba Street shows spectators dressed in mourning clothes. Altars honoring the dead are mixed in with booths feeding the living. Marigolds, candles, and skulls are all part of the decorations. According to Market Square artist Yolix Luna, all items on the altars are symbolic. The three candles represent light, faith, and hope. (Courtesy of Joanne Gonzales.)

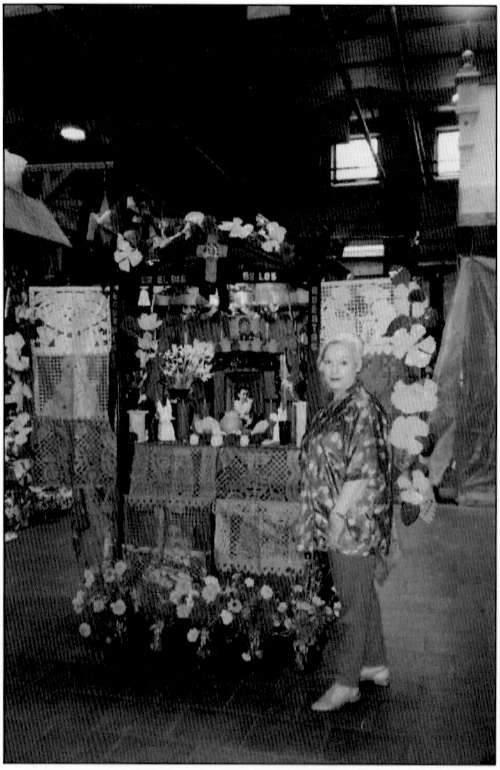

This 1991 Day of the Dead altar was designed by Yolix Luna, owner of Muñecas Etc. The altar honors her mother, Leonor L. de Cardero. Luna makes many of the decorations herself and uses a combination of artificial and fresh flowers. In the 1970s, Darson Persyn's farm provided flowers at the market for celebrating All Saints Day on November 1 and All Souls Day on November 2. (Courtesy of Yolix Luna.)

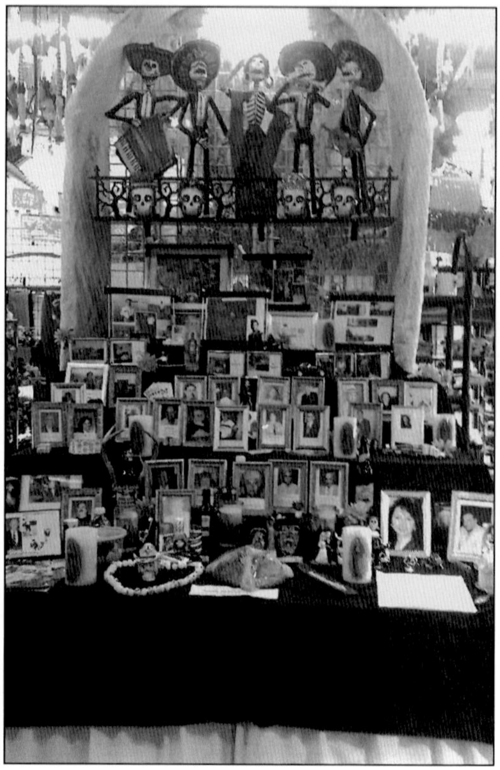

The community altar features the skeletons of a singer and her musicians. They are used to draw attention to the photographs of loved ones and friends. The photographs are surrounded by items representing the departed ones' favorite foods, drinks, games, sports, and other worldly goods they left behind. Market Square features one of the largest altar exhibitions in San Antonio. (Courtesy of Thelma Gonzalez.)

Ten

Market Square Today

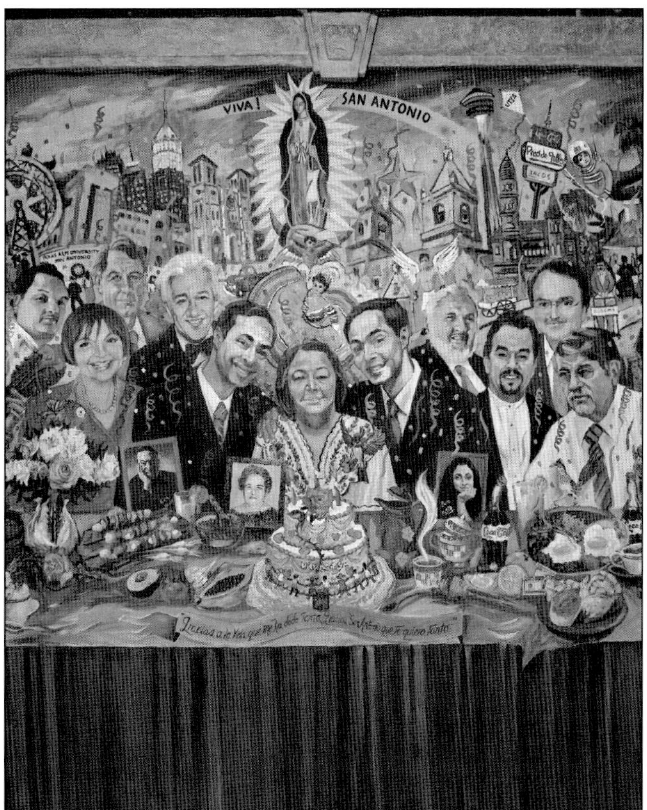

In 2018, San Antonio celebrates its 300th anniversary, and Market Square celebrates 118 years since the completion of Municipal Market House, establishing the area as a market in 1900. This mural at Pico de Gallo pays tribute to the success of San Antonio. Rosie Castro (center) and sons Julian (mayor, 2009–2014) and Joaquín are joined by community leaders; the city's iconic landmarks surround their images. (Photograph by Al Rendon; courtesy of La Familia Cortez Restaurants.)

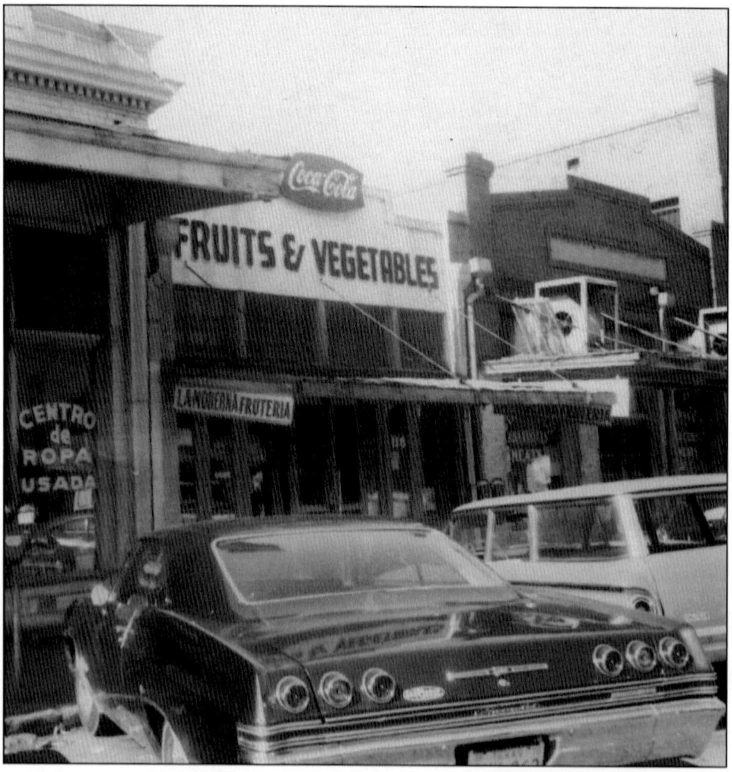

In 1970, Centro de Ropa Usada (used clothing center) was at 114 Produce Row, La Moderna Fruitera was at 116 Produce Row, and Coon Lee's was at 120 Produce Row. City directories listed Sam Lung doing business at 116 Produce Row in 1927 and Jan Yuen occupying that space between 1942 and 1943. In 1977, 102, 106 ½, 108, and 114–122 Produce Row were vacant. Plaza Novelty was at 112 Produce Row. Currently, El Merkadito is listed at 112 Produce Row. (Courtesy of Texana Division, San Antonio Public Libraries.)

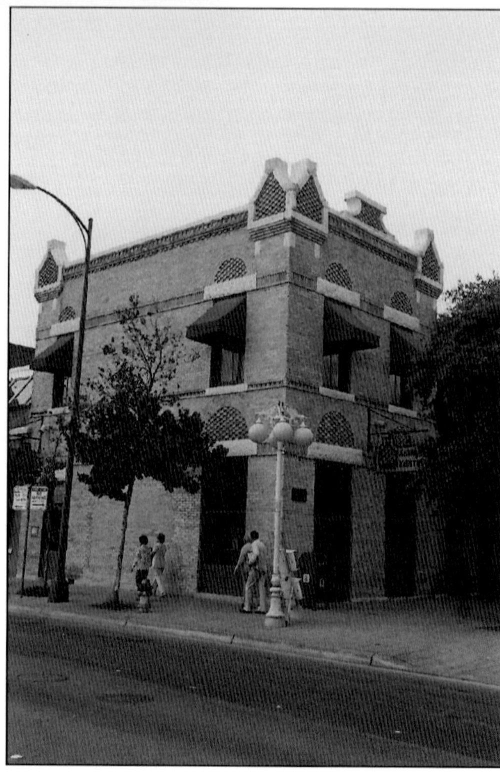

The building at 102–104 Produce Row was photographed for the Downtown Resources Survey in 1981. In 1941, a building permit for remodeling was issued to Alex J. Uhl. Businesses from the 1920s to the 1970s were New Home Café, P.E. Flores, Modern Café, La Norteña, Garza Fruits, Las Cazuelas, and Lalos's. Currently, Cano Fruteria is at 102 Produce Row. (Courtesy of the San Antonio Conservation Society Foundation.)

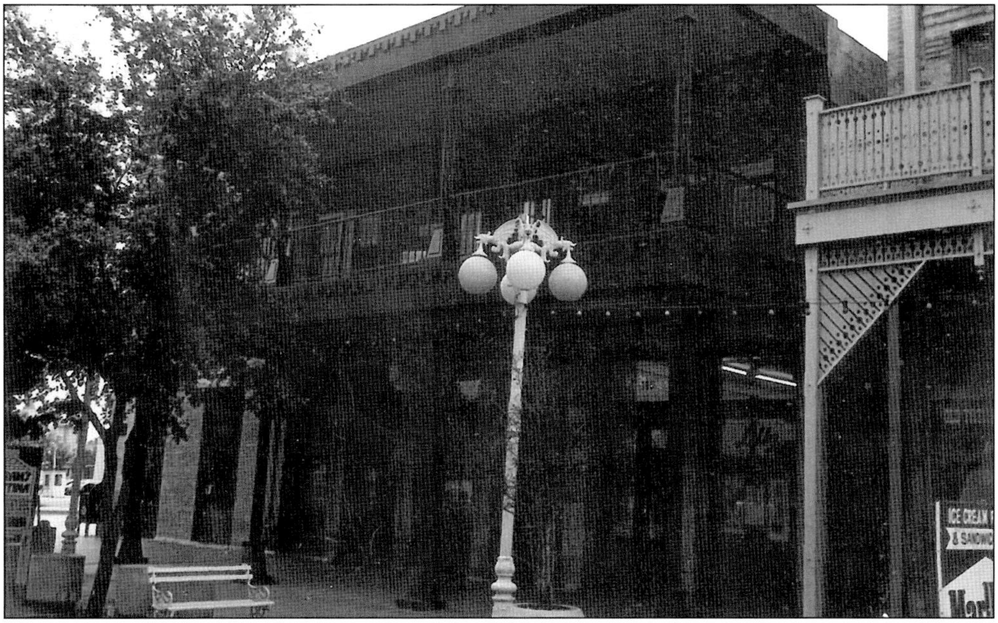

Botica Guadalupana, founded in 1893 at 106 Produce Row, was owned by pharmacist Daniel San Miguel. The doctors' offices included: 1920s, S. Guzman; 1940s, Saturnino Guzman Jr. and William Torres; and 1970s, Dr. Raul C. Villafana. In the 1940s, Teodula Mendez operated the Guadalupe Hotel at 106 ½ Produce Row. The building at 104–106 is currently Viriana Jewelry & Crafts and is listed at 104 Produce Row. (Courtesy of the San Antonio Conservation Society Foundation.)

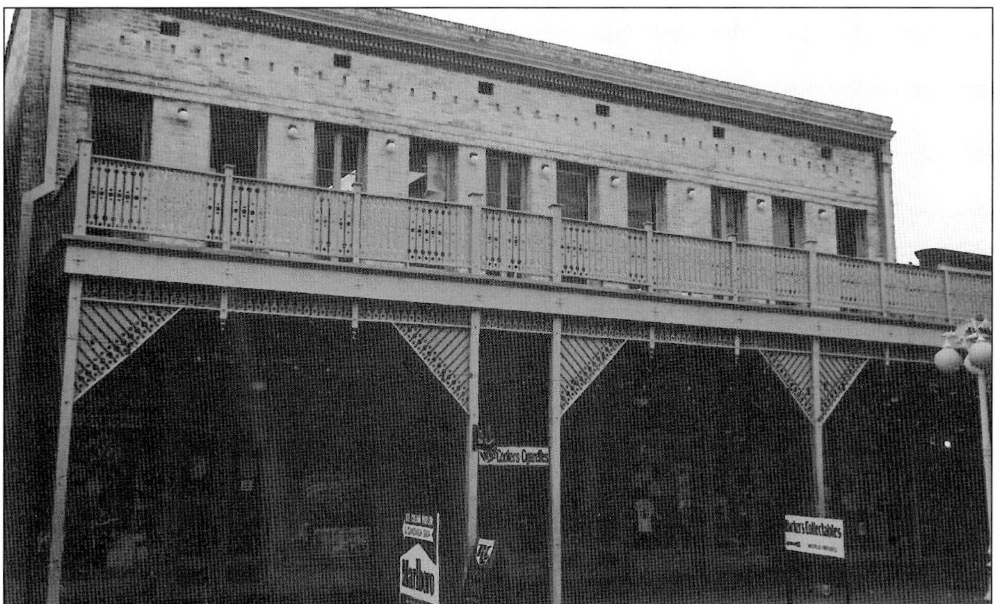

In the 1920s, 108–110 Produce Row housed Chong Fat and San Pedro Drug Store. In the 1940s, El Nopal Café, the drugstore, offices, and the San Pedro Hotel were in the building. In the 1970s, Alamo Meat & Fruit and Cadena's Fruit Stand were at 110 Produce Row. Today, El Mercado Glass Factory, The Cowboy Station, and General Market are listed at 110 Produce Row. (Courtesy of the San Antonio Conservation Society Foundation.)

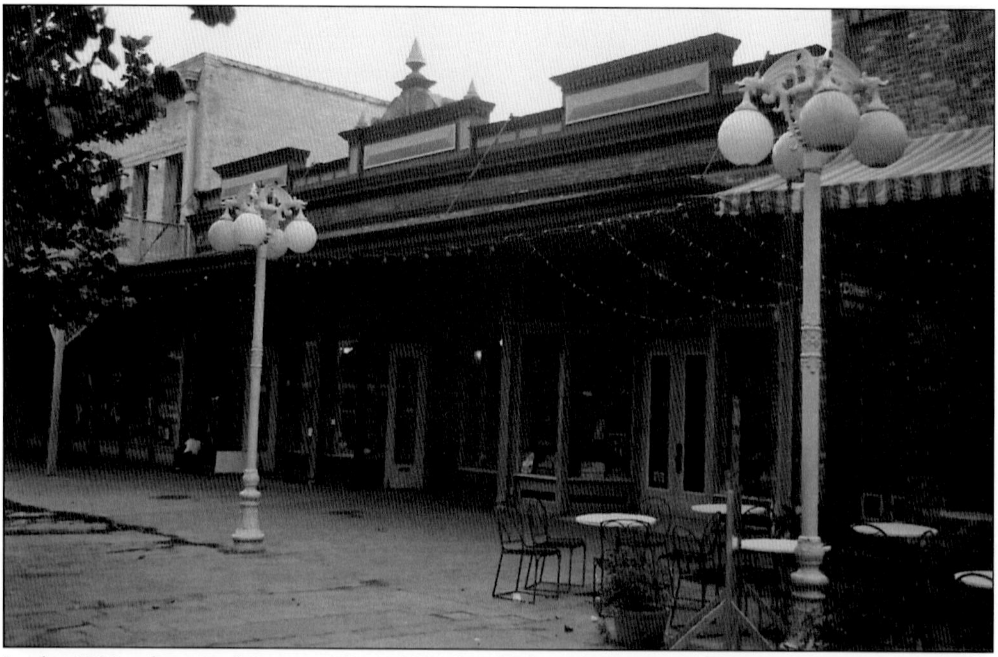

In the 1920s, the storefronts at 112–116 Produce Row were home to Wing Fat and Sam Lung. In the 1940s, Wing Fat, El Rancho Grande Fruit Stand, and Jan Yuen Grocery were doing business there. In 1968, Plaza Novelty was in the center and Arevalo's Fruit Stand and La Moderna were on the ends. El Merkadito and Casa Rivera are the current businesses located here. (Courtesy of the San Antonio Conservation Society Foundation.)

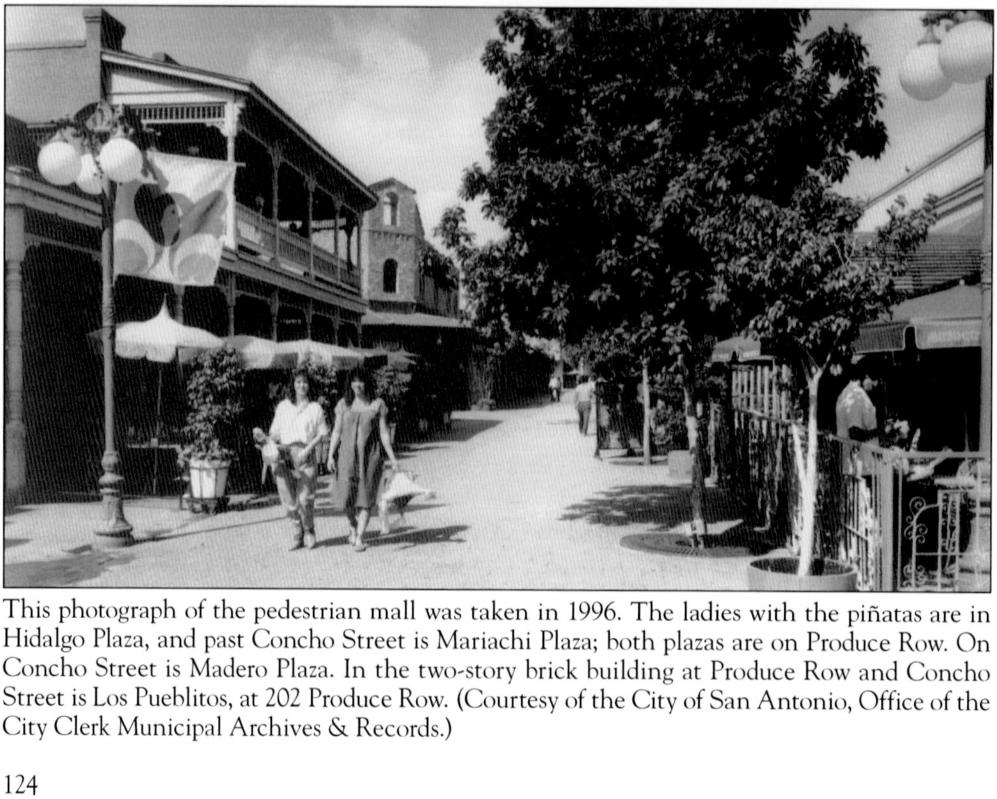

This photograph of the pedestrian mall was taken in 1996. The ladies with the piñatas are in Hidalgo Plaza, and past Concho Street is Mariachi Plaza; both plazas are on Produce Row. On Concho Street is Madero Plaza. In the two-story brick building at Produce Row and Concho Street is Los Pueblitos, at 202 Produce Row. (Courtesy of the City of San Antonio, Office of the City Clerk Municipal Archives & Records.)

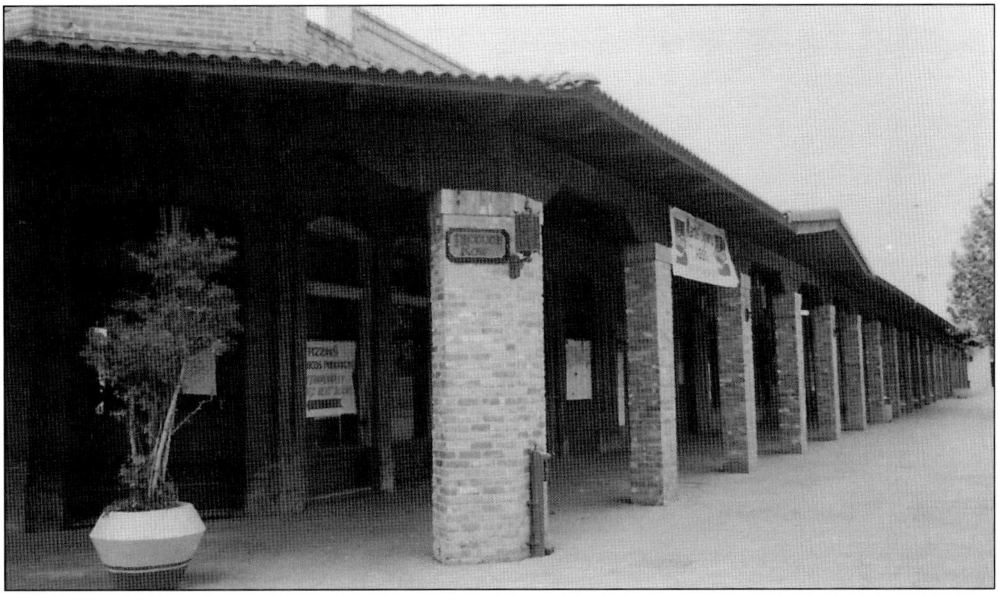

Frank Pizzini founded his store at 202 Produce Row in 1891. Pizzini came to San Antonio in the late 1870s from Mexico and went to work with an Italian merchant in Military Plaza. At one time, Pizzini was the largest importer of chilies and sold over 200 different herbs. The sign in the window in this 1980s photograph announces Pizzini's had moved next door. (Courtesy of the San Antonio Conservation Society Foundation.)

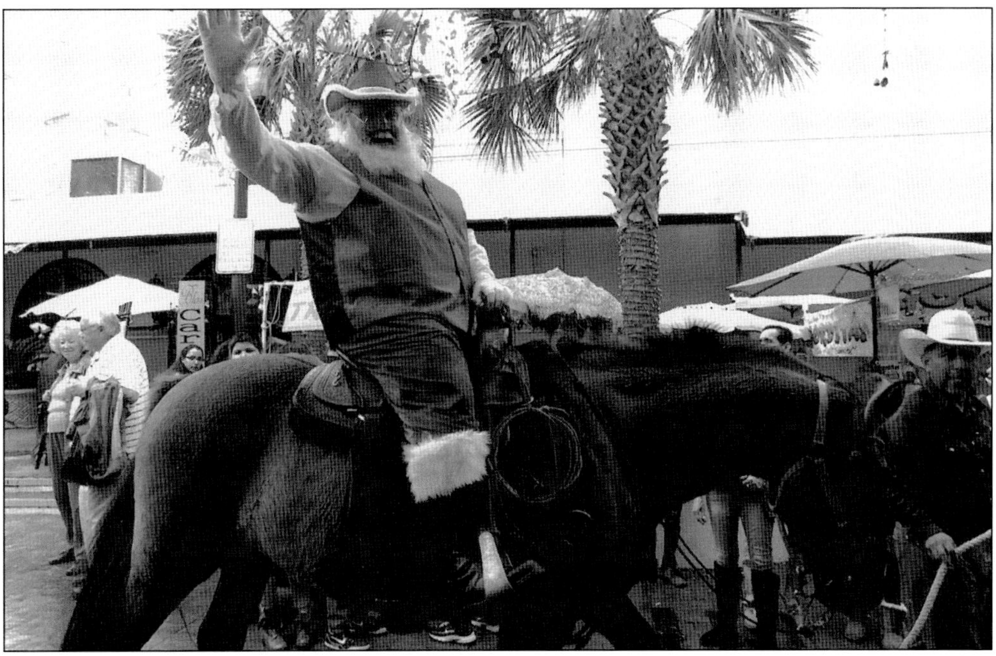

This book is a small sampling of Market Square history; there are still many stories that need to be told. If this book provokes curiosity to explore more of San Antonio and Market Square, then this project has served its purpose. As the saying goes, "All good things must come to an end." During the 2015 Blessing of the Animals Event, Santa Claus bids goodbye. *Hasta lluego*, until we meet again. (Author's collection.)

Merchants of Market Square

El Mercado:
Artes Metalicas
Casa Grande
Cozumel Arts & Crafts
De La Luz Imports
Don Roman Inc.
El Alebrije
El Mercado Snack Bar
El Taxqueñito
Forever Yours
Galeria Taxco
JB Leather Shop
Jesse's Jewelry
La Boutique International
La Morenita Imports
La Perla
Leather Creations
Little Bit of Texas
Little Mexico Imports
Magaly's
Maria's Imports
Maya Imports
Memories of Mexico
Mexico Lindo Imports
Mi Pueblito Arts & Crafts
Munchies
Muñecas Etc.
Naturaleza Celestial
Old Mexico Imports
Perales Mexican Imports
Silver Twins
Tesoro De Mexico
Texas Choice
Texas Toms

Farmers Market Plaza:
Angie's
Apparel and Hats
Baptismal Boutique
Boone's Café
Buendía Imports
Budweiser Souvenirs
Candy Bin
Clau's Beautiful Gifts
Chulerias
Del Sol
El Jumil–A Touch of Mexico
Fiesta Cut Outs
Fiesta Fun Company
Fiesta Mercado
Foreign Affairs
G's Gonzalez Gift Shop
Guatemala Mayan Designs
Gueros
House of Mexico Imports
Inca Treasures
Inspirational Art
International Market
J. Anthony's Leather Goods
Julia's Jewelry
La Plaza Imports
La Villa
Little Bit of Texas
Lone Star Souvenirs
Lorenza's
Magali's Silver International
Market General Store
Martin's Curios
Maruka's

Mexican Old Time Photos
More Plants Company
Nanny's Nook
Noah's Art Heavenly Safari
Olmeca Imports
Plaza Flowery
Pura Vida
Que Lindo Es Jalisco
Ranchero Grill & Tap
San Antonio Gift Shop
Scentchips
Shainy Designs
Silver Spur Tees
Sweety
Tejano Lou's
TAE
Texas Republic
The Texas General Store
The Treasure Box
Teriyaki Kitchen
Truque Imports
Turqueza
Vero's Café
Yesi's The Lit Dove

Market Square:
Casa Rivera
Centro de Artes Gallery
El Mercado Glass Factory Shop
El Merkadito
Fruteria Cano
General Market
La Margarita
Los Arcos Gifts
Los Pueblitos
Mi Tierra Café & Bakery
Plaza Taxco
SA Live Studio
The Cowboy Station at the Market
The Mariachi Bar
The Rustic Grape Wine Cellars
San Antonio Tricentennial Celebration Commission
Viva Villa Taqueria
Viriana Jewelry & Crafts
Univision Downtown Studio

Consistent with our mission to preserve history on a local level, this book was printed in South Carolina on American-made paper and manufactured entirely in the United States. Products carrying the accredited Forest Stewardship Council (FSC) label are printed on 100 percent FSC-certified paper.

MADE IN THE USA